1000 Words

———

Many hieroglyphic signs—phonetics are a very difficult language in themselves—have been used to give a pronunciation guide. We try to make it as simple as possible with the letters of the English language. We know that this method can not reproduce the finest nuances of pronunciation of a foreign language, but you will see that you will adapt yourself very quickly, as soon as you have the occasion to hear the Spanish language as it is spoken by Spaniards.

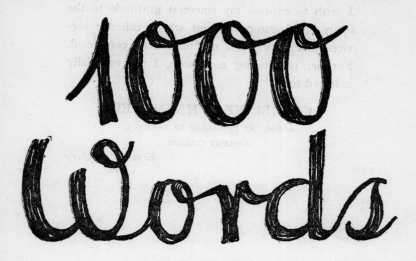

1000 Words

AND PHRASES

ESSENTIAL SPANISH

BY ERNST WALLENBERG

ESSENTIAL BOOKS

DUELL, SLOAN AND PEARCE

Publishers   New York

I wish to express my sincerest gratitude to the many collaborators without whose valuable services this book could not have been completed. For her painstaking assistance, I am especially indebted to

CATHERINE L. HAYMAKER,
ASSISTANT PROFESSOR OF SPANISH,
ADELPHI COLLEGE

Ernst Wallenberg

DRAWINGS BY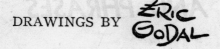

COPYRIGHT 1945 BY ESSENTIAL BOOKS

 199

PRINTED IN THE UNITED STATES OF AMERICA
BY J. J. LITTLE & IVES COMPANY, NEW YORK

1000 Words

SPANISH

Buenos	**días,**	**señorita**
booaynoss	deeas	sengyoreeta
Good	*morning,*	*young lady.*

Lesson One

Almost everyone knows, at least by name and reputation, one of the most celebrated California cities, Los Angeles. No matter how you pronounce Los Angeles, it is still a Spanish word, or better two Spanish words, meaning "the angels." Thus, it would not be true if you declared that you didn't know a word of Spanish or that you could think of no possible association you have with the Spanish language.

We could enumerate many more Spanish words with which you are undoubtedly well acquainted. Have you never heard of Don Juan, Sir John, who appears in Mozart's world-famous opera "Don Giovanni," beloved of a thousand and one girls in Spain? Although I cannot prove this fact, which was alleged by his servant Leporello, I am sure that you know, at least, what it means to be a Don Juan. Perhaps, too, you know a **señorita** in **Puerto Rico,** in other words, a Miss (or rather, a young lady) in Rich Harbor.

To be sure, we must know how to pronounce these few words correctly in Spanish; but when we know that, we know a great part of Spanish pronunciation.

los ángeles	Don Juan	señorita	puerto rico
loss anghaylays	donn hooan	sengyoreeta	pooerrto reeko
the angels	*Sir John*	*Miss*	*harbor rich*

By telling you that **Los Angeles** is pronounced "loss anghe-lays," I dare say I have shown you what, for a tongue accustomed to English, is the most difficult Spanish sound to pronounce. The Spanish g, followed by e or i, is a sound that does not exist in English. It is a very *guttural* sound, almost *gurgled* in the throat. If you succeed with the gurgled ge or gi (hay, hee), that is fine. But, if not, don't bother yourself too much about it; just substitute the sound h as in "house." The Spanish **j,** no matter what vowel sound succeeds it, has exactly the same sound h.

The heavy l e t t e r s s h o w which syllables are to be accentuated. In the English w o r d "Mary" the accent is on t h e first syllable. Using our pronunciation signs, it would look like this, **mayree.**

Juan	jugo	jardín	jota	jinete	jefe
hooan	hoogo	hardeen	hota	heenaytay	hayfay
John	*juice*	*garden*	*j* (Span)	*horseman*	*chief* or *boss*

	gente	general	gigante		
	hentay	haynayral	heegantay		
	people	*general*	*giant*		

To dream on this earth of *an angel,* **un ángel** (oon anghayl), or even of *angels,* **ángeles** (anghaylays), would be considered *a*

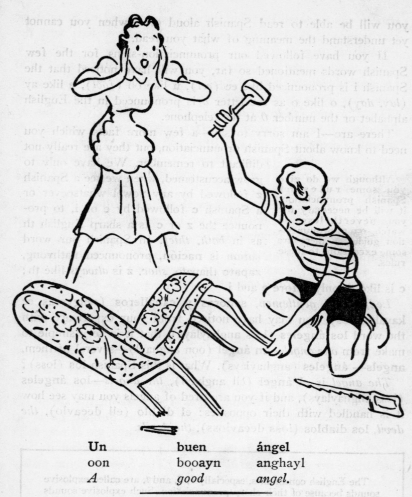

Un	buen	ángel
oon	boo**ayn**	ang**hayl**
A	*good*	*angel.*

vision, **una visión** (oona veezyon). To think of your *boss,*
jefe (hayfay), or of any one else as *an angel,* **un ángel** (oon
ang**hayl**), would be *an illusion,* **una ilusión** (oona eeloosyon).
Do you see how alike these words are in Spanish and English?
Only the pronunciation is very different. But when you know that
the written or printed letter **a** means an a as in the English word
art, you know for nearly every case the pronunciation of the
Spanish a. With very few exceptions, the same holds true of any
Spanish letter. That makes the pronunciation pretty simple, and

you will be able to read Spanish aloud even when you cannot yet understand the meaning of what you read.

If you have followed our pronunciation-signs for the few Spanish words mentioned so far, you will have noticed that the Spanish i is pronounced like ee (*eel*), u like oo (*fool*), e like ay (*lay, day*), o like o as the letter *o* is pronounced in the English alphabet or the number *0* at the telephone.

There are—I am sorry to say—a few more facts which you need to know about Spanish pronunciation, but they are really not difficult to remember. We have only to grow accustomed, when we see a Spanish z followed by any vowel whatsoever or a Spanish c followed by e or i, to pronounce the z or c as a sharp English th as in *bath, thief.* In Spanish our word *nation* is nación, pronounced nathyong, zapato thapato, *shoe.* z is *always* like th; c is like th only before e and i.

Although we do give you some r u l e s for Spanish pronunciation, it will be necessary for you, nevertheless, to watch o u r pronunciation guide, as there are some exceptions to these rules.

Ladies and gentlemen, señoras y caballeros (sengyoras ee kavalyayros), you may have noticed from your experience with the word los ángeles (loss anghaylays), that it is very simple to make from *one angel*—un ángel (oon anghayl)—several of them, angels— ángeles (anghaylays). What is this Spanish los (loss)?

The angel is el ángel (ell anghayl), *the angels*—los ángeles (loss anghaylays), and if you are tired of angels you may see how it is handled with their opposites: el diablo (ell deeavlo), *the devil,* los diablos (loss deeavloss), *the devils.*

The English consonants, especially *b*, *d*, and *t*, are called explosive sounds because of their sharp pronunciation. Such explosive sounds don't exist in Spanish. Therefore, these consonants must be softened in Spanish. B is almost like *v;* d, between vowels and at the end of words, is like the voiced *th* as in them. In our pronunciation guide we do not indicate this again and again as it would be nothing but confusing, especially so when you are not yet able to speak Spanish in the proper connected way. In the beginning every student breathes between each two words and these pauses change the pronunciation. Therefore, we give the pronunciation in the first sections word after word until we assume that you are familiar with the fluent reading and speaking.

Lesson Two

Damas y señores or **señoras y caballeros** (damas ee sengyorays sengyoras ee kavalyayros) *ladies and gentlemen*, when I last spoke to you, I did not behave properly. I was so anxious to introduce you to the Spanish language that I completely forgot to introduce myself to you.

I didn't even say "How do you do!" Don't be offended, for it is not good form in Spanish, when you are not very well acquainted with a person to ask him **¿Qué tal?** (kay tal) *How do you do? How are you?* But you will often hear it when good friends meet. Sometimes a Spaniard sees a friend of his on the street and calls **¡Hola, hombre!**

Spanish z is pronounced always like a sharp th as in "think"; for instance **z a p a t o** (thapato) *t h e s h o e.* j always like a **gurgling** spoken h—**Jerez** (hayreth).

(ola **o**mmbray)—*Hello man!* We would probably say, *Hello, fellow!* or just *Hello!*

No, I could not have said **Hola, hombre!** (ola ombray) to you. **h** is *never pronounced* in Spanish. Nor could I have said **¿Qué tal?** (kay tal). Not yet. I hope to do so later, if you will permit me. But what I *could* have said to you, without any hesitation, was

¡Buenos días, señor!	(booaynoss deeas sengyor)	*Good morning, sir!*
¡Buenos días, señora!	(booaynoss deeas sengyora)	*Good morning, madame!*
¡Buenos días, señorita!	(booaynoss deeas sengyoreeta)	*Good morning, young lady!*

Señorita is *the young lady* as long as she is *not married.* As soon as she *marries,* she becomes **señora,** even though she may remain a young lady for the next ninety years.

What did I say? Yes, **buenos días** literally translated means *good days.* **El día** (ell deea) the day, **los días** (loss deeas) *the days,* **un buen día** (óon booayn deea) a good day, **buenos días** (booaynoss deeas) *good days. Yes, sir—sí* **señor** (see sengyor)—*no, sir*—no, señor

Exclamation- and question-marks (! ?) are indicated twice in Spanish. Once at the beginning of the exclamation ¡ or question ¿ printed upside down and once at the end of the exclamation ! and the question ? printed just as in English.

(no sengyor), I can't

help saying it, you see. The Spaniard is not stingy; he does not wish you one good day, but many good days every day.

You should remember that ¡buenos días! (booaynoss deeas) is a morning greeting. It is like our *good morning,* which we say at any time of the morning until noon. Let us get accustomed very early to saying

Buenos días, señor or, **o** (o), **señora** or **señorita** or, **o** (o), when addressing many people at the same time.

¡Buenos días, señores!	(booaynoss deeas, sengyorays)	*Good morning, gentlemen.*
¡Buenos días, señoras!	(booaynoss deeas, sengyoras)	*Good morning, ladies.*
¡Buenos días, señoritas!	(booaynoss deeas, sengyoreetas)	*Good morning, young ladies.*

Speaking of ladies and girls, I must tell you that for the Spaniard as for all peoples of Latin descent, every living being, as well as every inanimate thing, is *either male or female.* We have one article *the* in English. In Spanish, the article is either **el** (ell), male, or **la** (la), female. Though there is no doubt about whether a person of whom we are speaking is male or female (he or she), we would be very much at a loss to decide whether a thing (it), for instance *a table,* **una mesa** (oona maysa), or *a chair,* **una silla** (oona seelya), belongs to the male or female sex. That is the great difference. We have seen

el día	**los días**	**la mesa**	**las mesas**
ell deea	loss deeas	la maysa	las maysas
the day	*the days*	*the table*	*the tables*
el vaso	**los vasos**	**la silla**	**las sillas**
ell vaso	loss vasos	la seelya	las seelyas
the glass	*the glasses*	*the chair*	*the chairs*

Till noon we know how to say *good morning,* **buenos días** (booaynoss deeas), but what happens after noon? The afternoon is **la tarde** (la tarday), and until evening, if we want to greet somebody, we say: ¡**Buenas tardes!** (booaynass tardays) *Good afternoon!*

After sunset, in the evening, **la noche** (la nochay), *the night* begins, and we have to say, *good nights,* ¡**buenas noches!** (booaynass noochays) instead of our *good evening* or *good night.* But don't forget to add, as a sign of good breeding, **señor** (sengyor), **señora** (sengyora), **señorita** (sengyoreeta) or **señores** (sengyorays), **señoras** (sengyoras), and let us keep in mind that the ñ with the little snake (tilde) above is always pronounced ny (y as in our English word *y(ear)*), ll as ly (as in *(va)l(ue)* and ch is always pronounced ch (as in *church*).

Un	**sombrero de paja**	**y la**	**bailarina**
oon	sommbrayro thay paha	ee la	baeelareena
A	*straw hat*	*and the*	*dancer.*

Lesson Three

For a time after we arrive in a Spanish-speaking country, we will be easily recognized as *foreigners,* **extranjeros** (aystranhayros). For although we may speak *the language,* **la lengua** (la lengwa), fluently, our accent will be noticed at once by every native we meet. We need not worry about that. There are, of course, many people who like to think they are more Spanish than the Spaniards themselves, and as that is a little foolish, they often turn out to be very funny indeed. When we speak in a foreign language, we cannot completely avoid making mistakes.

> **g** before **e** or **i** is, to be more exact, the English *h* with the throat closed somewhat, forming the sound in the roof of the mouth or hard palate. The Scotts say *loth* for lake and this *ih* is pronounced as the Spanish g before **e** and **i**, the Spanish **j** before every vowel. Our pronunciation v sign will be h for this sound.

What would the teachers do if there were no mistakes? All this means that you should take it easy, although it doesn't imply that you shouldn't aim toward a time when you won't make any mistakes at all.

You enter *a room,* **un cuarto** (oon kvarto), or you enter *a store,* **una tienda** (oona teeaynda). Because you are polite, you have learned to say **Buenos días, senorita,** when there is a girl in the room or in the store. **Buenos días, buenas tardes, buenas noches**

> **Vd. = usted** is pronounced oostayth, the ending th like in *them.*

(nochays). These are the words which will facilitate your first contacts in a foreign country. You pronounced these greeting words very well. No wonder then that you will be asked,

¿Habla usted español?
Avla oostayth ayspanyol
Do you speak Spanish?

¿Conoce usted a España?
konothay oostayth a ayspanya
Do you know Spain?

¿Conoce usted a Mexico o a Perú o a Puerto Rico o a Venezuela?
konothay oostayth a meheeko *o a* payroo o a pooerrto reeko o a vaynaythvayla

Do you know Mexico or Peru or Puerto Rico or Venezuela?

Since it wouldn't be true, you cannot say: **sí, señora** (see seng-yora) **o sí, señorita** (o see sengyoreeta) *Yes, madame or miss,* but you would admit very frankly: **todavía no** (tothaveea no) *not yet.* Or perhaps you might declare: **sí, señorita, un poco** (see sengyoreeta oon poko) *yes, miss, a little,* **hablo un poco** (avlo oon poko) *I speak a little.*

And if you have followed our pronunciation guide, it will not come as a surprise to you that the Spanish **v** and **b** are almost the same sound as the English *v.* That is a good rule, but, you know, the trouble with rules is that they always have exceptions. Therefore, although you should keep our rules in mind, you mustn't forget to look at our pronunciation-signs for quite a while yet.

S, s is always sharp no matter what its position in a word may be. **La casa** (kasa) *the house,* **el señor** (ell sengyor) *the gentleman.*

If you should ask me why a thing is pronounced in Spanish one way or another, you would embarrass me, because very often I couldn't answer you. I hope you'll *excuse me*—**¡perdone usted!** (perdonay oostayth).

If you find yourself *in a store,* **en una tienda** (enn oona teeaynda), you will only be able to guess what the salesman, **el vendedor** (ell venndaydor), *the employee*—**el dependiente** (ell daypenndyenntay—or if it is a girl, **la dependiente** (la daypenndyenntay), means in asking you,

¿Que se le ofrece a usted, señor? (kay say lay offressay a oostayth). You have probably guessed that this is, *What do you want?* or if we translate it literally, *What is offered you to you?*

You are not as yet able to answer this question, and so you will probably point to the items you are looking for. But then it is up to you to ask the question which seems the most important in any language: *How much is it?,* **¿cuánto es?** (kvannto ess).

It was *a handkerchief,* **un pañuelo** (oon pangyooaylo), *of silk,* **de seda** (de sayda), *of many colors,* **de muchos colores** (de moochos kolorays). And *the price*—**el precio** (ell praythyo)—is *two pesos*—**dos pesos** (doss paysos)—, but you discover you can't even count up to five. *Excuse me*—**perdone usted** (perrdonay oostayth)! It's all my fault. I allowed you to enter this store without even telling you the few numbers you have to know right at the beginning in order to be able to buy the little things you always need wherever you go.

¿Cuál es el precio? kval ess ell praythyo) *What is the price?*

Let us count then—¡contemos! (konnt*ay*moss)

1 un (oon) uno (oono)	7 siete (syaytay)
una (oona)	8 ocho (ocho)
2 dos (doss)	9 nueve (nooayvay)
3 tres (trays)	10 diez (deeayth)
4 cuatro (kvatro)	11 once (onnthay)
5 cinco (theengko)	12 doce (dothay)
6 Seis (sayees)	

The units of money in the various Spanish speaking countries are not the same. In many of the countries in South America, *the peso*—el peso (ell payso), is used. In Spain they count in *pesetas*—la peseta (la paysayta). When they speak of American money, they say el dólar (ell dolar) *the dollar*, los dólares (loss dolarays) *the dollars*. The English pound is la libra (la leebra), *the pounds* las libras (las leebras).

Some dollars are unos dólares (oonos dolarays), *some pesos*, unos pesos (oonos paysos), *some pesetas* unas pesetas (oonas paysaytas), *some pounds,* unas libras (oonas leebras).

One peso is un peso (oon payso), *two pesos* dos pesos (doss paysos), *three pesos* tres pesos (trays paysos). *The peseta* is feminine, therefore *one peseta,* una peseta (oona paysayta). And it is the same with the English pound. But from here on it is very easy, dos pesetas (doss paysaytas), dos libras (doss leebras), tres pesetas, cuatro dólares, cinco (theengko) pesetas, seis libras, siete pesos.

But this need not worry you too much, for wherever you spend money you will soon get accustomed to the currency, whether it is the *peso* in Argentina (arhenteena) the *Argentine Republic* or the *colon* in *Costa Rica* (kosta reeka), which, by the way, means *rich coast,* or the sucre (sookray) in Ecuador (aykvador) or the córdoba (kordova) in Nicaragua or the bolívar (boleevar) in Venezuela (vaynaythv*a*yla).

The main thing is *to have* good *money,* tener dinero (taynayr deenayro)—of any currency—and then you can be sure, you will be *all-right,* bien está (beeayn essta).

Make it a habit now whenever you see numbers up to twelve, to think of them in Spanish, and say them out aloud if you can do so without disturbing your neighbors: Uno, dos, tres, cuatro,

cinco, seis, siete, **ocho** (don't forget to pronounce **ocho**), **nueve,**
diez ($z =$ th), **once, doce** (ce $=$ thay).

I fully realize that you are accustomed to managing your affairs
on a larger scale, and later on you will be able to count in higher
numbers, in keeping with your usual style.

But for *to-day,* **hoy** (oee), I'll take my leave; not, however,
without saying to you

¡Hasta la vista!
asta la veesta
Till the sight, Till I see you again! or, as we put it:
Good bye!

¡Lea en alta voz!
laya enn alta voth

READ ALOUD

Los ángeles. Don Juan. Señorita, Puerto Rico. Juan, jugo,
jardin, jota, jinete, jefe, gente, general, gigante. Un ángel,
ángeles, jefe, una visión, una ilusión. Nación, zapata.

Señoras y caballeros. El ángel, los ángeles, el diablo, los diablos.
Damas y señores. ¿Qué tal? ¡Hola, hombre! ¡Buenas días, señor!
¡Buenos días, señora! ¡Buenos días, señorita! El día, los días, un
buen día. ¡buenos días! Si, señor. No, señor. ¡Buenos días,
señores! ¡Buenos días, señoras! ¡Buenos días, señoritas! El, la.
Una mesa, una silla. El día, los días, el vaso, los vasos, la mesa, las
mesas, la silla, las sillas. La tarde, buenas tardes. La noche, buenas
noches. ¡Buenas noches, señor!

Extranjeros. La lengua. Un cuarto, una tienda. Buenos dias,
buenas tardes, buenas noches. ¿Habla usted español? ¿Conoce
usted a España? ¿Conoce usted a Mexico o al Perú o a Puerto
Rico o a Venezuela? Si, señora, si, señorita. Todavía no. Si,
señorita, un poco, hablo un poco. ¡Perdone usted!

En una tienda, el vendedor, el dependiente, la dependiente. ¿Qué
se le ofrece a usted, señor? ¿Cuanto es? Un pañuelo, de seda, de
muchos colores, el precio, dos pesos. ¡Perdone usted! ¿Cuál es el
precio? ¡Contemos!

* 13 *

Lesson Four

No matter how many *illusions,* ilusiones (eeloosyonays), we may have, there is one fact we all realize, that, wherever we go, the first thing we investigate is whether we will have a roof over our head, to secure *a room,* un cuarto (oon kvarto), and, with that, something *to eat and drink,* comer y beber (komayr ee bayvayr).

If one cannot partake of a full-course *dinner,* una comida (oona komeeda), how refreshing it is to have at least *a cup of coffee,* una taza de café (oona tatha day kafay). Let us call *the waiter,* el camarero (ell kamarayro). We will just tell him briefly, since we cannot yet compose longer sentences:

¡Camarero,   un café con leche!
kamarayro   oongkafay kon laychay
Waiter,   *coffee with milk!*

Or do you prefer *black coffee,* un café negro (oongkafay naygro)?

From the tables around you perhaps you will be able to pick up what other people are saying to the waiter, as for instance

¿Tiene vino tinto?
teeaynay veeno teento
Have you wine colored? that is red wine?
¿Tiene cerveza?
teeaynay therrvaytha
Have you beer?

Give me—déme (daymay)

un vaso de cerveza   un vaso de vino
oon vaso thay therrvaytha   oon vaso thay veeno
a glass of beer   *a glass of wine*

una botella de vino
oona botellya thay veeno
a bottle of wine

Perhaps it is *a very hot day,* un día muy caluroso (oon deea mooy kalooroso), and *you are* very *warm,* usted tiene calor (oostayth teeaynay kalor). *You have warmth,* as it is expressed by the Spaniard. In any event, you are not in a mood for either *wine,* vino (veeno), *or,* o (o), *beer,* cerveza (therrvaytha), but you certainly would like some *pineapple juice,* jugo de piña (hoogo thay peenya) *juice of pineapple* or **una limonada** (oona leemonatha) *a (glass of) lemonade.*

By the way, **sea dicho de paso** (saya theecho thay paso), pineapple juice was first served in *South America,* **América del Sur** (amayreeka thell soor), and in the *West Indies,* **Antillas occidentales** (anteelyas oktheedentalays), before it came to *North America,* **América del Norte** (amayreeka thell nortay). A very Spanish drink is **la horchata** (la orrchata) *the orgeat,* a cool drink of almond milk, **el almendra** (ell almayndra) *the almond* water, *la almendra* (l'allmayndra), **el agua** (ell agva) *the water—and sugar*—**y azúcar** (ee athookar).

> **¿Qué toma usted?**
> kay toma oostayth
> *What do you take? or What will you have?*

Un café con leche (oongkafay con laychay) *coffee with milk* **o una horchata** (oona orrchata) *or orgeat* **o un jugo de piña** (o oon hoogo thay peenya) *or pineapple juice* **o un jugo de naranja** (o oon hoogo thay narangha) *or orange juice.*

¿Tiene usted ganas de comer algo?
teeaynay oostayth ganaz thay komayr algo
Have you wishes to eat something? Would you like to eat something?

> **¡Vamos a una fonda!**
> vamos a oona fonda
> *Let us go to a restaurant!*

*

tengo (tayngo) *I have*	**usted tiene** (oostayth teeaynay) *you have*
	¿Tiene usted? (teeaynay oostayth) *have you?*
tengo ganas (tayngo ganas) *I like*	**¿Tiene usted ganas?** (teeaynay oostayth ganas) *do you like?*
tomo (tomo) *I take*	**Usted toma** (oostayth toma) *you take*
	¿Toma usted? (toma oostayth) *do you take?*

¿Toma usted azúcar? (toma oostayth athookar) *Do you take sugar?*

¡Gracias, señora! (grathyas sengyora) *Thank you, madame!*
uso (ooso) *I use*   ¿usa usted? (oosa oostayth) *do you use?*
¿Usa usted azúcar? (oosa oostayth athookar) *Do you use sugar?*

*Do you want
sugar?*

*Do you take
sugar?*

Let us suppose that you were in a spending mood while you were in *the café*. El café (ell kafay) is the *coffee* and the *place* where *coffee* is the *main drink* served. Maybe some members of your family, la familia (la fameelya) *the family*, were with you; *the father*, el padre (ell pathray), *the mother*, la madre (la mathray) *the aunt*, la tía (la teea), and *the uncle*, el tío (ell teeo), *the brother*, el hermano (ell errmano) and *the sister*, la hermana (la errmana). You treated all of them to a *drink*, una bebida (oona bayveetha) and *a good dish*, un buen plato (oombooem plato). After all this, you are ready to leave and you say,

Words ending in a, e, i, o, u, or n, s are accentuated on the penult, the next to the last syllable, el padre (ell (pathray) *the father*; el hermano (ell errmano) *the brother*; la imahen (la eemahayn) *the picture*; Carlos (karloss) *Charles*. If a word is not accented on the penult the a c c e n t mark shows which syllable is to be stressed también (tammbyayng) *also*; ahí (aee) *here*.

¡Camarero, la cuenta!
kamarayro la kvennta
Waiter, the check (the bill)!

¿Cuánto es? (kvanto ess) *How much is it?*
16 pesos   dieciséis pesos (deeaytheesayees paysos)

Perhaps you understood him. You might have remembered that diez (deeayth) is *ten* and seis (sayees) is *six*. But to make absolutely sure,

¡Haga el favor de contar hasta veinte!
aga ell favor thay kontar asta vayeentay
Please   count up to twenty!   literally,
Make the favor to count

si usted gusta (see oostayth goosta) *if you please!*

¡Cuente usted hasta veinte!
kvenntay oostayth asta vayeentay
Count   up to twenty!

* 16 *

uno	dos	tres	cuatro	cinco	seis	ocho	nueve
oono	doss	trays	kvatro	thingko	sayees	ocho	nooayvay
1	*2*	*3*	*4*	*5*	*6*	*8*	*9*

diez	once	doce	trece	catorce	quince
deeayth	onthay	dothay	traythay	katorthay	kinthay
10	*11*	*12*	*13*	*14*	*15*

dieciséis	diecisiete	dieciocho
deeaytheesayees	deeaytheesyaytay	deeaytheeocho
16	*17*	*18*

diecinueve	veinte
deeaytheenooayvay	vayeentay
19	*20*

¡Muy bien, amigo!
mooy beeayn ameego
Very well, (my) friend!

But why did you forget 7 *seven*, siete (seeaytay)? I'll tell you. *Sometimes*, á veces (a vaythays), it is a lucky number. Bastante (bastantay) *enough!* ¿Qué tal? (kay tal) *How are you?* Bien, muy bien, señor. (beeayn, mooy beeayn sengyor), *Good, very well!* ¿Y usted? (ee oostayth) *And you?* ¡Mil gracias! (meel grathyas) *A thousand thanks*, muy bien (mooy beeayn) *very well.*

¡Hasta la vista!
asta la veesta
Good bye!

Translate into Spanish

The angels, Sir John, Miss, harbor rich, John, juice, garden, horseman, chief or boss, people, general, giant. An angel, angels, a vision, an illusion, nation, shoe. Ladies and gentlemen. One angel, angels. The angel, the angels, the devil, the devils. How do you do? How are you? Hello, man (Hello, my boy—). Good morning, sir! Good morning, madame! Good morning, young lady! The young lady. The days, a good day, good days. Yes, sir! No, sir! Good morning, gentlemen! Good morning, ladies! Good morning, young ladies! A table, a chair, the day, the days, the glass, the glasses, the table, the tables, the chair, the chairs. The afternoon. Good afternoon! The night, good evening, good night.

Lesson Five

One of the reasons why we are so interested in going to a foreign country is that we want to come in contact with something new, something unknown. This may be *the people*—la gente (la hayntay), or *the country,* el país (ell paees), itself. And we like to pretend, even if only to ourselves, that *for a little while,* un poco de tiempo (oom poko thay teeaympo) *a little of time,* we are like *a king*—un rey (oon ray), *a duke,* un duque (oon dookay) or *a count,* un conde (oongkonday), traveling incognito in a foreign land.

The plural ending of nouns is s. Nouns ending on a consonant take the ending -es, el señor (ell sengyor), los señores (loss sengyorays); el rey (ell ray), los reyes (loss rayays) *the king, the kings.* Nouns ending in z change from z to c to form the plural: una vez (oona vayth) *once;* dos veces (doss vaythays) *twice.*

But we will soon see that we cannot go very far without giving our *name,* un nombre (nommbray). We must get involved, whether we like it or not, with some kind of red tape. There is *the passport,* el pasaporte (ell pasaportay); there is *a check,* un cheque (oon chaykay) or a *registered letter,* una carta certificada (oona karta therrteefeekatha). For any of these things we have to answer the question *What is your name?* ¿Cómo se llama usted? (komo say lyama oostayth) *How do you call yourself?*

A name, un nombre (oon hommbray), is the very least that a person must keep in mind, and it is the thing he knows best how to write. That is very important to know for *the signature* —la firma (la feerma). But it is not always enough, for very often one is obliged *to spell,* deletrear (daylaytrayar), the name.

Thus, it would be very embarrassing if we did not know the Spanish *A-B-C,* el alfabeto (ell alfabayto). Knowing the names of the Spanish letters, many difficulties of the pronunciation will disappear.

La primera letra es a A (la preemayra laytra ess a) *the first letter is a.*

La segunda letra es b B (la saygoonda laytra ess bay) *the second letter is b.*

La tercera letra es c C (la terrthayra laytra ess thay) *the third letter is c.*

La cuarta letra es d D (la kvarta laytra ess day) *the fourth letter is d.*

La quinta letra es e, E (la keenta laytra ess ay) *the fifth letter is e.*

The Spanish alphabet has a few letters more than the English. These *thirty,* **treinta** (trayeenta), *letters,* **letras** (laytras), are:

a	called	a	pronounced as		in *art*
b	"	bay	"	"	in *boy*
c	"	thay	"	"	unvoiced th before e and i, otherwise like k
ch	"	chay	"	"	in *church*
d	"	day	"	like d	
e	"	ay	"	"	ay as in *day*
f	"	effay	"	"	f
g	"	hay	"	"	gurgling h as in *h(ouse)* before e and i, otherwise like g as in *gift*
h	"	athay	not pronounced at all		
i	"	ee	pronounced like ee in eel		
j	"	hota	"	"	h in house, but gurgling
k	"	ka	"	"	k
l	"	ellay	"	"	l
ll	"	ellyai	"	"	ly as l in value
m	"	emmay	"	"	m
n	"	ennay	"	"	n
ñ	"	ennyai	"	"	ny as (u)n-i(on)
o	"	o	"	"	o in the alphabet or 0 at the telephone
p	"	pay	"	"	p
q	"	koo	"	"	k
r	"	ayray	"	"	r, but rolling and dramatic
rr	"	erray	"	"	rr, but rolling and dramatic
s	"	essay	"	"	s, always *sharp* as in *s(ay)*
t	"	tay	"	"	t, but softer
u	"	oo	"	"	oo as in *(f)oo(l)*
v	"	vay	"	"	v as in *v(olume)*
x	"	ekkis	"	"	x as in *(e)x(ile)*
y	"	ee greeayga	"	"	y as in *year* or seldom ee as in *eel*
z	"	thayta	"	"	like unvoiced th as in *th(ief),* *(th)under*

By and by you will know *the Spanish A-B-C,* **el abecedario español** (ell abaythaydaryo), very well and there will be no difficulty in using it. If your first *name,* **nombre** (nommbray) is *Elisabeth,* you will *spell,* **deletrear** (daylaytrayar), it in Spanish:

E -l -i -s -a-b -e -t -h
ay-ellay-ee-essay-a-bay-ay-tay-achay

¿Cómo se llama Vd. (usted)?	**Me llamo Pedro**
komo say lyama oostayth	may lyamo paythro
What is your name?	*Me I call Peter (I call myself Peter)*
Llamo (lyamo) *I call*	**llama Vd. (usted)** (lyama oostayth) *do you call*

Vd. se llama (oostayth say lyama) *you call yourself*
me llamo (may lyamo) *I call myself*
¡Deletree su nombre! (daylaytrayay soo nommbray) *Spell your name!*

P - e - d - r - o
pay-ay-day-ayray-o

Miss Elisabeth is **Doña Elisabeth** (donnya ayleezavayt) and *Mr. Pedro (Peter)* is **Don Pedro** (donn paythro).

Don and **Doña** are to be prefixed only to the Christian names, **nombres** (nommbrays), to *the surname,* **el apellido** (ell apelyeedo), prefix **Señor, señora, señorita,** *Mr., Mrs., Miss.*

Me llamo Pedro Pérez (may lyamo paythro payrayth) *My name is Mr. Pedro Perez.*
Mi apellido es Pérez (mee apelyeedo ess payrayth) *My surname is Perez.*

P - e - r - e - z
pay-ay-ayray-ay-thayta

It makes a very nice game to try to spell the signs you see along *the street,* **la calle** (la kalyay). Then for a change you can read *the numbers of the houses,* **los números de las casas** (loss noomayroz thay las kasas). **La primera casa tiene el número uno** (la preemayra kasa teeaynay ell noomayro oono) *the first house has the number one, the number of the first house is one.*

But what about this one, **Calle Victoria 21?**

* 20 *

—¡Qué	calor	hace!	Tengo calor
kay	kalor	athay	tayngo kalor
How	*hot*	*it is!*	*I am warm.*

—Yo	también.	¡Qué	novidad!
yo	tambeeayn	kay	noveedad
I	*too.*	*What*	*news?*

That's not difficult at all. You remember how to say the *number 20,* el número veinte (ell noomayro vayeentay), and you remember that *1* is uno (oono). Then you know *at once,* de una vez (day oona vayth), that *twenty-one* is veinte y uno (vayeentay ee oono) *twenty and one.*

21	veinte y uno	(vayeentay ee oono)
22	veinte y dos	" " doss)
23	veinte y tres	" " trays)
24	veinte y cuatro	
25	veinte y cinco	

26 veinte y seis
27 veinte y siete
28 veinte y ocho
29 veinte y nueve
30 treinta (trayeenta)

And now you can ask anybody on the street

¿Dónde está la calle de la Concordia 34?
   donnday essta la kalyay thay la konnkoordya trayeenta ee kvatro
   Where is street of the concord 34? Where is 34 Concord Street?

Diez minutos de aquí.
deeayth meenootoz thay akee.
Ten minutes from here.

Vaya Vd. (usted) dos calles a la derecha después una calle a la izquierda.
vaya oostayth thoss kalyays a la dayrecha thespooess oona kalyay alla eethkyerrtha
Go two streets to the right and then one street to the left.

Una cuadra (oona kvathra) *one block*, dos cuadras (doss kvathras) *two blocks*. Dos cuadras a la derecha (doss kvathras a la dayrecha), dos cuadras a la izquierda (doss kvathras a la eethkyerrtha) *two blocks to the right, two blocks to the left.*

Very often one of the very polite Spaniards will offer to guide you. And you, even more polite, will say "Please, don't trouble yourself." Don't you wish you knew how? I'll tell you.

¡No se moleste! (no say molaystay) or ¡No se incomode! (no say eenkomothay) *Don't trouble yourself!*

Perhaps he will say to you:

¡Vaya Vd. con dios, señorita!
vaya oostayth konn dyoss sengyoreeta
Go with God, my lady!

And you think: This fellow is *all right*—muy bueno (mooy booayno)

You found the way to your friend's home very easily. You enter *the house of your friend,* la casa del amigo (la kasa dell ameego) or *la casa de la amiga* (la kasa della ameega) and

* 22 *

you ask, **¿Cómo está Vd.?** (komo eesta oostayth) *How are you?* **¿Cómo está la familia?** (komo essta la fameelya) *How is the family?* **¿Cómo están en casa?** (komo esstan enn kasa) *How are they all in the house?* **¡Bien, gracias!** (beeayn grathyas) *Well, thanks!* **¿Y Vd.?** (ee oostayth) *And you?*

¡Qué calor hace! (kay kalor athay) *What a heat it makes! How hot it is!*

¿Una orchata (oona orchata)? *An orgeat,* that's a good idea.

¿Quiere Vd. beber? (kyayray oostayth bayvayr) *Will you (have a) drink?*

¡Sí, seguramente! (see saygooramente) *Yes, certainly!*

Now I'll leave you with your friend. But don't forget *the letters,* **las letras** (las laytras), and *the numbers,* **los números** (loss noomayros) *up to thirty-nine—***hasta treinta y nueve** (asta trayeenta ee nooayvay).

The Spanish accent mark shows y o u which sound is to be emphasized in speaking. Some words are written both with and without accents in order to show the difference in t h e i r meaning; **más** = *more,* **mas** = *but.* **¿Qué?** = *what?;* **que** = *that, than, which.*

¡Hasta la vista!
asta la veesta
Good bye!

¡Lea en alta voz!
laya   enn   alta   voth
READ ALOUD

Un, uno, una,—dos, tres, cuatro, cinco, seis, siete, ocho, nueve, diez, once, doce. El peso, la peseta. El dolar, los dolares, la libra, las libras, unos dolares, unos pesos, unas pesetas, unas libras. Un peso, dos pesos, tres pesos. Una peseta, dos pesetas, dos libras, tres pesetas, cuatro dolares, cinco pesetas, seis libras, siete pesos.

Argentina, Costa Rica, sucre, Ecuador, cordoba, bolivar, Venezuela. Tener dinero. Bien esta. Hoy. ¡Hasta la vista!

Ilusiones, un cuarto, comer y beber, una taza de café, el camarero. ¡Camarero, un café con leche! Un café negro. ¿Tiene vino tinto? ¿Tiene cerveza? Deme un vaso de cerveza, un vaso de vino, una botella de vino.

Un día muy caluroso, usted tiene calor. Vino, cerveza, jugo de piña or una limonada. Sea dicho de paso.

Lesson Six

If you have nothing else to do and *you have money*, **Vd. tiene dinero** (oostay teeaynay deenayro), what a pleasure it is to go shopping, to go *to a store*, **a una tienda** (a oona teeaynda).

The other day, **ha poco** (a poko) = **hace poco** (athay poko), we bought *a many-colored handkerchief of silk*, **un pañuelo de seda de muchos colores** (oon pangyooaylo they sayda thay moochos kolorays), and you took that opportunity to notice that the Spanish *"de"* corresponds to our English *"of."* **El sombrero** (ell sommbrayro) is *the hat*, and *a felt hat* is *a hat of felt*, **un sombrero de fieltro** (oon sommbrayro thay feeayltro) ; a straw hat, which you need very badly in these southern districts, is **un sombrero de paja** (oon sommbrayro day paha), *a hat of straw* (by the way this "aw" in "straw" is like the Spanish sound o, as it is frequently pronounced.)

The hats, **los sombreros** (loss sommbrayros) are for both ladies and gentlemen, and

> **Hay sombreros de muchos colores para señoras y señores**
> **aee** sommbrayroz thay moochos kolorays para sengyoras
> ee sengyorays
> *There are hats of many colors for ladies and gentlemen.*

But to win the good-will of all my lady readers, I want to introduce them to items which only they use. *For instance*—**por ejemplo** (porr ehemmplo): *the hand-bag*, **el bolso de mano** (ell bollso thay mano), and let us not forget *the mirror*, **el espejo** (ell espayho) which, I am told, means more than food *to a lady*, **a una señora o a una señorita** (a oona sengyora o a oona sengyoreeta). For this reason one of the greatest inven-

Feminine words beginning with an **accentuated** a or ha, are used with masculine articles. **El agua** (ell agva) *the water;* **el hambre** (ell ammbray) *the hunger;* but **la amiga** (la ameega) *the friend* f. (beginning with an **unaccentuated** a).

tions of all time is *the pocket mirror*, **el espejo de bolsillo** (ell espayho thay bollseellyo). This word will be no *riddle*, **adivinanza** (atheeveenantha), when I tell you that **el bolsillo** (ell bollseellyo) is *the pocket*, **los bolsillos** (loss bollseellyos) *the pockets* and **espejo** (espayho), of course, is *mirror*, therefore **el espejo de bolsillo** is *the pocket mirror.*

* 24 *

When you are looking for *a hat,* **un sombrero** (oon somm-brayro), or *a blouse,* **una blusa** (oona bloosa), or *stockings,* **medias** (maydeeas), or for *a shirt,* **una camisa** (oona kameesa), *the color of the hat,* **el color del sombrero** (ell kolor dell sommbrayro), *the color of the shirt,* **el color de la camisa** (ell kolor thay la kameesa), etc., will be an important consideration.

el sombrero	ell sommbrayro	*the hat*
del sombrero	dell sommbrayro	*of the hat*
los sombreros	loss sommbrayros	*the hats*
de los sombreros	day loss sommbrayros	*of the hats*
la camisa	la kameesa	*the shirt*
de la camisa	day la kameesa	*of the shirt*
las camisas	las kameesas	*the shirts*
de las camisas	day las kameesas	*of the shirts*
el señor	ell sengyor	*the gentleman, sir*
del señor	dell sengyor	*of the gentleman, sir*
los señores	loss sengyorays	*the gentlemen, sirs*
de los señores	day loss sengyorays	*of the gentlemen, sirs*
la señora	la sengyora	*the lady*
de la señora	day la sengyoras	*of the lady*
las señoras	las sengyoras	*the ladies*
de las señoras	day las sengyoras	*of the ladies*

Déme un sombrero negro.
daymay oon sommbrayro
  naygro
Give me a black hat.

Déme una camisa blanca.
daymay oona kameesa blanka
Give me a white shirt.

If you are going to a very sunny country, I am quite sure, *ladies and gentlemen,* **señoras y caballeros** (sengyoras ee ka-vallyayros), that you will prefer *hats with large brims,* **sombreros de ala ancha** (sommbrayroz thay ala ancha), to *hats with small brims*—**sombreros de ala angosta** (sommbrayroz thay ala angosta).

Mi sombrero es negro (mee sommbrayro ess naygro), **tu sombrero es blanco** (too sommbrayro ess blanko), **su sombrero es marrón** (soo sommbrayro ess marron), *my hat is black, your hat is white, his or her hat is brown.*

Mis guantes son amarillos,	**mis camisas son azules.**
mees gvantays sonn amareellyos,	mees kameesas sonn athoolays
My gloves are yellow,	*my shirts are blue.*
Tus guantes son marrones,	**tus camisas son blancas.**
toos gvantays sonn marronays,	toos kameesas sonn blankas
Your gloves are brown,	*your shirts are white.*
Sus guantes son rojos,	**sus camisas son negras.**
soos gvantais sonn rohoss,	soos kameesas sonn naygras
His, her, their/gloves are red,	*his, her, their/shirts are black.*
/ *and your*/	/*and your*/

mi	**mis**	**tu**	**tus**	**su**	**sus**
mee	mees	too	toos	soo	soos
/		/		/	
my		*your*		*his, her, their* and *your*	

Esta mujer tiene una blusa blanca, tiene la cara morena, es muy hermosa y muy amable (aysta moohayr teeaynay oona bloosa blanka teeaynay la kara morayna ess mooy errmosa ee mooy amavlay), *this woman has a white blouse; (her face is dark brown) she has a brunette complexion; she is very beautiful and very amiable.*

We have heard so much of the beauty and the charm of Spanish women, **estas mujeres** (aystas moohayrays), *these women with their black veils,* **con el velo negro** (konn ell vaylo naygro), which fall over *the forehead,* **la frente** (la frenntay). It is a picture, *a painting,* **un cuadro** (oon kvathro), which, once seen, you will never forget: *these ladies and girls,* **estas señoras y señoritas** (aystas sengyoras ee sengyoreetas), coming from *church,* **iglesia** (eeglaysya), or a *cathedral,* **catedral** (kattaythral), *with the large veil,* **con la mantilla** (kon la mannteellya) as this veil is called, flowing down from a large *comb,* **el peine** (ell payeenay), in the hair. Only *strangers,* **los extranjeros** (loss aystranhayross), wear hats.

¿Es Vd. español? (ays oostayth ayspangyol) *Are you a Spaniard?*

¿Es Vd. española? (ays oostayth ayspangyola) (*to a lady*)

No, señor, soy de Nueva York.
no sengyor, soee thay nooayva york
No, sir, I am from New York.

Yo soy americano, mi amigos también.
yo soee amayreekano mee ameegoss tammbyenn
I am American; my friends also.

¿Y ustedes? Nosotros somos todos ingleses.
ee oostaythays? nosotross sommoss tothoss eenglaysays
And you? We are all Englishmen.

ser (sayrr)—*to be* **soy** (soee) *I am*
                        eres (ayrays) *you are (familiar)*
                        es (ess) *he is, she is*
                        Vd. es (oostayth ess) *you are*
                        somos (sommoss) *we are*
                        sois (soees) *you are*
                        son (sonn) *they are*

Does Spanish never use our personal pronouns I, you, etc.?
Yes, it does, in order to emphasize the person meant, or when
addressing somebody in the formal way. It is well to keep in
mind that this is the way to address a native Spaniard if one is not
very well acquainted with him.

These personal pronouns are:

yo (yo) **tú** (too) **él** (ayl) **Vd., usted** (oostayth) **ella** (ellya)
I   *you* (very *he*   *you*   *she*
        fam. form)

nosotros (nosotross) **vosotros** (vosotross) **ellos** (ellyoss)
we   *you* (familiar form *they* (masculine)
                       used when addressing
                       many people)

ellas (ellyas) **Vds., ustedes** (oostaythays)
they (feminine) *you* (when addressing several persons)

This word "usted" has an interesting history. You have often
heard people speak of the famous Spanish court which set the
fashion for all courts over a period of
centuries. Almost every action was
strictly formalized and the courtesy that
is discussed so much even in these modern times has come down to us through
the customs cultivated to their highest degree by the Spanish court
when Spanish kings ruled the world. It is from this time on that

All interrogative words
(questioning) are accent-
ed; **¿qué?** (kay) =
what? **¿Cómo?** (komo)
= *how?* **¿Dónde?**
(donnday) = *where?*

people who were not well-known were addressed by **usted** (abbreviated **Vd.**) or if more than one, **ustedes** (abbreviated to **Vds.**). The word "usted" stands for **vuestra merced** (vooaystra merrthayth) and the translation of this phase would be the old English title *"Your Grace," "Your honor."*

So we can understand why with **usted** (or the plural form **ustedes**), *Your Grace* or *Your Graces,* we use the third person and why this form it is not always used.

The personal nouns are not needed so much in Spanish because the endings of the verb show what person is meant. But when we wish to emphasize the person we mean, we say:

yo tengo (yo tenngo)	*I have*
tú tienes (too teeaynays)	*you have* (familiar)
él tiene (ell teeaynay)	*he has*
ella tiene (ellya teeaynay)	*she has*
	(it has)
Vd. tiene (oostayth teeaynay)	*you have*
nosotros tenemos (nosotross taynaymoss)	*we have*
vosotros tenéis (vosotross taynayees)	*you have* (fam.)
ellos tienen (ellyos teeaynayn)	*they have* m.
ellas tienen (ellyas teeaynayn)	*they have* f.
Vds. tienen (oostaydays teeaynayn)	*you have* (to several persons).

There is hardly anyone who is not at least a little curious. It is only a question of how well we are able to control our curiosity. We all know people who are always asking us questions, with one question coming after another, like a shower we cannot avoid. Fortunately, these very inquisitive people ask a second question without waiting for a reply to the first. And there is nothing to be done about it. You must simply be patient.

People of this kind fall into different types. Have you never met Mr. or Mrs. "Where—is—it?" or Mr. or Mrs. "Who—is—it"? They are *always,* **siempre** (syemmpray), looking for something or at something; *every few minutes,* **cada cinco minutos** (katha theengko meenootoss), they turn to something else.

Everyone in the house, **todos en casa** (tothoss enn kasa)—is approached. Whether it is just *a pencil* they need—**un lápiz** (oon lapeeth) or *a pen,* **una pluma** (oona plooma), or *a fountain pen,* **una pluma fuente** (oona plooma fooenntay), we see them des-

* 28 *

perately looking around: *Where is it?*—¿Dónde está eso? (donn-day aysta esso).

¿Donde está mi lápiz, mi pluma, mi pluma fuente?
donnday essta mee lapeeth, mee plooma, mee plooma fooenntay.
Where is my pencil, my pen, my fountain pen?

And *a second later,* y un segundo más tarde (ee oon say-goondo mas tarrthay), they can't find any *paper,* papel (pa-**payl**), to write on. *Where is the paper?*—¿Dónde está el papel? (donnday essta ell papell). ¿Dónde hay papel? (donnday aee papel) *Where is some paper?* Hay = *there is.*

I think *it is late,* es tarde (ays tarrthay). We shall end *our lesson,* nuestra lección (nooaystra lekkthyong).

¿Qué hora es? (kay ora ess)—*what time is it?*

Es la una (ess la oona), *it is one o'clock.* **No, son las tres** (no sonn las trays), *no, it is three o'clock.* **Son las cuatro** (sonn las kvatro), *4 o'clock;* **son las cinco** (sonn las theengko)—*5 o'clock.*

¡Vamos a dar un paseo por Buenos Aires!
vamoss a dar oon pasayo porr booaynoss aeerays
Let us take a walk through Buenos Aires!

ℒea en alta voz!
laya   enn   alta   voth

READ ALOUD

¿Tiene usted ganas de comer algo? ¡Vamos a una fonda! Tengo, usted tiene. ¿Tiene usted? Tengo ganas. ¿Tiene usted ganas? Tomo, usted toma, ¿toma usted? ¿Toma usted azúcar? ¡Gracias, senora! Uso ¿Usa usted azúcar?

El café, la familia, el padre, la madre, la tía, el tío, el hermano, la hermana, una bebida, un buen plato. ¡Camarero, la cuenta! ¿Cuanto es? Dieciseis pesos. ¡Haga el favor de contar hasta veinte! Si usted gusta. ¡Cuente usted hasta veinte!

Uno, dos, tres, cuatro, cinco, seis, ocho, nueve, diez, once, doce, trece, catorce, quince, dieciseis, diecisiete, dieciocho, diecinueve, veinte. ¡Muy bien, amigo! Siete, á veces. Bastante. ¿Qué tal?

Translate into Spanish

Foreigners. The language. A room, a store. Good morning, good afternoon, good evening, good night. Do you speak Spanish? Do you know Spain? Do you know Mexico or Peru or Puerto Rico or Venezuela? Yes, madame or miss. Not yet. Yes, miss, a little. I speak a little. Excuse me!

In a store, the employee. What do you want? How much is it? A handkerchief of silk, of many colors. The price, two pesos. What is the price? Let us count!

1, 2, 3, 4, 5, 6, 7, 8, 9, 10, 11, 12. The peso, the peseta, the dollar, the dollars, pound, the pounds, some dollars, some pesos, some pesetas, some pounds, one peso, two pesos, three pesos.

The Argentine Republic, Costa Rica, to have money, all right. Today. Good bye!

Illusions, a room, to eat and drink, a dinner, a cup of coffee, the waiter. Waiter, coffee with milk! Black coffee. Have you red wine? Have you beer? Give me a glass of beer, a glass of wine, a bottle of wine.

A very hot day, you are warm, wine, beer, pineapple juice or a (glass of) lemonade. By the way, South America, West Indies, North America, the orgeat, the almond, the water and sugar. What do you take? Or what will you have? Coffee with milk or orgeat or pineapple juice or orange juice.

Would you like to eat something? Let us go to a restaurant! I have, you have, have you? I like. Do you like? I take, you take. Do you take? Do you take sugar? Thank you, madame! I use. Do you use? Do you use sugar? Do you want sugar? Do you take sugar?

The café, the family, the father, the mother, the aunt, the uncle, the brother, the sister, a drink, a good dish. Waiter, the check (the bill)! How much is it? 16 pesos. Ten, six. Please count up to twenty. If you please! Count up to twenty! 1, 2, 3, 4, 5, 6, 8, 9, 10, 11, 12, 13, 14, 15, 16, 17, 18, 19, 20. Very well, my friend. 7. Sometimes. Enough. How are you? Good, very well. And you? A thousand thanks, very well! Good bye!

¡Haga el favor de repetir!

aga	ell	favor	thay	raypayteer
have	*the*	*favor*	*to*	*repeat*
		Please repeat.		

Review

los ángeles	loss anghelays	*the angels*
señorita	sengyoreeta	*miss*
jugo	hoogo	*juice*
jardín	hartheen	*garden*
jefe	hayfay	*chief, boss*
gente	hentay	*people*
general	haynayral	*general*
un ángel	oon anghayl	*an angel*
una ilusión	oona eeloosyong	*an illusion*
nación	nathyong	*nation*
zapato	thapato	*shoe*
señoras y caballeros	sengyoras ee kaval-yayros	*ladies and gentle-men*
el diablo	ell deeavlo	*the devil*
¡Buenos días, señor!	booaynoss deeas senyor	*Good morning, sir!*
el día	ell deea	*the day*
los días	loss deeas	*the days*
si, señor	see sengyor	*yes, sir*
no, señor	no sengyor	*no, sir*
una mesa	oona maysa	*a table*
una silla	oona seelya	*a chair*
el vaso	ell vaso	*the glass*
la tarde	la tarthay	*the afternoon*
la noche	la nochay	*the night*
la lengua	la lengwa	*the language*
un cuarto	oon kvarto	*a room*
una tienda	oona teeaynda	*a store*
¿Habla usted español?	avla oostayth ayspanyol	*Do you speak Spanish?*
¿Conoce usted a España?	konothay oostayth a ayspanya	*Do you know Spain?*
todavía no	tothaveea no	*not yet*
¡Perdone usted!	perdonay oostayth	*Excuse me!*
a una tienda	a oona teeaynda	*in a store*
el vendedor	ell venndaydor	*the salesman*
el dependiente	ell daypenndyayn-tay	*the employee (male)*

la dependiente	la daypenndyayn-tay	*the employee* (female)
¿Qué se le ofrece a usted, señor?	kay say lay ofressay a oostayth sengyor	*What do you want?*
¿Cuanto es?	kvannto ess	*How much is it?*
un pañuelo	oon panyooaylo	*a handkerchief*
de seda	day saytha	*of silk*
de muchos colores	day moochos kolorays	*of many colours*
¿Cuál es el precio?	kval es ell praythyo	*What is the price?*
¡Contemos!	konntaymoss	*Let us count!*
el peso	ell payso	*the peso*
el dólar	ell dolar	*the dollar*
unos dólares	oonos dolarays	*some dollars*
unas pesetas	oonas paysaytas	*some pesetas*
bien está	beeayng essta	*all-right*
tener dinero	taynayr deenayro	*to have money*
hoy	oee	*today*
¡Hasta la vista!	asta la veesta	*Good bye!*
comer y beber	komayr ee bayvayr	*to eat and drink*
una comida	oona komeetha	*a dinner*
una taza de café	oona tatha thay kafay	*a cup of coffee*
¡Camarero, un café con leche!	kamarayro oongkafay kon laytshay	*Waiter, coffee with milk!*
un café negro	oongkafay naygro	*black coffee*
¿Tiene vino tinto?	teeaynay veeno teento	*Have you red wine?*
¿Tiene cerveza?	teeaynay therrvaytha	*Have you beer?*
déme!	daymay	*give me!*
un vaso de cerveza	oon vaso thay therrvaytha	*a glass of beer*
una botella de vino	oona botellya thay veeno	*a bottle of wine*
un día muy caluroso	oon deea mooy kalooroso	*a very hot day*
jugo de piña	hoogo thay peenya	*pineapple juice*
una limonada	oona leemonatha	*a (glass of) lemonade*
sea dicho de paso	saya theecho thay paso	*by the way*
América del Sur	amayreeka thell soor	*South America*
Antillas occidentales	anteelyas oktheedentalays	*West Indies*
América del Norte	amayreeka thell nortay	*North America*

1000 Words

SPANISH

¿Dónde están mis botones?
donday esstan mees botonays
Where are my buttons?

Lesson Seven

My uncle, **mi tío** (me teeo) (I will never forget him) was always looking around for his *collar,* **el cuello** (kwellyo), for his *necktie,* **la corbata** (la korrvata), his *buttons,* **los botones** (loss bottonays). He would look *on the table*—**sobre la mesa** (sobray la maysa), *under the table,* debajo de la mesa (day-baho thay la maysa), *in the wardrobe*—en el armario (enn ell armareeo).

> ¿Dónde está su cuello, su corbata?
> donnday essta soo kwellyo, soo korrvata
> *Where is his collar, his necktie?* (also *your collar, your necktie*)
> ¿Dónde están sus botones?
> donnday aystán soos botonays
> *Where are his buttons?*

And it usually happened at *a critical moment*—en un momento crítico (enn oon momennto kreeteeko), when the whole family was waiting to pay an important visit which had to be made *on time*—a tiempo (a tyaympo). It was difficult not to get excited. No wonder we tried to find a remedy. We bought *a dozen shirts*—una docena de camisas (oona dothayna thay kameesas), *with collars and cuffs*—con cuellos y puños (konn kwellyoss ee poonyoss), attached, so that the possibility of having to go searching for the buttons and collars would not come up again.

So we thought! But the result was entirely different. The next time we were ready to go out, my uncle shouted all over the house:

> ¿Quién tiene mis camisas?
> kyayn teeaynay mees kameesas
> *Who has my shirts?*

> ¿Dónde está mi camisa nueva?
> donnday essta mee kameesa nooayva
> *Where is my new shirt?*

And exploration for the shirt began anew, de nuevo (day nooayvo). *I tell you,* le digo a Vd. (lay deego a oostayth)—*we had a fine time*—nos divertimos mucho (nos deeverrteemoss moocho). Compared with *my uncle,* mi tío (mee teeo), *that aunt of ours,* aquella tía nuestra (akellya teea nooaystra), did not mean much. She searched for her *eyeglasses,* los lentes (loss lenntays), *six or eight times a day,* de seis hasta ocho veces al día (day sayees asta ocho vaythays al deea).

Most Spanish adjectives end in o in the masculine form, in a in the feminine form, and in the plural form in -os or -as.

una vez (oona vayth) *once* de una vez (day oona vayth) *at once*

dos veces (doss vaythays) a la vez (a la vayth) *by turns,*

tres veces (trais vaythays) *three times*

cuatro veces (kvatro vaythays) *four times*

and so forth—etcétera (aytthaytera)

cada vez (katha vayth) *each time*

más de una vez (maz thay oona vayth) *more than once, frequently*

tal vez (tal vayth) *perhaps* a veces (a vaythays) *sometimes*

We talked a good deal about our *uncle* and our *aunt,* los tíos (loss teeoss), they were so amusing. But we must not forget that *there is,* hay (aee), *something,* alguna cosa (algoona kosa), of this in every one of us. How often are *parents,* los padres (loss pathrays), bothered by the overflow of *questions from children,* las preguntas de los hijos (las praygoontas thay loss eehoss), and even *the grandfather,* el abuelo (ell avooaylo), and *the grandmother,* la abuela (la avooayla), *the grandparents,* los abuelos (loss avooayloss), *sometimes,* a veces (a vaythays), *lose patience,* la paciencia (la pathyaynthya).

But besides the unnecessary questions, there are, *without doubt,* sin duda (seen dooda), many which are absolutely necessary ones and without which we could not get along.

Especially in a foreign country must we know about *where—* ¿dónde? (donnday), and *how—*¿como? (komo)—and *who—* ¿quién? (kyayng). When we see something new, are we not curious to know what it is? ¿Qué es eso? (kay ess esso)—*what is that?* ¿Qué hay? (kay aee)—*what is the matter?* ¿Para qué sirve esto? (para kay seerrvay aysto)—*what is it for?* (Literally: *for what serves this?*)

We ask, preguntamos (praygoontamoss) *a gentleman,* a un señor (a oon sengyor) or *a lady,* a una señora o a una señorita (a oona sengyora o a oona sengyoreeta). And the gentleman or the lady *answers,* contesta (konntaysta).

I ask a lady *the lady answers me*

pregunto a una señora la señora me contesta

praygoonto a oona sengyora la sengyora may koontaysta

Even without our mentioning it, you have probably noticed that the Spanish **a** is the English *to*. We say, *The brother has given a present to the sister*. In Spanish that would be: **el hermano ha dado un regalo a la hermana** (ell errmano a thatho oon raygalo a la errmana). This English *to* and likewise this Spanish **a** are important in pointing the direction; that is, indicating toward whom or toward what a person or a thing is moved. There is only one difference with regard to the use of **a** in Spanish when speaking of persons and countries: this is in the objective (accusative) form, where *to* is not used in English. We know the Accusative in English is always the same as the Nominative, just as it is in Spanish where things are concerned. But where persons and countries are concerned, the Dative and Accusative are alike in Spanish, as you may see in the following lines.

N. **el cuadro** (ell kvathro)	*the picture*
G. **del cuadro** (dell kvathro)	*of the picture*
D. **al cuadro** (al kvathro)	*to the picture*
A. **el cuadro** (ell kvathro)	*the picture*
N. **los cuadros** (loss kvathross)	*the pictures*
G. **de los cuadros** (de loss kvathros)	*of the pictures*
D. **a los cuadros** (a loss kvathross)	*to the pictures*
A. **los cuadros** (loss kvathross)	*the pictures*
N. **la camisa** (la kameesa)	*the shirt*
G. **de la camisa** (de la kameesa)	*of the shirt*
D. **a la camisa** (a la kameesa)	*to the shirt*
A. **la camisa** (la kameesa)	*the shirt*
N. **las camisas** (la kameesas)	*the shirts*
G. **de las camisas** (de las kameesas)	*of the shirts*
D. **a las camisas** (a las kameesas)	*to the shirts*
A. **las camisas** (las kameesas)	*the shirts*
N. **un cuadro** (oon kvathro)	*a picture, a painting*
G. **de un cuadro**	*of a picture, of a painting*
D. **a un cuadro**	*to a picture, to a painting*
A. **un cuadro**	*a picture, to a painting*
N. **cuadros**	*pictures, paintings*
G. **de cuadros**	*of pictures, paintings*
D. **a cuadros**	*to pictures, paintings*
A. **cuadros**	*pictures, paintings*

But, as you remember, *for persons and countries* the direct and the indirect objects are alike in Spanish:

N.	el padre (ell pathray)	*the father*
G.	del padre (dell pathray)	*of the father*
D.	al padre (al pathray)	*to the father*
A.	al padre (al pathray)	*the father*
N.	los padres (loss pathrays)	*the fathers*
G.	de los padres (de loss pathrays)	*of the fathers*
D.	a los padres (a loss pathrays)	*to the fathers*
A.	a los padres (a loss pathrays)	*the fathers*
N.	la madre (la mathray)	*the mother*
G.	de la madre	*of the mother*
D.	a la madre	*to the mother*
A.	a la madre	*the mother*
N.	las madres (las mathrays)	*the mothers*
G.	de las madres	*of the mothers*
D.	a las madres	*to the mothers*
A.	a las madres	*the mothers*

La madre pregunta al padre
la mathray praygoonta al pathray
The mother asks the father

los hijos preguntan a los padres
loss eehoss praygoontan a loss pathrays
the children ask the parents

Do you remember:

¿Conoce Vd. a España o al Perú?
konothay oostayth a esspangya o al payroo
Do you know Spain or Peru?

España (esspangya)	*Spain*	Perú (payroo)	*Peru*
de España	*of Spain*	de Perú	*of Peru*
a España	*to Spain*	al Perú	*to Peru*
a España	*Spain*	al Perú	*Peru*

Lesson Eight

Anyone, **cualquiera** (kvalkeeayra), *this or that person*, **esta o aquella persona** (essta o akellya perrsona), who speaks *one or more foreign languages*, **una o más lenguas extranjeras** (oona o mas layngwas aystranhayras), will tell you that you will find *the same kind*, **las mismas clases** (las meezmas klasays) *the same classes*, of people all over the world, with really only very slight differences. Much of the generalizing that goes on concerning foreign peoples has come from not knowing these people. *We don't know each other*, **no nos conocemos** (no noss konothaymoss).

Many misunderstandings would be avoided if we could overcome this handicap that comes from not understanding each other. At the beginning, understanding comes most easily through language, the most effective medium that *mankind*, **el hombre** (ell ommbray), has for *getting together*, **juntarse** (hoontarsay), with others.

z always like *th*, c before e and i, j always like h, g before e and i. G before a, o, u = g (as in *gift*). If the Spaniard wants to keep the g hard before an e or i, he inserts a silent u between the g and the e or i. **La guerra** (la gvayrra) *the war*. Sometimes the u is meant to be pronounced—in that case he uses a so-called trema, two dots above the u. For instance **la vergüenza** (la vayrgooayntha) *the shame*.

As soon as you can make yourself understood, though that may be little enough *in the beginning*, **al principio** (al preentheepyo), you will realize the difference, for you will come in contact with many people you could never have met otherwise and with many things you would otherwise never have seen.

¡Juntémonos! (hoontaymonoss), *Let us get together!*

Since you don't have a command of as many words in a foreign language as you have in your mother tongue, make it a principle always to express yourself *as simply as possible*, **tan simple como sea posible** (tang seemplay komo saya posseevlay). This gives you two advantages.

First, **primero** (preemayro), you have a better chance of getting what you want. Don't forget that the conventional forms were introduced to make life easier, not to complicate it. You have probably encountered people who try so hard to be *so polite*, **tan cortés** (tang korrtays), that they never come to the point. What do they accomplish with all their politeness? They make you tired! Certainly, when it becomes a matter of routine and *you can speak Spanish*, **Vd. habla español** (oostayth avla ayspangyol), *as well as English*, **tan bien como el inglés**, (tam byayng komo ell eenglays), it will be very nice to ask a policeman, "Would you be so kind as to tell me how I could find the way to City Hall?" But if you have to prepare this question in Spanish first, and get all confused, standing there in front of the policeman, it is better to ask him simply and pleasantly,

¿Cuál es el camino del ayuntamiento?
kval ess ell kameeno dell ayoontamyennto
What is the way to City Hall?

or even shorter:

¿Dónde está el ayuntamiento?
donnday essta ell ayoontamyennto
Where is City Hall?

¿Qué distancia hay? (kay theestanthya aee) *What distance is it? How far is it?*

¿Adónde quiere Vd. ir? (adonnday kyayray oostayth eer),
Where do you want to go?

¿Adónde va Vd? (adonnday va oostayth), *Where do you want to go?*

No está lejos de aquí, está muy cerca.
no essta layhoz thay akee essta mooy therrka
It is not far from here, it is very near.

¡Vaya Vd. derechito!   **a la derecha!**   **a la izquierda!**
vaya oostayth thayrecheeto   a la thayrecha   a la eethkyerrtha
Go straight ahead!   *to the right!*   *to the left!*

Do you see how often the Spanish **a** corresponds to the English *to?* **¿Dónde?** (donnday) *Where?* **¿Adónde?** (adonnday) *Where to?* **A la derecha** (a la thayrecha) *to the right.*

I asked you to express yourself as simply as possible. I said *first*, that *it is easier*, **primero es más fácil** (preemayro ess mas fatheel), *second*, **segundo** (saygoondo), it is necessary for us *to consider*, **pensar** (pennsar), what *is more important*, **más importante** (mas eemporrtantay), and what is *less important*, **menos importante** (maynoss eemporrtantay).

* 39 *

Lesson Nine

Whether we realize it or not, all our statements, all our actions are judged through comparisons. What is *much*, **mucho** (mootsho), for one is *little*, **poco** (poko), for another one. If *I have a hundred dollars in the (my) pocket*, **tengo cien dólares en el bolsillo** (tenngo thyenn dolarays enn ell bollseellyo), I feel that *I have much money*, **tengo mucho dinero** (tenngo moocho theenayro). I almost fancy that *I am a rich man*, **soy un hombre rico** (soy oon ommbray reeko). And you'll laugh at me and say, *What's the matter with you?* **¿Qué hay?** (kay ay). *A hundred dollars!* **¡Cien dólares!** (thyenn dolarays), why, *that's nothing to me*, **eso no es nada para mí** (esso no ess natha para mee). *I have more money than you*, **tengo más dinero que Vd.** (tenngo maz theenayro kay oostayth). *I am richer than you all*, **soy más rico que todos vosotros** (soy marreeko kay tothoss vosotross). And I know a lady who has a hundred dollars, just as I have —you see, I associate only *with very rich people*, **con la gente muy rica** (konn la hayntay mooy reeka). This lady does not impress me at all when she says:

All Spanish nouns are either masculine or feminine. There is a neuter article **lo** (lo), but is used only with **adjectives** when they are used as **nouns**.
lo bueno (lo booayno),
lo bonito (lo boneeto).

Taken all together, *you are still all poor* people, **todos vosotros sois pobres** (tothoss vosotross soees povrays); *I have a great deal of money*, **tengo muchísimo dinero** (tayngo moocheeseemo theenayro); *I am the richest lady in the world*, **soy la señora más rica del mundo** (soy la sengyora mas reeka dell moondo).

Only too often we find ourselves listening to a heated discussion about *the beauty*, **la hermosura** (la errmosoora), *of women*, **de las mujeres** (de las moohayrays); about *dresses*, **vestidos** (vaysteethoss); about the good or bad *qualities of men*, **la cualidad, las cualidades de los hombres** (la kvaleethath lass kvaleethathayz thay loss ommbrays), about *quantities of objects*, **las cuantidades de las cosas** (las kvanteethathayz thay las kosas) etc.

I wouldn't dare give you any advice about how to handle all these questions, but in my opinion it is well to say to a lady: *You are not only beautiful*, **Vd. no solo es hermosa** (oostayth no solo ess errmosa); *you are more beautiful than the Venus of Milo*,

Mi	**amigo**	**¿Qué**	**tal?**
mee	ameego	kay	tal
My	*friend,*	*how*	*are you?*

Vd. es más hermosa que la Venus de Milo (oostayth ess mas errmosa kay la vaynooz thay meelo); *you are the most beautiful lady I have ever seen,* **Vd. es la señora más hermosa que he visto** (oostayth ess la sengyora mas errmosa kay ay veesto). And if *the winner of a beauty contest,* **la reina del certamen de belleza** (la rayeena thell therrtamayn thay bellestha), happens to be passing by, and your friend herself can't help saying: *What a beauty!* **¡Qué hermosa!** (kay errmosa), it is well to keep silent or, better still, to say: I don't know, I don't like her!

hermoso, hermosa	**más hermoso, más hermosa**
errmoso errmosa	mas errmoso, mas errmosa
beautiful	*more beautiful*

el más hermoso, la más hermosa
ell mas errmoso, la mas errmosa
the most beautiful.

Ladies and gentlemen, **señoras y caballeros**, (sengyoras ee kavallyayross), I completely forgot, for the moment, that I was telling my experiences exclusively to the men, although we were not *alone*, **solos** (soloss). No, *we men are not alone*, **nosotros los hombres no estamos solos** (nosotross loss ommbrays no esstamoss soloss). *There are many women here*, **hay muchas mujeres aquí** (ay moochas moohayrays akee). After having gone so far in telling you *my secrets*, **mis secretos** (mees saykraytoss), what can I do now but declare:

Todas ustedes señoras son las más hermosas, tanto una como otra.

tothas oostaythays sengyoras sonn las mas errmosas tanto oona komo otra

All you ladies are the most beautiful, one as much as another.

¿Qué oigo? (kay oeego) *What do I hear?* **¿Qué veo?** (kay vayo). *What do I see?* **¿Qué hay?** (kay ay). *What is the matter?* A *revolution*, **una revolución** (oona revoloothyong).

The ladies cry: Don't serve us these commonplaces! *It has been a long time*, **hace mucho tiempo** (athay moocho tyemmpo), since we first learned that each of us is *the most beautiful* lady, *the nicest, the most charming, the best*, **la más hermosa** (la mas errmosa), **la más simpática** (la mas seempateeka), **la más encantadora** (la mas ennkanntadora), **la óptima** (la oppteema), and so on. And *by the way*, **sea dicho de paso** (satha thayeecho thay paso) *who is Venus?* **¿Quién es esta señora Venus?** (kyenng ess essta sengyora vaynoos). I will tell you; she is a lady of long ago, *the most beautiful* woman of an age *long past*, **la hermosura más antigua** (la errmosoora mas anteegva), *the oldest beauty.*

B and V sound almost alike. But avoid in Spanish altogether the English explosive sounds; t h e y don't e x i s t in Spanish. Therefore, d may v e r y often sound like the soft English "th" as you hear it in "although"; **nada** almost like natha = nothing. Also t is not explosive at all, it is very soft.

And the man, is he *nothing*, **nada** (natha)? Let us pretend *we are great*, **somos grandes** (somoss granndays), or that *one* of us *is greater than the other one*, **uno es más grande que el otro** (oono ess mas grannday kay ell otro). We are all looking for *the greatest*

* 42 *

man, **el hombre más grande** (ell **h**ommbray mas gra**nn**day), I hope *not in vain*, **no en vano** (no enn vano).

We characterize or differentiate persons and things by their *qualities*, **cualidades** (kvaleethathays), and you have noticed how these qualifying or descriptive words (adjectives) are handled in Spanish in connection with the principal words (nouns). To show the difference between two or more persons and between two or more things of the same kind, the adjective is placed *after* the principal word; for instance, **paño negro** (pangyo naygro) *black cloth;* **paño rojo** (pangyo roho) *red cloth.* But certain adjectives which are used in connection with steady qualities are put before the word, especially if they attribute an inherent quality to an object or person. Study the examples. **La dulce miel** (la **d**oolthay meeayl), *the sweet honey,* **la blanca nieve** (la blanka neeayvay), *the white snow.*

Adjectives not ending in **o** (masc.) or **a** (fem.) have only **one form for both genders.** e. g. **verde** (vayrday) g r e e n, **el verde vestito** (ell vayrday vaysteeto) *the green clothes;* **la tinta verde** (la teenta vayrday) *the green ink.*

dulce	más dulce	el más dulce, la más dulce
doolthay	mas doolthay	ell mas doolthay, la mas doolthay
sweet	*sweeter*	*the sweetest*, m. and f.

rico, a	más rico, a	el más rico, la más rica
reeko, a	mas reeko, a	ell mas reeko, la mas reeka
rich	*richer*	*the richest*

pobre	más pobre	el más pobre, la más pobre
povray	mas povray	ell mas povray, la mas povray
poor	*poorer*	*the poorest*

Todo eso es facilísimo, es lo más fácil del mundo.
totho esso ess fatheeleeseemo, ess lo mas fatheel dell moondo
All that is most easy; it is the easiest in the world.

When people are inclined toward exaggeration, this **isimo** is repeated very often, **fortísimo** (forrteeseemo) *very, very strong;* **simplísimo** (seemmpleeseemo) *very, very simple;* **bonísimo** (boneeseemo) *very, very good;* **malísimo** (maleeseemo) *very, very bad.*

I am as happy as you are, **yo soy tan feliz como Vds.** (yo soy tang fayleeth komo oostaythes) that all this follows very regular grammatical rules.

tan ancho como largo	**tan estrecho como corto**
tang ancho komo larrgo	tang esstrecho komo korrto
as broad as long	*as narrow as short*

Irregular adjectives are

bueno, a	**mejor**	**óptimo**
booayno, a	mayhor	oppteemo
good	*better*	*best*

malo	**peor**	**pésimo**
malo	payor	payseemo
bad	*worse*	*worst*

grande	**mayor**	**máximo**
granday	mayor	makseemo
great	*greater*	*greatest*

pequeño	**menor**	**mínimo**
paykayngyo	maynor	meeneemo
small	*smaller*	*smallest*

mucho	**más**	**muchísimo**
moocho	mas	moocheeseemo
much	*more*	*most*

poco	**menos**	**poquísimo**
poko	maynoss	pokeeseemo
little	*less*	*least*

¡Hasta más ver!	**¡Hasta luego!**
asta mas vayr	asta looaygo
I'll see you later!	*Good-bye!*

Lesson Ten

¿Cómo está Vd.? (komo essta oostayth) *How are you?* How often we use these words and how rarely do we take them seriously! We do not realize that they may be very important. *It is almost impossible,* es casi imposible (ess kasee eemposeevlay) for us to know what we mean when we answer, bien, gracias (byayng grathyas), *well, thank you,* when we know that this answer *is not true,* no es verdad (no ess vayrthath). The way we feel, we would like to say what only our best friends—los buenos amigos (loss booaynoss ameegoss) *the good friends,* would be interested in: No estoy muy bien (no esstoy mooy byayng), *I am not very well. Not to be in good health,* no ser sano (no sayrr sano) *is very disagreeable,* es muy desagradable (ess mooy daysagradavlay).

¿Qué tiene Vd.? (kay teeaynay oostayth) *What is the matter with you?,* the doctor asks. Tengo una indigestión (tenngo oona eendeehaystyong) *I am suffering from indigestion.* Estoy enfermo (esstoy ennferrmo) *I am sick.* We all hope that the ill health is only temporary and that it will pass very soon. When we recover and are healthy again, we hope that our good health will last forever. *We are well, we feel well,* estamos bien (esstamoss byayng).

From a knowledge of his language, we see that the Spaniard has a strong instinctive feeling as to what, as far as mankind can predict, is a temporary fact and what is fact that has duration or is permanent. We assume this from the fact that in Spanish there are two words for *to be,* ser and estar (sayrr and esstar), ser expressing a permanent fact and estar a temporary fact. We must first become acquainted with the difference between the two and soon we will begin to feel it.

Estar, the Latin word "stare" (*to be standing*), could be translated as *to be in a place, to be in a situation,* and if we understand that, we realize at once why we must say: el señor esta aquí, (ell sengyor essta akee) *the gentleman is here.* That means, his place is here. But *to be* is being used in another sense—and then it is in Spanish ser (sayrr)—if we say *of a good man,* de un buen hombre (day oon booayn ommbray): es bueno (ess booayno), *he is good,* or *of a good woman,* de una buena mujer (day oona booayna moohayr): es buena (ess booayna) *she is good*, implying that he or she cannot be anything but good, and this in an absolutely permanent sense.

Therefore

(yo) soy	(yo soy)	*I am*
(tú) eres	(ayrays)	*you are*
(él) es	(ess)	*he, she, it is*
Vd. es		*you are*
(nosotros) somos	(somoss)	*we are*
(vosotros) sois	(soees)	*you are*
(ellos, ellas, Vds.) son	(sonn)	*they are, you are* (addressing several persons).

You will not feel offended *if I tell you once more*, si le digo a Vd. una vez más (see lay theego a oostayth oona vayth mas) that in addressing a person we usually use the equivalent of *your grace* or *your honor* which is usted (oostayth) = Vd., or, when addressing several persons, *your honors*, ustedes (oostaythays) = Vds. Think of it. In Spanish-speaking countries you are "your honor" without passing any examination!

Vd. es inglés (oostayth ess eenglays), *you are an Englishman;* eres Americano (ayrays amayreekano), *you are an American.* And to more than one person: sois Alemanes, Españoles, Franceses (soees alaymanays, ayspangyolays, franthaysays), *you are Germans, Spaniards, Frenchmen.* These last are the forms used only by friends.

Somos de América, de Francia, de Alemania, de Bolivia, de Chile.
somoss thay amayreeka, thay franthya, thay alaymanya, thay boleevya, thay cheelay.
We are from America, from France, from Germany, from Bolivia, from Chile.

Nosotros todos estamos aquí.
nosotross tothoss esstamoss akee
We are all here.

Excuse me, excúseme or perdone Vd. (exkoosaymay or perrdonay oostayth). I had completely forgotten that you told me that you did not feel very well; no estoy muy bien (no esstoy mooy byayng) *I am not very well;* Vd. no está muy bien (oostayth no essta mooy byayng) *you do not feel very well*, and that you

Este	pañuelo de seda,	¿cuanto es?
Esstay	panyooaylo thay saytha	kvanto ess
This	*silk handkerchief,*	*how much is it?*

have seen *a doctor*, **un doctor** (oon dokktor). What did he say?

I can see right at the beginning that you do not intend to spare me the tiniest detail of what the doctor told you.

The doctor has told me, **el médico me ha dicho** (ell maytheeko may a theecho). But forgetting my *good training*, **la educación** (la aythookathyong), *I take the liberty*, *I allow myself*, **tomo licencia, me permito** (tomo leethenthya may perrmeeto) to interrupt you.

Dispense Vd. si le interrumpo.
deespensay oostayth see lay eenterroompo
Pardon me if I interrupt you.

You, *always polite*, **siempre cortés** (syemmpray korrtays)— do not say anything except

¡No hay de qué!	**¡De nada!**	**¡No importa!**
no ay thay kay	day natha	no eemporrta
It doesn't matter!	*that's nothing!*	*no matter at all!*

For all these expressions we usually say simply, "*Not at all.*"

It is very disagreeable, **es muy desagradable** (ess mooy daysagrathavlay), but I must tell you something; I did not understand what you said. **El doctor me ha dicho** (ell dokktor may a theecho), *the doctor has said:* why, *suddenly*, **de repente** (day raypenntay), this **ha** for *has?* All along I understood that the word for *have* is **tener** (taynayr). **Tengo paciencia** (tenngo pathyennthya), *I have patience, but what is too much is too much*, **lo qué es demasiado, es demasiado** (lo kay ez thaymasyatho ez thaymasyatho). There are two forms for *to be*, **ser** (serr) and **estar** (esstar). And now, *to have* is not only **tener** (taynayr), **tengo, tienes, tiene, tenemos, tenéis, tienen** (tenngo, teeaynays, teeaynay, taynaymoss, taynayess, teeaynayn), but also a second word. We must have an explanation.

Lesson Eleven

Do not get excited! *Take it easy!* **Tenga calma** (tennga kalma), **tenga paciencia** (tenga pathyenthya)! We will explain everything. When you are speaking of what you have or do not have, whether it's money or anything that money can buy or even things that money cannot buy, anything that has become your property, you say, just as you did before, **tengo** (tenngo). **Tengo dinero** (tenngo theenayro), *I have money. My congratulations to you,* **mis congratulaciones** (mees kongratoolathyonays)! **Tengo dos ojos y oídos** (tenngo thoss ohoss ee thoss oeethoss), *I have two eyes and two ears.* **Tú también tienes dos ojos** (too tammbyayng teeaynayz thoss ohoss, *you also have two eyes. Isn't that so?* **¿No es verdad?** (no ez vayrthath).

The other Spanish word for *to have* is **haber** (avayr) and that is only used together with another verb, as an auxiliary.

(yo) he dicho	(ay theecho)	*I have said*
(tú) has dicho	(as)	*you have said*
(él) dicho ha	(a)	*he*
(ella) dicho		*she* } *has said*
(Vd.) ha dicho	(a)	*you have said*

(nosotros) hemos	(aymoss)	*we have said*
(vosotros) habeis	(avayees)	*you have said*
(ellos, ellas Vds.) han dicho	(an)	*they have said, you have said*

El médico ha dicho (ell maytheeko a theecho) *the doctor has said;* **el doctor me ha dicho** (el dokktor may a theecho) *the doctor has told me.* **Tengo dinero** (tenngo theenayro) *I have money;* **he tenido dinero** (ay tayneetho theenayro) *I have had money,* which is not a great help now, but anyway, the *memory is better (more) than nothing* at all, **reminiscencia es más que nada** (raymeeneesthaynthya ess mas kay natha). **Tengo la reminiscencia** (tenngo la raymeeneesthaynthya) *I have memories.* (I have the memory.)

He hablado	(ay avlatho)	*I have spoken*
Vd. ha contestado	(a konntesstatho)	*you have answered*
hemos comprado	(aymoss kommpratho)	*we have bought*
habéis vendido	(abayees vayndeetho)	*you have sold*

* 49 *

Vd. ha consultado al médico
oostayth a konnsooltatho al maydeeko
You have consulted the doctor.

But, mas (mas), it was I who interrupted you. *Now tell me,* digame ahora (deegamay aora), *all about it,* en todas partes (enn todas partays), from the time you entered *the waiting room,* la sala de espera (la sala day espayra) till you left *the doctor's house,* la casa del doctor (la kasa dell dokktor).

¡Qué lástima! (kay lasteema) *what a pity* it would be if we tried to prevent some people from talking about their sufferings. *There are many people,* hay mucha gente (ay moocha henntay) for whom *nothing,* nada (natha) is more refreshing than to be able to talk about their troubles to anyone who happens along. There is one good thing about these people. They talk and talk, but they don't notice when you are not listening to them. Only *you* or somebody else *must be there.* Usted debe estar ahí (allí) (oostayth daybay esstar aee) (allyee).

¡Ahora continue, por favor!
aora konnteenooay porr favor
And now continue, please!

En mi reloj son las cuatro de la tarde.
enn mee rayloh sonn las kvatro day la tarrday
According to my watch it is four o'clock in the afternoon.

Mañana por la mañana he de estar en casa.
mangyana porr la mangyana ay day esstar eng kasa
Tomorrow morning I have to be at home.

¿Cuándo? A las diez de la mañana, si es posible.
kvando a las deeayth day la mangyana see ess poseeblay
When? At ten o'clock in the morning if it is possible.

Hoy es lunes (oy ez looness) *today is Monday. The week begins very well,* la semana empieza muy bien (la saymana emm-pyaytha mooy beeayn) said a man once, when he got news *on a Monday morning,* el lunes por la mañana (ell looness porr la mangyana) that all of his money was lost.

¿A cuántos estamos hoy? (a kvanntos esstamoss oy) *what's the date?* ¿Qué día del mes es hoy? (kay deea dell mess ess oy) *what day of the month is today? Wait a minute,* espere un minuto (esspayray oon meenooto): *yesterday was Sunday,* ayer fué domingo (a-yayr fooay domeengo); *and the day before yesterday,*

anteayer (anntaya-yayr) was *pay day*, **día de pago** (deea day pago). *I never forget pay day*, **no olvido nunca** el día de pago (no ollveedo noongka ell deea day pago). *The day before yesterday was Saturday*, **anteayer fué sábado** (anntayayayr fooay sabado); *it was the 31st of October*, **fué el 31** (trayeenta ee oono) **de octubre** (fooay ell trayeenta ee oono day okktoobray). *Therefore*, **por eso** (porr esso), *yesterday was Sunday, the first of November*, **ayer fué domingo el primero de noviembre** (ayayr fooay domeengo ell preemayro day novyembray); *and today is Monday, the second of November*, **hoy es lunes el dos de noviembre** (oy ess looness ell doss day novyemmbray).

¿Cuáles son los días de la semana?
kvalays sonn los theeas day la saymana
What are the days of the week?

Los días de la semana se llaman:
loss theeas day la saymana say lyaman
The days of the week are called (in Spanish: call themselves):

lunes	(looness)	*Monday*
martes	(martess)	*Tuesday*
miércoles	(myerr koless)	*Wednesday*
jueves	(hooayvess)	*Thursday*
viernes	(vyerrness)	*Friday*
sábado	(sabatho)	*Saturday*
domingo	(domeengo)	*Sunday*

el mes	**la semana**	**el día**
ell mess	la saymana	ell theea
the month	*the week*	*the day*

los meses	**las semanas**	**los días**
loss maysess	las saymanas	loss theeas
the months	*the weeks*	*the days*

El primer mes del año es enero (ell preemayr mess thell angyo ess aynayro) *the first month of the year is January;* **el segundo mes del año es Febrero** (ell saygoondo mess thell angyo ess faybrayro) *the second month of the year is February.* **Los otros meses se llaman** (loss otross maysess say lyaman) *the other months are called:*

Marzo	(martho)	*March*
Abril	(avreel)	*April*
Mayo	(mayo)	*May*

Junio	(hoonyo)	*June*
Julio	(hoolyo)	*July*
Agosto	(agossto)	*August*
Setiembre	(saytyemmbray)	*September*
Octubre	(okktoobray)	*October*
Noviembre	(novyemmbray)	*November*
Diciembre	(deethyemmbray)	*December*

el primero de Enero	(ell preemayro thay aynayro)	*January 1st*
el dos de Enero	(ell doss thay aynayro)	*January 2nd*
el tres de Mayo	(ell tress thay mayo)	*May 3rd*
el veinte y uno de Junio	(ell vayeentay ee oono dai hoonyo)	*June 21st*
el treinta y uno de Abril	(ell trayeenta ee oono thay avreel)	*April 31st*

No, you couldn't say that, because it doesn't exist, for, as we know, *the month of April has only thirty days*, **Vd. no puede decirlo porque el mes de Abril tiene solo treinta días** (oostayth no pooaythay daytheerlo porrkay ell mess de avreel teeaynay solo trayeenta theeas). *The thirtieth of April is the last day of the month of April*, **el treinta de Abril es el último día del mes de Abril** (ell trayeenta thay avreel ess ell oolteemo theea thell mess thay avreel).

estar				**ser**		
(esstar)				(serr)		
estuve				**fuí**		
(esstoovay)	*I was*			(fooee)	*I was*	
estuviste				**fuiste**		
(esstooveestay)	*you were*			(fooeestay)	*you were*	
estuvo				**fué**		
(esstoovo)	*etc.*			(fooay)	*etc.*	
estuvimos				**fuimos**		
(esstooveemoss)				(fooeemoss)		
estuvisteis				**fuisteis**		
(esstooveestayees)				(fooeestayees)		
estuvieron				**fueron**		
(esstoovyayron)				(fooayron)		

If you omit from **estuve** (esstoovay) *I was*, *the first syllable* **es, la primera sílaba** (la preemayra seelava), then *you have* **Vd. tiene** (oostayth teeaynay) the past tense of the verb **tener** (taynayr).

tuve (toovay)		*I had*
tuviste (tooveestay)		*you had*
tuvo (toovo)		
tuvimos (tooveemoss)		*we had*
tuvisteis (tooveestayees)		
tuvieron (toovyayron)		

¡Lea en alta voz!

READ ALOUD

Bien, muy bien, señor. ¿Y usted? ¡Mil gracias! Muy bien.
!Hasta la vista!
¿Como se llama usted? La firma, deletrear, el alfabeto. La primera
letra es a. La segunda letra es b. La tercera letra es c. La cuatra
letra es d. La quinta letra es e. Treinta letras. a, b, c, ch, d, e, f,
g, h, i, j, k, l, ll, m, n, ñ, o, p, q, r, rr, s, t, u, v, x, y, z. El abecedario español.
¿Como se llama Vd. (usted)? Me llamo Pedro. Llamo.
¿Llama Vd. (usted)? Vd. se llama. Me llamo. ¡Deletree su nombre! Doña Elisabeth. Don Pedro. El apellido. Me llamo Pedro
Pérez. Mi apellido es Pérez. La calle, los números de las casas.
La primera casa tiene el número uno. Calle Victoria 21. El número
veinte. De una vez, veinte y uno, veinte y dos, veinte y tres, veinte
y cuatro, veinte y cinco, veinte y seis, veinte y siete, veinte y ocho,
veinte y nueve, treinta. ¿Dónde está calle de la Concordia 34?
Dies minutos de aquí. Vaya Vd. (usted) dos calles a la derecha
y pues una calle a la izquierda. Una cuadra, dos cuadras, dos
cuadras a la derecha, dos cuadras a la izquierda.
¡No se moleste! ¡No se incomode! Vaya Vd. (usted) con
Dios, señorita. Muy bien. La casa del amigo. La casa de la amiga.
¿Cómo está Vd.? ¿Cómo está la familia? ¿Cómo están en casa?
¡Bien, gracias! ¿Y Vd.? ¡Qué calor hace! Una orchata. ¿Quiere
Vd. beber? ¡Si, seguramente! Las letras, los números, hasta
treinta y nueve. ¡Hasta la vista!

Lesson Twelve

Although I would like to, I cannot spare any more time to hear what you have asked the doctor and what the doctor has asked you. As you, with whom I have just had this conversation, are *the richest girl in the city,* la muchacha más rica de la ciudad (la moochacha mas reeka thay la theeoodad) there is no doubt (*without doubt*) (sin duda, seen dooda) that you went *to the best physician in town,* al mejor médico de la ciudad (al mayhor maydeeko thay la theeoodad).

What are the doctor's office hours? ¿Cuándo tiene consulta el doctor? (kvanndo teeaynay koonsoolta ell dokktor). ¿Cuándo son las horas de consulta del médico? (kvanndo sonn las oraz thay konnsoolta thell maydeeko). They begin *at half past three in the afternoon,* a las tres y media de la tarde (a las tress ee maydya thay la tarrthay) and *he is there until a quarter to six,* está ahí hasta las seis menos cuarto (essta aee asta las sayees maynoss kvarto).

A little while after three, poco después de las tres (poko thayspooays thay las tress) *I am in the waiting room,* estoy en la sala de espera (esstoy enn la sala thay esspayra). *Many people are there,* mucha gente está ahí (moocha henntay essta aee). *It is ten minutes to four,* son las cuatro menos diez (sonn las kvatro maynoss deeayth) *before I can enter the doctor's room,* cuando puedo entrar en el cuarto del doctor (kvando pooaytho enntrar enn ell kvarto thell dokktor).

He says to me, me dice (may deethay):
Tell me, what do you have? What is the matter? ¿Dígame, qué tiene Vd.? (deegamay kay teeaynay oostayth). But first *take a seat,* tome Vd. asiento (tomay oostayth asyennto); *sit down,* siéntese Vd. (seeenntaysay oostayth).

I tell him, le digo (lay theego):
I eat very little, como muy poco (komo mooy poko); *my eyes and ears ache,* me duelen los ojos y los oídos (may dvaylayn loss ohoss ee loss oeethoss); *I have a pain in my throat, in my head and in my shoulder,* me duele la garganta, la cabeza, la espalda (may dvaylay la gargannta la kavaythas la esspalda). *My whole body,* todo el cuerpo (totho ell kverrpo), *is not right,* no

* 54 *

Un muchacho alegre y una muchacha hermosa.
oon moochacho alaygray ee oona moochacha errmosa
A merry boy and a beautiful girl.

está bueno (no esta booayno). *I ache in every limb*, **me duelen todos los miembros** (may dvaylayn tothoss loss myemmbross), *the breast*, **el seno** (ell sayno); *the cheek*, **el carillo** (ell kareellyo); *the legs*, **las piernas** (las pyerrnas); *the chest*, **el pecho** (ell paycho); *the fingers*, **los dedos** (loss thaythoss); *the feet*, **los pies** (loss peeays); *the neck*, **el cuello** (ell kvellyo); *the hands*, **las manos** (las manoss); *the chin*, **la barba** (la barrba); *the nose*, **la nariz** (la nareeth); *the forehead*, **la frente** (la frenntay).

For some time I have noticed that *I have a heart*, **tengo un corazón** (tenngo oon korrathonn), *a liver*, **un hígado** (oon eegatho), and *nerves*, **nervios** (nerrvyoss).

Translate into Spanish

For a little while a king, a duke, a count, a name, the pass- port, a check, a registered letter. What is your name? How do you call yourself? The signature, to spell, the Spanish A-B-C. The first letter is a A, the second letter is b B, the third letter is c C, the fourth letter is d D, the fifth letter is e E. Thirty. a, b, c, ch. d, e, f, g, h, i, j, k, l, ll, m, n, ñ, o, p, q, r, rr, s, t, u, v, x, y, z. The Spanish A-B-C.

What is your name? I call myself Peter. I call, do you call? You call yourself. Spell your name! The surname. My name is Mr. Peter Perez. My surname is Perez. The street, the numbers of the houses. The first house has the number one. Number twenty. At once, twenty-one, 22, 23, 24, 25, 26, 27, 28, 29, 30. Where is 34 Concord Street? Ten minutes from here! Go two streets to the right and then one street to the left. One block, two blocks to the right, two blocks to the left. Don't trouble yourself! Go with God, my lady! All right! The house of your friend. How are you? How is the family? How are they all in the house? Well, thanks! How hot it is! An orgeat. Will you have a drink? Yes, certainly! The letters, the numbers up to thirty-nine. Good bye!

You have money, to a store, a many colored handkerchief of silk, the hat, a felt hat (a hat of felt), a straw hat, the hats. There are hats of many colors for ladies and gentlemen. For instance, the handbag, the mirror, the pocket mirror, to a lady, the pocket, the pockets, a blouse, a shirt, the colour of the hat, the color of the shirt.

A friend of mine, **un amigo mio** (oon ameego meeo) *has told me*, **me ha dicho** (may a theecho): *Go to a dentist*, **vaya Vd. al dentista** (vaya oostayth al dennteesta). *I was there*, **fuí allá** (fooee allya), and he told me, *there's nothing wrong*, **no hay nada** (no aee natha). *What do you think of that?* **¿qué piensa Vd. de eso?** (kay pyennsa oostayth thay esso).

The doctor answers, **el doctor contesta** (ell dokktor konntessta): *Show me your tongue*, **enséñeme Vd. la lengua** (ennsaynyaymay oostayth la lenngva). *It is not coated*, **no está sucia** (no essta soothya). Then he makes an examination. *I am examined by the doctor*, **soy examinado por el médico** (soy ekksameenatho porr ell maytheeko), and he asks me once more:

How about your appetite? **¿Qué tal de apetito** (kay tal thay apayteeto). And I say: *I eat very little*, **(yo) como muy poco** ((yo) komo mooy poko); *just two eggs*, **apenas dos huevos** (apaynaz thoss ooayvoss), *coffee*, **café** (kaffay), *bread and butter*, **pan y mantequilla** (pan ee manntaykeellya), *some fried fish*, **algun pescado frito** (algoon pesskatho freeto), *a fruit*, **frutas** (frootas), *jam and marmalade*, **jalea y marmelada** (halaya ee marrmaylatha). *That is all for breakfast*, **eso es todo para el desayuno** (esso ess totho para ell thessayoono).

Now we have to make you acquainted with a very important fact—a fact which is, indeed, not so easy to understand, at first, for one who does not speak a Romance language. Spanish, like many other Romance languages, is spoken in so-called "connected" speech. That means that the Spaniards, in speaking their language, contract one word with the following word. They do not separate one word from the other as we do in English. Even when we speak English very quickly we do not contract two words into almost one. This liaison, interrupted only by breathing pauses or by any kind of punctuation such as a comma, colon, question mark, etc., has a great influence on the pronunciation. Take, for instance, the word **tan**, pronounced tang, meaning: *so;* **tan bueno**, *so good*, is pronounced tambooayno. We avoid demonstrating this again and again by making a connection sign (‿) between pronunciation guide words, because it would annoy you to see such a repetition. But don't wonder when you see that word endings are different in the pronunciation guide. It is not inconsistent at all, but it shows you how you have to connect the words with each other. The th in a liaison is always the voiced th, as in *them*. In the same manner, Spanish **d** between words is pronounced almost like voiced *th* as in *them*.

Then at noon I have my lunch, a very light one too, just to eat a little, soup, two mutton chops, some vegetables, potatoes, a dessert. Entonces, a mediodía, tomo mi almuerzo muy legero, solamente para comer un poco, sopa, dos chuletas, legumbres, patatas (papas), postres. (enntonnthays a maythyotheea komo mee almooerrtho mooy layhayro, solamenntay para komayr oon poko, sopa, dos choolaytas, laygoombrays, patatas (papas), postrays).

Between four and five I just take a cup of tea,
Entre las cuatro y las cinco tomo solamente una taza de té,
enntray las kvatro ee las theenko tomo solamenntay oona tatha
    thay tay

some cake and toast.
torta y tostadas.
torrta ee tostathas

At seven o'clock I don't eat much, only my regular dinner
A las siete no como mucho, solamente mi comida regulare
a las syaytay no komo moocho solamenntay mee komeetha ray-
    goolaray

of six courses.
de seis platos.
thay sayees platoss

That is all I eat during the day. Isn't that a shame, doctor?
Eso es todo lo que como durante el día. ¿No es (una) lástima, doctor?
esso ess totho lo kay komo thoorantay ell deea. no ess oona las-
    teema, dokktor

The doctor, a very intelligent man, says: *That is not a shame.* Eso no es lástima (esso no ess lasteema); *that's a scandal,* es un escándalo (ess oon esskanndalo); *I know what's the matter with you,* sé lo que le pasa a Vd. (say lo kay lay pasa a oostayth). *You do not work.* Vd. no trabaja (oostayth no travaha). Work, my dear, and *don't think of your complaints,* no piense en su enfermedad (no pyennsay enn soo ennferrmaythath). Work *as much as* you eat, tanto como (tannto komo). *You eat too much and you work too little,* Vd. come demasiado y trabaja muy poco (oostayth komay thaymasyatho ee travaha mooy poko). *That's my advice to you,* este es mi consejo (esstay ess mee konnsayho). With a patient like you, an unscrupulous doctor could live *all his life*, **toda la vida** (tótha la veetha), giving you *a prescription*, **una receta** (oona raytháyta) every day, *a spoonful every hour*, **una cuchara cada hora** (oona koochara katha ora). *No, young lady*, **no señorita** (no senngyoreeta), *I am sorry to say*, **siento decir** (syennto thaytheer) *you are absolutely healthy*, **Vd. está absolutamente sana** (oostayth essta apsolootamenntay sana).

Work is the best medicine.
El trabajo es la mejor medicina.
ell travaho ess la mayhor maytheetheena

Translate into Spanish

The hat, of the hat; the shirt, of the shirt; the gentleman; of the gentleman; the lady, of the lady; the hats; of the hats; the shirts, of the shirts; the gentlemen, of the gentlemen; the ladies, of the ladies. Give me a black hat. Give me a white shirt.

My hat is black, your hat is white, his or her hat is brown. My gloves are yellow, my shirts are blue. Your gloves are brown, your shirts are white. His, her, their, your gloves are red, his, her, their, your shirts are black.

This woman has a white blouse. These women. A picture. These ladies and girls. Church, cathedral, with the large veil, a large comb.

Are you a Spaniard? No, sir, I am from New York. I am American, my friends also. And you? We are all Englishmen! I am, you are (familiar), he is, she is, you are. We are, you are, they are (without personal pronoun). I, you (familiar), he, she, you, we, you (familiar), they (m.), they (f.), you.

Your Grace, Your Graces. I have, you have (familiar), he has, she has, you have; we have, you have (fam.), they have (m.), they have (f.), you have.

Every few minutes. Everyone in the house. A pencil, a pen, a fountain pen. Where is it? Where is my pencil, my pen, my fountain pen? And a second later: where is some paper?

My uncle, the collar, the necktie, the buttons on the table, under the table, in the wardrobe. Where is his collar? Where is his necktie? Where are his buttons? At a critical moment, on time, a dozen shirts with collars and cuffs.

Who has my shirts? Where is my new shirt? Anew. I tell you. We had a fine time. That aunt of ours, the eyeglasses, four or eight times a day.

Once, twice, three times, four times, five times, each time, perhaps, at once, by turns, more than once (frequently), sometimes.

Uncle and aunt, something, the questions from children. The grandfather, the grandmother, the grandparents, the patience, without doubt. Where? How? Who? What is it?

¡Lea en alta voz!

Vd. tiene dinero. A una tienda. Un pañuelo de seda de muchos colores, el sombrero, un sombrero de fieltro, un sombrero de paja, los sombreros. Hay sombreros de muchos colores para señoras y señores. Por ejemplo: el bolso de mano, el espejo, el espejo de bolsillo, a una señorita, el bolsillo, los bolsillos, una blusa, una camisa, el color del sombrero, el color del bolsillo, el color de la camisa.

El sombrero, del sombrero; la camisa, de la camisa; el señor, del señor; la señora, de la señora; los sombreros, de los sombreros; las camisas, de las camisas; los señores, de los señores; las señoras, de las señoras. Deme un sombrero negro. Deme una camisa blanca.

Mi sombrero es negro, tu sombrero es blanco, su sombrero es marrón. Mis guantes son amarillos, mis camisas son azules. Tus guantes son marrones, tus camisas son blancas. Sus guantes son rojos, sus camisas son negras.

Esta mujer tiene una blusa blanca. Estas mujeres. Un cuadro. Estas señoras y señoritas. Iglesia, catedral, con la mantilla, el peine.

¿Es Vd. español? ¿Es Vd. una española? No, señor, soy de Nueva York. Yo soy american, mi amigos también. ¿Y Vds.? Nosotros somos todos ingleses. Soy, eres, es, Vd. es, somos, sois, son. Yo, tu, el, Vd. (usted), elle, nosotros, vosotros, ellos, ellas, Vds. (ustedes).

¡Haga el favor de repetir!

la horchata	la orrtshata	*the orgeat*
el almendra	ell almayndra	*the almond*
el agua, fem.	ell agva	*the water*
y azúcar	ee athookar	*and sugar*
¿Qué toma usted?	kay toma oostayth	*What do you take?* *What will you have?*
o	o	*or*
un jugo de naranja	oon hoogo thay narangha	*orange juice*
¿Tiene usted ganas de comer algo?	teeaynay oostayth ganas thay ko- mayr algo	*Would you like to eat something?*
¡Vamos a una fonda!	vamos a oona fonda	*Let us go to a res- taurant!*
tengo	tayngo	*I have*
usted tiene	oostayth teeaynay	*you have*
tomo	tomo	*I take*
usted toma	oostayth toma	*you take*
¡Gracias, señora!	grathyas sengyora	*Thank you, ma- dame!*
uso	ooso	*I use*
el café	ell kafay	*the café* and *the coffee*
la familia	la fameelya	*the family*
el padre	ell pathray	*the father*
la madre	la mathray	*the mother*
la tía	la teea	*the aunt*
el tío	ell teeo	*the uncle*
el hermano	ell errmano	*the brother*
la hermana	la errmana	*the sister*
una bebida	oona bayveetha	*a drink*
un buen plato	oon booayn plato	*a good dish*
¡Camarero, la cu- enta!	kamarayro la kvennta	*Waiter, the check (or the bill)!*
¿Cuanto es?	kvanto ess	*How much is it?*
¡Haga el favor de contar hasta veinte!	aga ell favor thay kontar asta vay- eentay	*Please count up to twenty!*

¡Muy bien, amigo!	mooy byayng ameego	Very well (my) friend!
bastante	bastantay	enough
mil gracias	meel grathyas	a thousand thanks!
el país	ell paees	the country
un poco de tiempo	oon poko thay tyaympo	for a little while
un rey	oon ray	a king
un duque	oon dookay	a duke
un conde	oon konday	a count
el pasaporte	ell pasaportay	the passport
un cheque	oon chaykay	a check
una carta certificada	oona karta therrteefeekatha	a registered letter
¿Como se llama usted?	komo say lyama oostayth	What is your name?
un nombre	oon nombray	a name
la firma	la feerma	the signature
deletrear	daylaytrayar	to spell
el alfabeto	ell alfabayto	the Spanish A-B-C
la primera letra es a A	la preemayra laytra ess a A	the first letter is a A
el abecedario español	ell abaythaydaryo espangyol	the Spanish A-B-C
me llamo Pedro	may lyamo paythro	I call myself Peter
¡Deletree su nombre!	daylaytrayay soo nommbray	Spell your name!
el apellido	ell apelyeetho	the surname
la calle	la kalyay	the street
los números de las casas	loss noomayroz thay las kasas	the numbers of the houses
¿Dónde está calle de la Concordia 34?	donnde essta kalyay thay la konnkorrdya trayeenta ee kvatro	Where is 34 Concord Street?
diez minutos de aquí	deeayth meenootos thay akee	10 minutes from here
vaya Vd. (usted)	vaya oostayth	go!
después	dayspooays	then
una calle a la izquierda	oona calyay al eethkyerrtha	one street to the left
una cuadra	oona kvathra	one block
¡No se moleste!	no say molaystay	Don't trouble yourself!
¡vaya Vd. con Diós!	vaya oostayth kon dyoss	go with God!
la casa del amigo	la kasa dell ameego	the house of the friend

¿Cómo está la familia?	komo aysta la fameelya	How is the family?
bien, gracias	byayn grathyas	well, thanks!
¡Qué calor hace!	kay kalor athay	How hot it is!
¿Quiere Vd. beber?	kyayray oostayth bayvayr	Will you have a drink?
¡si, seguramente!	see saygooramentay	yes, surely!
Vd. tiene dinero	oostayth teeaynay theenayro	you have money
a una tienda	a oona tyayntha	to a store
un pañuelo de seda	oon panyooaylo thay saytha	a handkerchief of silk
un sombrero de fieltro	oon sommbrayro thay fyayltro	a hat of felt, a felt hat
un sombrero de paja	oon sommbrayro thay paha	a hat of straw
de muchos colores	de moochoss kolorays	of many colors
para señoras y señores	para sengyoras ee sengyorays	for ladies and gentlemen
por ejemplo	porr ehemmplo	for instance
el bolso de mano	ell bollso thay mano	the handbag
el espejo	ell ayspayho	the mirror
el espejo de bolsillo	ell espayho thay bollseellyo	the pocket mirror
una blusa	oona bloosa	a blouse
medias	maydyas	stockings
una camisa	oona kameesa	a shirt
mi sombrero es negro	mee sommbrayro ess naygro	my hat is black
tu sombrero es blanco	too sommbrayro ess blanko	your hat is white
su	soo	his, her
marrón	marrong	brown
amarillo	amareellyo	yellow
azule	athoolay	blue
mis guantes	meez gvantays	my gloves
rojo	roho	red
sus guantes	sooz gvantays	his, her, their, your gloves
Esta mujer tiene una blusa blanca	aysta moohayr teeaynay oona bloosa blanka	This woman has a white blouse
le frente	la frenntay	the forehead
un cuadro	oon kvathro	a painting
iglesia	eeglaysya	church
catedral	kataythral	cathedral
con la mantilla	konn la manteelya	with the large veil

el peine	ell payeene	the large comb
los extranjeros	loss aystrannhayros	the strangers
¿Es Vd. español?	ays oostayth ayspangyol	Are you a Spaniard?
¿Es Vd. española?	ays oostayth ayspangyola	Are you a Spaniard? (female)
no, señor, soy de Nueva York	no sengyor soee thay nooayva york	no, sir, I am from New York
también	tammbyayng	also
siempre	syaympray	always
cada cinco minutos	katha theengko meenootoss	every few minutes
todos en casa	tothoss enn kasa	everyone in the house
el lápiz	ell lapeeth	the pencil
la pluma fuente	la plooma fooenntay	the fountain pen
¿dónde está eso?	donnday aysta ayso	where is it?
el papel	ell papayl	the paper
el cuello	ell kvellyo	the collar
la corbata	la korrvata	the necktie
el botón	ell botong	the button
sobre	sobray	on
debajo de	dayvaho day	under
en el armario	enn ell armaryo	in the wardrobe
á tiempo	a tyaympo	in time
la docena	la dothayna	the dozen
con cuellos y puños	konn kvellyoss ee poonyoss	with collars and cuffs
¿Quién?	kyayn	Who?
mi camisa nueva	mee kameesa nooayva	my new shirt
de nuevo	day nooayvo	anew
le digo a Vd.	lai theego a oostayth	I tell you
nos divertimos mucho	noz theeverrteemoss mootsho	we had a fine time
los lentes	loss layntays	the eyeglasses
una vez	oona vayth	once
cada vez	katha vayth	each time
más de una vez	maz thay oona vayth	more than once, frequently
tal vez	tal vayth	perhaps
á veces	a vaythays	sometimes
alguna cosa	algoona kosa	something
la pregunta	la praygoonta	the question
el abuelo	ell avooaylo	the grandfather
la abuela	la avooayla	the grandmother
la paciencia	la pathyaynthya	the patience

1000 Words
SPANISH

¿Qué hay?	¿Qué ha sucedido?
kay **ay**	a soothaydeedo
What is the matter?	*What has happened?*

Hoy todavía	**no**	hay accidentes.
oy tothav**ee**a	no	ay aktheethenntays
There have been	*no*	*accidents so far today.*

* 65 *

Lesson Thirteen

I am sorry, but I can no longer hide the fact that the endings of words are the most important part of the Spanish language. For verbs there are three kinds of endings, **ar** as in **hablar** (avlar), *to speak;* **–er** as in **comer** (komayr), *to eat;* and **ir** as in **vivir** (veeveer), *to live.*

hablo	(avlo)	*I speak*	**como**	(komo)	*I eat*
hablas	(avlas)	*etc.*	**comes**	(komays)	*etc.*
habla	(avla)		**come**	(komay)	
hablamos	(avlamoss)		**comemos**	(komaymoss)	
hablais	(avlaees)		**coméis**	(kommayees)	
hablan	(avlan)		**comen**	(komayn)	

vivo	(veevo)	*I live*
vives	(veevays)	*etc.*
vive	(veevay)	
vivimos	(veeveemoss)	
vivís	(veevees)	
viven	(veevayn)	

There is no difficulty for an American to get along with his English anywhere in the British Empire and neither is it difficult for an Englishman in the United States of America, even though there are some differences in many respects. And it is likewise with the Spanish language: a Castilian-speaking Spaniard (and Castilian is the only universally accepted Spanish standard) will never have any difficulties in comprehension in Spanish America. There are minor differences in pronunciation. For instance, **y** before vowels is pronounced in several South American countries, such as Venezuela or Argentina, like j as in the word *jewel.* They pronounce **yo**—that means *I*—jo; but if you would pronounce **yo** the Castilian way, yo, nobody would notice it very much. In many South American countries, ll has not the Castilian pronunciation, like our *ly,* but simply y. **Cavallo,** *horse,* is, in those countries, pronounced kavayo and **caballero,** *gentleman,* is kavayayro. There are some countries in South America which omit, in the Past Participle, the pronunciation of the letter d. They say for **amado,** *loved,* amao; for **comprado,** *bought,* komprao. But, if you speak in the Castilian way, **amado** and **comprado,** they will know that you talk of love and business.

You will remember how easy it was to form the past tense by using the auxiliary verb **haber** (avayr): *I have spoken,* **he hablado** (ay avlado). *Without* any more *difficulty*, **sin dificultad** (seen deefeekooltath), you will be able to form the past of other verbs when I tell you that, for instance, for **dudar** (doothar), *to doubt*, the past participle is **dudado** (doothatho); and so on:

tomar			**tomado**	
(tomar)	*to take*		(tomatho)	*taken*
pagar			**pagado**	
(pagar)	*to pay*		(pagatho)	*paid*
ganar			**ganado**	
(ganar)	*to gain, earn*		(ganatho)	*gained, earned*
trabajar			**trabajado**	
(travahar)	*to work*		(travahatho)	*worked*

Ado is the ending for all verbs that end in **ar.** For the verbs that end in **er** and **ir** it is **ido** (eetho).

comer			**comido**	
(komayr)	*to eat*		(komeetho)	*eaten*
vivir			**vivido**	
(veeveer)	*to live*		(veeveetho)	*lived*
vender			**vendido**	
(vayndayr)	*to sell*		(vendeetho)	*sold*
beber			**bebido**	
(baiayvayr)	*to drink*		(bayveetho)	*drunk*
temer			**temido**	
(taymayr)	*to fear*		(taymeetho)	*feared*
correr			**corrido**	
(korrayr)	*to run*		(korreetho)	*run*
partir			**partido**	
(parteer)	*to start*		(parteetho)	*started*
interrumpir			**interrumpido**	
(eenterroompeer)	*to interrupt*		(eenterroompeetho)	*interrupted*
recibir			**recibido**	
(raytheeveer)	*to receive*		(raytheeveetho)	*received*

And now combining our past participles with the auxiliary verb we have the past tense:

he comido
(ay komeetho)   *I have eaten*
has tomado
(as tomatho)   *you have taken*
ha, Vd. ha partido
(a, oostayth a parteetho)   *he, she, it has started*
hemos recibido
(aymoss raytheeveetho)   *we have received*

habeis corrido	
(avayees korreetho)	*you have run*
Vds. han ganado	
(oostaythayth ann ganatho)	*they, you have gained*
hube dicho	
(oovay deecho)	*I had said*
hubiste olvidado	
(ooveestay ollveethatho)	*you have forgotten*
hubo olvidado	
(oovo ollveethatho)	*he had forgotten*
hubimos olvidado	
(ooveemoss ollveethatho)	*we had forgotten*
hubisteis olvidado	
(ooveestayees ollveethatho)	*you had forgotten*
hubieron olvidado	
(oovyayron ollveethatho)	*they had forgotten*

Dicho (deecho), *said, told*, comes from **decir** (daytheer), *to tell, to say*. That is one of the irregular verbs with which you will get acquainted *by and by*, **de paso** (day paso).

Let us talk *a minute*, **un minuto** (oon meenooto), about the way we learn a language. It is not true that we can pick up a language without working and studying.

Haber (avayr), *to have* is an auxiliary verb used with other verbs. Only in one form is it to be used independently: i.e. **hay** (aee) *there is, there are;* **había** (aveea) *there was, there were;* **hubo** (oovo) *there was, there were.*

If you have ever observed *a child*, **un niño** (oon neenyo), you know that from his first attempts to speak *his mother tongue*, **la lengua de su madre** (la lengva thay soo mathray), he tries to form *words*, **palabras** (palavras). *These words*, **estas palabras** (estas palavras), it is true are often understood, **son comprendidas** (sonn kommprenndeethas), only *by the mother of the baby*, **por la madre del nene** (porr la mathray dell naynay). She is sure that the baby is telling her *long stories*, **cuentos largos** (kventoss largoss). When nobody else can understand the child she is sure of it, even when it utters that word which is the first word that every baby produces, *the word "mamma,"* **la palabra de mama** (la palavra thay mama).

Yes, indeed, *in the eyes of our loving mother*, **en los ojos de nuestra madre amanda** (enn loss ohoz thay nooesstra mathray amanda), *we are all wonderful children*, **nosotros somos todos niños maravillosos** (nosotross somoss tothos neenyoss maraveelyososs), and *geniuses*, **genios** (haynyoss). *Later on*, **más tarde** (mas tarthay), life shows us that either our mother made a mistake or the world doesn't recognize *our greatness*, **nuestra grandeza** (nooestra grandestha). *Maybe*, **puede ser** (pooaythay serr), it is because we have in the meantime learned to form *sentences*, **sentencias** (senntennthyas), and we cannot deny that it is not always *gold*, **de oro** (day oro), that many people talk as soon as they are able to form sentence after sentence. If it were gold, how rich do you think the nonsense-talkers would be? It is really hard to imagine.

But after all, *you are hungry*, **Vd. tiene hambre** (oostayth teeaynay ambray); let us have our meal. Later I will tell you something about doing so in the Spanish way.

Today let us go home, *let us take our meal*, **comemos** (komaymoss), and later on, *let us go to bed*, **vamos a dormir** (vamoss a dorrmeer). Sleeping we forget all. But, please, don't do that with all you have learned.

¡Buenas noches! (booaynas nochays), *Good night!*
¡Qué duerma bien! (kay dooerrma byayng), *Sleep well!*
¡Qué descanse! (kay dayskannsay), *Rest well!*
Descansar (dayskansar), *to rest.*

¡Lea en alta voz!

Usted, Ustedes. Yo tengo, tu tienes, el tiene, ella tiene, Vd. tiene; nosotros tenemos, vosotros teneis, ellos tienen, ellas tienen, Vds. tienen.

Cada cinco minutos. Todos en casa. Un lápiz, una pluma. ¿Dónde está eso? ¿Dónde está mi lápiz, mi pluma? Y un segundo más tarde: ¿Dónde está el papel?

Mi tío, el cuello, la corbata, los botones, sobre la mesa, debajo de la mesa, en el armario. ¿Dónde está su cuello, su corbata? ¿Dónde están sus botones? En un momento crítico, á tiempo, una docena de camisas con cuellos y puños.

¿Quién tiene mis camisas? ¿Dónde está mi camisa nueva? De nuevo. Le digo a Vd. Nos divertimos mucho. Aquella tía nuestra, los lentes, cuatro hasta ocho vece al día.

Una vez, dos veces, tres veces, cuatro veces, cada vez, tal vez, de una vez, a la vez, más de una vez, á veces.

Lesson Fourteen

One of the most surprising facts I have come across is that so many people, and among them very *intelligent men and women*, **hombres y mujeres inteligentes** (ommbrays ee moohayrays eentelleehenntays), are very anxious to find out what is going to happen to them *in the* distant *future*, **en el futuro** (enn ell footooro). They will not believe that perhaps we are very fortunate that we do not know, at any moment, what the next will bring forth. We constantly look for wonders and do not realize that the most wonderful and mysterious things are present right around us all the time. Without giving it a thought, they take for granted the fact that *the sun rises and sets every day*, **el sol sale y se pone todos los días** (ell sol salay ee say ponay tothoss loss deeas), that *nature*, **la naturaleza** (la natooralestha), has its own ways. No matter how many facts scientists unearth, the ultimate secrets of nature will remain unknown. An old Latin saying goes: Ignoramus, ignorabimus, *we are ignorant and we shall be ignorant*, or as the Spanish say: **Ignoramos e ignoraremos** (eegnoramoss ay eegnoraraymoss).

> Before a masculine noun, the adjectives **bueno** (b o o a y n o) *good*, **malo** (malo), *bad* drop the **o**, e.g. **un buen asiento** (oon booayn asyaynto) *a good seat;* **un mal hombre** (oon mal ommbray), *a bad man.* They preserve it when they are placed after the noun.

I think we can safely say that everyone has problems. And as each man thinks his problem *the most important thing on earth*, **la cosa más importante del mundo** (la kosa mas eemporrtantay dell moondo), *he is inclined*, **es inclinado** (ess eenkleenatho), to believe in *fortune tellers*, **decidores de la buena ventura** (daytheedorays thay la booayna venntoora); literally: *tellers of the good future*. The Spaniard, in his language, makes a very fine distinction between what is a fact, what may be *a fact*, **un hecho** (oon aycho), what is certain, what will be almost certain, and what is possible and what is not.

Facts are stubborn things. The Spaniard says: *There is nothing so obstinate as a fact*, **no hayo nada tan terco como un hecho** (no ayo natha tann terrko komo oon aycho). You see, there are two words for *future* in Spanish, **el futuro** and **la ventura** (ell footooro and la vayntoora). **El futuro** is what we may possibly know; **la**

Una flora,   **una florecita,**   **señora,**   **por una**
oona flora   oona floraytheeta   sengyora   porr oona
A flower,   *a little flower,*   *lady,*   *for a small*

perra chica.
oona perra cheeka
copper coin (penny).

ventura is our future, our fortune, which, of course, is absolutely uncertain in spite of all fortune tellers.

I once had *the occasion*, **la ocasión** (f.) (la okkasyong), to hear what *a* very popular *fortune teller had prophesied to a girl*, **una decidora de la buena ventura hubo profetizado a una muchacha** (oona daytheedora thay la booayna vayntoora oovo profayteethado a oona moochacha). She had said:

Vd. cruzará una calle y entrará en una casa. Vd. encontrará
oostayth kroothara oona kallyay ee enntrara enn oona kasa
oostayth ennkonntrara
You will cross a street and enter a house. You will meet

en esta casa un amigo, este amigo hablara con Vd. Volverá
enn essta kasa oon ameego esstay ameego avlara konn oostayth
vollvayra
a friend in this house. This friend will talk to you. You will return

a casa. Vd. comerá. Vd. recibirá una carta muy importante.
a kasa. oostayth komayra. oostayth raytheeveera oona karta
mooy eemporrtantay
to your home. You will eat. You will receive a very important letter.

Esta carta decidirá su ventura.
essta karta daytheedeera soo vayntoora.
This letter will decide your fortune.

I met the girl *a few days later*, **unos días más tarde** (oonoss deeas mas tarday), and she said: The fortune teller told me:

Crusaré una calle (krootharay oona kallyay) *I shall cross a street*. It was true, **he crusado una calle** (ay kroothado oona kallyay) *I have crossed a street*. **Entraré en una casa** (enntraray enn oona kasa) *I shall enter a house*. Absolutely right; **yo he entrado en una casa y encontrado un amigo** (yo ay enntrado enn oona kasa ee ennkonntrado oon ameego) *I have entered a house and I have met a friend*. And just think of it, *this friend spoke to me*, **este amigo ha hablado conmigo** (esstay ameego a avlado konnmeego). The fortune teller *has told me*, **me ha dicho** (may a deecho): **encontraré un amigo que hablará conmigo** (ennkonntraray oon ameego kay avlara konnmeego), *I shall meet a friend who will speak to me*. **Volveré a casa** (vollvayray a kasa) *I shall return home*. So I did; **he vuelto** (ay vooellto) *I have returned*. **Comeré** (komayray) *I shall eat;* **he comido** (ay komeetho) *I have eaten*. And now this settles the question. You remember what he said: **recibiré una carta** (raytheeveeray oona karta) *I shall receive a letter.* What do you think of this? **He recibido una carta muy importante** (ay raytheeveedo oona karta mooy eemporrtantay) *I have received a very important letter.* **Esta carta, asi ha dicho, decidirá mi ventura** (essta karta, asee a deecho, daytheedeera mee venntoora), *This letter, so he said, will decide my fortune.* My boss wrote me that he is sorry, but I should look for another job. Isn't that important? You'll see; I'll find a better job. That settles it. I shall go to the fortune teller again for further details.

I did not try to convince the girl that I could have predicted things like that to her every day. She wouldn't have believed me. But *we will be*, **seremos** (sayraymoss), very grateful to her anyway, *because*, **porque** (porrkay), even if she hasn't told us about *the future*, **la ventura** (la venntoora), *of our life*, **de nuestra vida** (day nooesstra veetha), she taught us verbs.

Mis amigos queridos, mi amigo querido, mi querida amiga,
mees ameegoss kayreethoss, mee ameego kayreetho, mee kayreetha ameega
My dear friends, my dear friend (m. and f.),

lo comprenderéis todo, si os lo habré dicho todo.
lo kommprenndayrayees totho see os lo avray deecho totho
you will understand everything if I shall have told you everything.

habré recibido	(avray raytheebeetho)	*I shall have received*
habrás dicho	(avraz theecho)	*you will have said*
habrá comprendido	(avra kommprenndeetho)	*he, she, it will have understood*
habremos pasado	(avraymoss pasatho)	*we will have passed*
habréis trabajado	(avrayees travahatho)	*you will have worked*
habrán tomado	(havrann tomatho)	*they will have taken*

Lesson Fifteen

Vd. no habrá olvidado (oostayth no avra ollveethatho) *you will not have forgotten:* **tengo dinero** (tenngo theenayro) *I have money;* **no tengo dinero** (no tenngo theenayro) *I have no money;* **tendré dinero** (tenndray theenayro) but *I shall have money;* **lo ganaré** (lo ganaray) *I shall earn it.* **Mi hermano lo ha ganado hace mucho tiempo** (mee errmano lo a ganatho athay moocho tyemmpo) *my brother earned it a long time ago.* **¿Está feliz?** (essta fayleeth), *To be happy? Are you happy?* **¡No lo sé!** (no lo say) *I do not know!*

tener (taynayr)		*to have* (as a property)
tengo (tenngo)		*I have*
tuve (toovay)		*I had*
he tenido (ay tayneetho)		*I have had*
tendré (tenndray)		*I shall have*
tendrás (tenndras)		*you will have*
tendrá (tenndra)		*etc.*
tendremos (tenndraymoss)		
tendréis (tenndrayees)		
tendrán (tenndran)		

Translate into Spanish

What is it for? We ask a gentleman or a girl or a woman. The brother has given a present to his sister. The mother asks the father. It is late, our lesson. What time is it? It is one o'clock. It is three o'clock, four o'clock, five o'clock. Let us take a walk through Buenos Aires!

This or that person. One or more foreign languages. The same kind, we don't know each other. Mankind, in the beginning, let us go together! First, you can speak Spanish. You can speak Spanish as well as English. What is the way to City Hall? Where is City Hall? How far is it? Where do you want to go? It is not far from here, it is very near. Go straight ahead, to the right, to the left.

estar (esstar)	to be (in a place)
estoy (esstoy)	I am
estuve (esstoovay)	I was
he estado (ay esstado)	I have been
ser (sayr)	to be (permanent)
soy (soy)	I am
fuí (fooee)	I was
he sido (ay seetho)	I have been

estaré (esstaray)	I shall be	seré (sayray)
estarás (esstaras)	etc.	serás (sayras)
estará (esstara)		será (sayra)
estaremos (esstaraymoss)		seremos (sayraymoss)
estaréis (esstarayees)		seréis (sayrayees)
estarán (esstaran)		serán (sayran)

hablar (avlar)	to speak
hablaré (avlaray)	I shall speak
hablarás (avlaras)	etc.
hablará (avlara)	
hablaremos (avlaraymoss)	
hablaréis (avlarayees)	
hablarán (avlaran)	

comer (komayr)	to eat
comeré (komayray)	I shall eat
comerás (komayras)	etc.
comerá (komayra)	
comeremos (komayraymoss)	
comeréis (komayrayees)	
comerán (komayran)	

vivir (veeveer)	to live
viviré (veeveeray)	I shall live
vivirás (veeveeras)	etc.
vivirá (veeveera)	
viviremos (veeveeraymoss)	
viviréis (veeveerayees)	
vivirán (veeveeran)	

Lesson Sixteen

When we talk of Spanish speaking countries, we cannot help thinking of Carmen's country and of her "toreador," **de su torero** (thay soo torrayro) *of her bullfighter.* *These bullfighters,* **estos toreros** or **estos toreadores** (esstos torrayross esstos torrayathorays) are the heroes of the Spanish people.

¿Quiere Vd. ir a una corrida de toros?
kyayray oostayth eer a oona korreetha thay toross.
Do you want to go to a bullfight?

Compraremos una entrada para una corrida de toros.
kommpraraymoss oona enntratha para oona korreetha thay toross
We will buy a ticket for a bullfight.

La corrida empezará a las cuatro y media en punto de la tarde.
la korreetha emmpaythara a las kvatro ee maythya enn poonto thay la tarrthay
The fight will begin at half past four in the afternoon.

Las puertas de la plaza se abrirán dos horas antes.
las pooerrtas thay la platha say avreeran doss oras antays
The doors of the place will be opened (the Spaniards say: *will open themselves*) *two hours earlier.*

Veremos los picadores (vayraymoss loss peekathorays). *We shall see the picadores (the fighters on horseback);* **Vds. verán los espadas que matarán los toros** (oostaythays vayran loss esspaythas kay mataran loss toross) *you*

Santo (sangto), *saint* very often drops the last syllable "to" e.g. San Fernando (san ferrnando), San Francisco (san frantheesko).

(to many persons) *will see the fighters, the espadas who will kill the bulls,* and before them, **los banderilleros que trabajan con sus banderillas** (loss banndayreelyayross kay travahan konn soos bandayreelyas), *the men with the small darts with a bannerol* which they thrust into the shoulders and neck of the bull. Let us not forget *the* poor *bulls,* **los toros** (loss toross) and *the audience,* **el público** (ell poobleeko).

"El mundo es de los atrevidos" (ell moondo ess thay loss atrayveethoss) is *an old Spanish proverb,* **un viejo proverbio español** (oon vyayho proverrbyo esspangyol). Literally translated, it is,

"*The world is of the courageous ones.*" We would say, "The courageous rule the world." But let us dwell a little upon this expression. *It is necessary,* es necesario (ess naythessaryo), first to decide, primero pensar (preemayro pennsar) *first to think,* what *the word "courage,"* la palabra de coraje (la palavra thay korrahay), means. It has nothing to do with *impudence,* la impudencia (la eempoodennthy) or forwardness or arrogance. To say what we feel is *the truth,* la verdad (la verrthath) and *to act,* actuar (aktooar) according to our ideals, that, *I should like to say,* me gustaría decir (may goostareea daytheer), *is courageous,* eso es atrevido (esso ess atrayveetho).

Su casa can mean *his house, her house, their house* or *your house.* If it is necessary to be very accurate, one says su casa de él (soo kasa thay ell) *his house;* su casa de ella (soo kasa thay ellya) *her house;* su casa de Vd. (soo kasa thay oostayth) *your house;* su casa de ellos (soo kasa thay ellyoss) *their house;* su casa de ellas (soo kasa thay ellyas) *their house* (fem.).

Have courage! ¡Tenga valor! (tennga valor) *Be plucky!* ¡Sea valeroso! (saya valayroso) *Come, cheer up!* ¡Vamos! (vamoss) ¡Valor! (valor). Whenever you have *the occasion,* la ocasión (la okkasyong), *to speak Spanish,* de hablar español (day avlar esspangyol), *or to read Spanish,* o de leer español (o thay layayr esspangyol), *do not say,* no diga (no deega) *I haven't the courage to do it,* no tengo valor para hacerlo (no tenngo valor para athayrlo); *I can't do it,* no puedo hacerlo (no pooaytho athayrlo). *I don't believe it,* no lo creo (no lo krayo).

puedo	(pooaytho)	*I can*	podemos (pothaymoss)	*we can*
puedes	(pooaythays)	*etc.*	podéis (pothayees)	*etc.*
puede	(pooaythay)		pueden (pooaythayn)	

Have you noticed this lo: hacerlo (athayrlo) lo creo? (lo krayo)? In Spanish it is sometimes used for the English *it,* and sometimes also for *so.* Again and again *we have shown you,* le hemos mostrado a Vd. (lay aymoss mosstratho a oostayth) that it is absolutely impossible to translate word for word from English into Spanish because the ways of expressing the same idea are very different in the two languages. We may sometimes say "I can't do so." The Spaniard always says, "I can't do it." *But if you were to ask,* pero si Vd. preguntaría (payro see oostayth praygoontareea), "Is there no word in Spanish for the word 'so'?" I would have to answer, debo contestar (dayvo konntesstar). *I must answer, "Certainly, it is,* **Así, ciertamente eso es así** (thyerrtamenntay esso ess asee). But knowing under what circumstances you use it, **pero cuando Vd. debe usarlo** (payro kvando oostayth dayvay oosarlo) *but when you must use it,* is a matter of practice."

This feeling for the Spanish language, this knowing when and where to use each word in its exact sense, will come to you *by and by,* **de paso** (day paso).

Here are more examples of the difference in the ways of expression. We say: *Spanish is spoken.* The Spaniard usually says, *Spanish speaks itself,* **se habla español** (say avla esspangyol). It is the style often used for public notices: *Se alquila* (say alkeela). *It rents itself* is our *for rent.*

Se alquila habitación amueblada.
say alkeela aveetathyong amooayvlatha
Furnished room for rent.

Se alquila habitación sin amueblar.
say alkeela aveetathyong seen amooayvlar
Unfurnished rooms to let.

Se prohibe fumar.
say proeevay foomar
It is forbidden to smoke (No smoking).

Se prohibe la entrada.
say proeevay la enntratha
It is forbidden to enter (*No admittance*).

Se suplica cerrar la puerta.
say soopleeka therrar la pooerrta
It is requested to close the door (*Please close the door*).

Se suplica no tocar.
say soopleeka no tokar
It is requested not to touch (*Please do not touch*).

But it is quite wrong, **estaría Vd. en un error** (esstareea oostayth enn oon error) *you would be wrong* (in an error), to think that you cannot express an idea up to its final nuance in Spanish just as you can in English, for the difference lies only in the idiomatic form. *They are right,* **tienen razón** (teeaynayng rathong) *just as we are right,* **exactamente como nosotros tene-**

Cuente usted   **hasta veinte.**
quayntay oostayth   asta vayeentay
Count up to   *twenty.*

¿Por qué? Tengo solamente   **cinco duros.**
porr kay? tenngo solamenntay   theengko dooross
Why? I have only   *five dollars.*

mos razón (ayksaktamenntay komo nosotross taynaymoss rathong).

In English, the endings of words do not play the great part in determining meaning that they do in Spanish. We have seen that *I shall speak* is **hablaré** (avlaray), *you will rent*, **alquilarás** (alkeelaras). This is the familiar form used only for very intimate friends. And now, because it is really very simple, let us see how we would say, *I would speak.*

Grande, before nouns beginning with a consonant, **b e c o m e s gran** (grann) e.g. **un gran maestro** (oon grann maaystro), *a great master.* And it is just the same with the number **ciento** (thyaynto), e.g. **cien pesetas** (thyayng paysaytas), *hundred pesetas.*

For regular verbs you have nothing to do but to add to the infinitive form the endings **ía, ías, ía, íamos, íais, ían.** *I should speak,* **hablaría** (avlareea); *you would send,* **mandarías** (manndareeas); *he would sell,* **vendería** (venndayreea); *we should buy,* **compraríamos** (kommprareeamoss); *you would live,* **viviríais** (veeveereeaees); *they would understand,* **comprenderían** (kommprenndayreean).

hablar	(avlar)	*to speak*
hablaría	(avlareea)	*I should speak*
hablarías	(avlareeas)	*etc.*
hablaría	(avlareea)	
hablaríamos	(avlareeamoss)	
hablaríais	(avlareeaees)	
hablarían	(avlareean)	
comer	(komayr)	*to eat*
comería	(komayreea)	*I should eat*
comerías	(komayreeas)	*etc.*
comería	(komayreea)	
comeríamos	(komayreeamoss)	
comeríais	(komayreeaees)	
comerían	(komayreean)	
vivir	(veeveer)	*I live*
viviría	(veeveereea)	*I should live*
vivirías	(veeveereeas)	*etc.*
viviría	(veeveereea)	
viviríamos	(veeveereeamoss)	
viviríais	(veeveereeaees)	
vivirían	(veeveereean)	

This polite way of speaking, **este modo cortés de hablar** (esstay motho korrtayz thay avlar), *is very easy,* **es muy fácil** (ess mooy fatheel), even when using irregular verbs. As soon as you see the endings **ía, ías, ía, íamos, íais, ían,** you can be sure *without* any *doubt*, **sin duda** (seen dooda), that you have this form, I should, you would etc., *before you*, **enfrente de Vd.** (ennfrenntay thay oostayth).

¡ Lea en alta voz !

Esta o aquella persona. Una o más lenguas extranjeras. Las mismas clases, no nos conocemos. La humanidad, al principio. ¡Nos juntamos! Primero, Vd. habla español. Vd. habla español tan bien como inglese. ¿Cuál es el camino del ayuntamiento? ¿Dónde está el ayuntamiento? ¿Qué distancia hay? ¿Adónde quiere Vd. ir? ¿Adónde va Vd.? No está lejos de aquí, está muy cerca. ¡Vaya Vd. derechito! A la derecha! A la izquierda!

¿Dónde? ¿Adónde? Primero es más fácil. Segundo, pensar, el más importante, menos importante. Mucho, poco. Tengo cien dólares en mi bolsillo. Tengo mucho dinero. Soy un hombre rico. ¿Qué hay? Cien dólares, eso no es nada para mi. Tengo más dinero que Vd. Con la gente muy rica, vosotros todos vosotros sois pobres. Soy la señora más rica del mundo.

La hermosura de las mujeres, vestidos, las cualidades de los hombres, las cuantidades de cosas. Vd. es más hermosa que la Venus de Milo. Vd. es la señora más hermosa que he visto. ¡Qué hermosura! Hermoso, más hermoso, el más hermoso. Nosotros los hombres no estamos solos. Hay muchas mujeres aquí. Mis secretos. Vds. todas señoras son las más hermosas, una como otra. ¿Qué veo? ¿Qué hay? Una revolución. ¿Qué oigo? Hace mucho tiempo, la más hermosa, la más simpatica, la más encantadora, la óptima. ¿Quién es está señora Venus?

Lesson Seventeen

The other day, **el otro día** (ell otro deea), you said to me: *I would like to see a bullfight*, **querría ver una corrida de toros** (kerreea vayr oona korreetha thay toross). *Would you buy me a ticket? Don't forget*, **¿Compraría Vd. una entrada? No lo olvide** (kommprareea oostayth oona enntratha no lo ollveethay). *I haven't forgotten it*. **No lo he olvidado** (no lo ay ollveethatho).

I shall always keep my promise.
Yo cumpliré siempre mi promesa.
yo koompleeray syemmpray mee promaysa.

¿Vd. también?	**¿Y mi querida, tu también?**
oostayth tammbyayng	ee mee kayreetha too tammbyayng
You too?	*And my dear, you too?*

Vosotros todos, os convido; vosotros todos seréis convidados por mi.
vosotross todoss oss konnveetho vosotross tothoss sayrayees konnveethathos porr mee

You all, I invite you; all of you will be invited by me.

And if we don't want to specify the particular person, I, you, he or she, who gives an invitation or who speaks or who does something, we use in English the indefinite pronoun "one"; sometimes we, they or you. In Spanish the Reflexive is very often used for this form. Therefore: **se habla** (say avla) *one speaks, it is spoken;* **se convida** (say konnveetha) *they invite, one invites.*

¿A qué hora se visitan las corridas de toros?
a kay ora say veeseetan las korreethas thay toross
At what time (hour) do they go (visit) to the bullfights?

It is not forgotten, **No se olvida** (no say ollveetha) (*one doesn't forget*). *Here is the ticket*, **aquí está la entrada** (akee essta la enntratha)!

¿O prefiere Vd. ir a las corridas de caballos?
o prayfeeayray oostayth eer a las korreethas thay kavallyoss
Or do you prefer to go to the horseraces?

¿Le gustan a Vd. más las corridas de caballos que las corridas de toros?
lay goostan oostayth mas las korreethas thay cavallyoss kay las korreethas thay toross
Do you like horseraces better than bullfights?

* 82 *

Billete para una corrida de toros.
beelyaytay para oona korreetha thay toross
Ticket for a bull-baiting.

Plaza de Toros de Madrid.
platha thay toross thay mathreeth
Bull ring (place) of Madrid.

Tendido ocho	**sol y sombra**
tenndeetho ocho	sol ee sommbra
Row (of seats) 8	*sun and shadow*
Balconcillo	**delantera**
ballkonntheelyo	daylanntayra
Balcony	*front seat*

Seis pts. (pesetas) quince cts. (céntimos)
sayees paysaytas keenthay thennteemoss
Six pesetas fifteen céntimos.

2ª (segunda) Corrida de abono
saygoonda korreetha thay abono
Second subscription bullfight 1939.

What is 1939 in Spanish? You remember *39*, **treinta y nueve** (trayeenta ee nooayvay); you remember: **uno** (oono) *1;* **dos** (doss) *2;* **tres** (tress) *3;* **cuatro** (kvatro) *4;* **cinco** (theenko) *5;* **seis** (sayees) *6;* **siete** (syaytay) *7;* **ocho** (ocho) *8;* **nueve** (nooayvay) *9;* **diez** (deeayth) *10;* **once** (onnthay) *11;* **doce** (dothay) *12;* **trece** (traythay) *13;* **catorce** (katorrthay) *14;* **quince** (keenthay) *15;* **dieciséis** (deeaytheesayees) *16;* **diecisiete** (deeaytheesyaytay) *17;* **dieciocho** (deeaytheeocho) *18;* **diecinueve** (deeaytheenooayvay) *19;* **veinte** (vayeentay) *20.*

tres y dos son cinco
tress ee doss sonn theenko
3 + 2 = 5

siete y tres son diez
syaytay ee tress sonn deeayth
7 + 3 = 10

uno y quince son dieciséis
oono ee keenthay sonn deeaytheesayees
1 + 15 = 16

diecisiete y diez son veinte y siete
deeaytheesyaytay ee deeayth sonn vayeentay ee syaytay
$17 + 10 = 27$

veinte	(vayeentay)	*20*
treinta	(trayeenta)	*30*
treinta y uno	(trayeenta ee oono)	*31*
treinta y dos	(trayeenta ee doss)	*32*
etc.		

cuarenta	(kvarennta)	*40*
cincuenta	(theenkvennta)	*50*
sesenta	(saysennta)	*60*
setenta	(saytennta)	*70*
ochenta	(ochennta)	*80*
noventa	(novennta)	*90*
ciento	(thyennto)	*100*

veinte y cuatro menos doce son doce
vayeentay ee kvatro maynoss dothay sonn dothay
$24 - 12 = 12$

cuarenta y dos menos treinta y tres son nueve
kvarennta ee doss maynoss trayeenta ee tress sonn nooayvay
$42 - 33 = 9$

ochenta y ocho menos treinta y nueve son cuarenta y nueve
ochennta ee ocho maynos trayeenta ee nooayvay sonn kvarennta
    ee nooayvay
$88 - 39 = 49$

dos por dos son cuatro   **uno por uno es uno**
doss porr doss sonn kvatro   oono porr oono ess oono
$2 \times 2 = 4$ $1 \times 1 = 1$

tres por siete son veinte y uno
tress porr syaytay sonn vayeentay ee oono
$3 \times 7 = 21$

seis por seis son treinta y seis
sayees porr sayees sonn trayeenta ee sayees
$6 \times 6 = 36$

Do not make any mistakes in counting! That might be expensive, so it is better to get acquainted right away with the numbers. If a merchant says **catorce** (katorrthay) *14*, it would be better to think he had said **cuatro** (kvatro) *4* than **cuarenta** (kvarennta) *40*. "Divide et impera" is a Latin motto. It is a rule for rulers; it means *"Divide and rule."* In Spanish it is:

"Divide y gobierna" (deeveethay ee govyerrna). If we put it in a more formal way, it is, **divida Vd. y gobierne** (deeveetha oostayth ee govyerrnay). But leave that to rulers and spend your time dividing numbers instead of countries.

diez dividido por dos son cinco
dyayth deeveetheetho porr thoss sonn theenko
$10 \div 2 = 5$

veinte y ocho dividido por siete son cuatro
vayeentay ee ocho deeveetheetho porr syaytay sonn kvatro
$28 \div 7 = 4$

setenta y cinco dividido sor cinco son quince
saytennta ee theenko deeveetheetho porr theenko sonn keenthay
$75 \div 5 = 15$

   ¿Tengo razón? (tenngo rathong). *Am I right?* **¿O estoy en un error?** (o esstoy enn oon error). *Or am I wrong?* **¿Me equivoco?** (may aykeevoko) *Am I wrong?* **¿Qué dice Vd?** (kay deethay oostayth) *What do you say?* **Lo creo** (lo krayo) *I think so.* **Muy bien** (mooy byayng). *All right.* **¡Qué no haya más que decir sobre eso!** (kay no a-ya mas kay daytheer sovray esso). *Let us say no more about it!* **Me digo a mi mismo** (may deego a mee meesmo) *I say to myself;* **no te lo digo a ti** (no tay lo deego a tee) *I do not say it to you.*

   100—**ciento** (thyennto)
   1000—**mil** (meel)
   1939—**mil novecientos treinta y nueve** (meel novaythyenntos trayeenta ee nooayvay).

*   *
*

Lesson Eighteen

Los viejos buenos tiempos son siempre elogiados por nuestros mayores a los jóvenes. No sabemos nunca si tienen razón o no.

*

Los viejos buenos tiempos son siempre elogiados por nuestros
loss veeayhoss booaynoss tyemmposs sonn syemmpray ayloheeathoss porr nooesstross
The good old times are always being praised by our

mayores a los jóvenes. No sabemos nunca si tienen razón o no.
ma-yorays a loss hovaynays. no savaymoss noonka see teeaynayn rathong o no
elders to the youngsters. We are never sure whether they are right or not.

*   *

Estaríamos en un error si no admitiésemos que la edad contribuye mucho a nuestra felicidad. Pero no podemos olvidar que alguna vez y al mismo tiempo hubo guerra o revolución o barbarismo en alguna parte del mundo. Y ciertamente hubo mucha gente que no gozó de los buenos tiempos en tanto que en otras partes del mundo todos podían gozar las bendiciones de la paz.

*

Estaríamos en un error si no admitiésemos que la edad contribuye
esstareeamoss enn oon error see no admeeteeaysaymoss kay la aythath konntreevooyay
We would be wrong if we did not admit that the time we live in may contribute

mucho a nuestra felicidad. Pero no podemos olvidar que alguna vez
moocho a nooesstra fayleetheethath. payro no pothaymoss ollveethar kay algoona vayth
a great deal to our happiness. But we cannot forget that at one

y al mismo tiempo hubo guerra o revolución o barbarismo
ee al meesmo tyemmpo oovo gerra o rayvoloothyonng o barbareesmo
and the same time there may exist war or revolution or barbarity

en alguna parte del mundo y ciertamente hubo mucha gente
enn algoona partay dell moondo ee thyerrtamenntay oovo
    moocha henntay
*in some part of the world, and certainly there may be a great many
    people*

que no gozó de los buenos tiempos en tanto que en otras
kay no gotho thay loss booaynoss tyemmposs enn tanto kay enn
    otras
who do not enjoy the good life, even while in other

partes del mundo todos podían gozar las benediciones de la
partays dell moondo tothoss podeeann gothar las benaydeethyon-
    ays thay la
parts of the world everyone is able to enjoy the blessings of

paz.
path
peace.

*   *

Con respecto al individuo, debemos decir que la felicidad no
existiria si no existiera la desventura. El hombre que vive siempre
feliz no apreciaría su felicidad si no supiera lo que significa el
serinfeliz.

*

Con respecto al individuo, debemos decir que la
konn resspekkto al eendeeveedoo-o dayvaymoss daytheer kay la
With regard to the individual, we must realize that

felicidad no existiria si no existiera la desventura. El
fayleetheedath no ekkseesteereea see no ekkseestyayra la dess-
    venntoora ell
happiness would not exist if misfortune were not also present. The

hombre que vive siempre feliz no apreciaría su felicidad
ommbray kay veevay syemmpray fayleeth no apraythyareea
    soo fayleetheedath
man who is always happy would not appreciate his happiness

si no supiera lo que significa el ser infeliz.
see no soopyayra lo kay seegneefeeka ell sayr eenfayleeth
since he would not know what it meant to be unhappy.

*   *

Casi todo el mundo tiene buenos días, buenas horas y malos
días y malas horas. Pero la minoría de los seres humanos difiere
de la mayor parte en lo que (ellos) pueden hacer con su felicidad
o con su desventura.

*

Casi todo el mundo tiene buenos días, buenas horas y malos días
kasee totho ell moondo teeaynay booaynoss deeas booaynas oras
ee maloss deeas
Almost everyone has good days, good hours and bad days

y malas horas. Pero la minoría de los seres humanos
ee malas oras. payro la meenoreea thay loss sayrays oomanoss
and bad hours. But the minority of human beings

difiere de la mayor parte en lo que (ellos)
deefyayray thay la ma-yor partay enn lo kay (ellyoss)
differ from the greater part (majority) in what they

pueden hacer con su felicidad o con su desventura.
pooaythayn athayr konn soo fayleetheethath o konn soo dess-
venntoora
are able to make of their happiness as well as of their misfortune.

No es solamente el sacar partido a cualquiera situación, no importa cuán trágica sea, sino que el gran problema es el uso que haremos de las memorias.

No es solamente el sacar partido a cualquiera
no ess solamenntay ell sakar parteetho a kvalkyayra
It is not enough simply to make the best of a

situación, no importa cuán trágica sea, sino que. El
seetooathyong no eemporrta kvann traheeka saya seeno kay ell
situation, no matter how tragic it may be. The

gran problema es el uso que haremos de las memorias.
grann problayma ess ell ooso kay araymoz thay las maymoryas
great problem is the use we make of memories.

* *

El que¯sufra las experiencias más fantásticas, las felices o las desventuradas, parece olvidarlas todas un minuto después de los acontecimientos. Se convierten en meros hechos que son enumerados. Pero hay otros para quienes el hecho más insignificante se convierte en experiencia que le toca el corazón. Y es esto lo que debemos llamar vida.

*

El que sufra las experiencias más fantásticas, las felices
ell kay soofra lass expayryennthyas mas fanntasteekas, lass
fayleethays
One person who goes through the most amazing experiences, happy

(Continued on Page 90.)

Vivi feliz   **en mi cuartito (en mi pequeño cuarto).**
veevee fayleeth   enn mee kvarteeto (enn mee paykayngyo kvarto)
I live happily   *in my small room.*

Yo sé que la gente rica   **tiene pequeño**
yo say kay la henntay reeka   tyaynay paykayngyo
I know that wealthy people   *have a small room*

en sus cuatro cuartos   **pero no son tan**
enn soos kvatro kvartoss   payro no sonn tan
among their four rooms,   *but they are not so*

felices como yo.
fayleethays komo yo
happy as I am.

o las desventuradas parece olvidarlas todas un minuto después
o las dessvenntoorathas paraythay ollveetharlas toothas oon
  meenooto thesspooess
or unhappy seems to forget them a moment after they

de los acontecimientos. Se convierten en meros hechos que son
thay loss akonntaytheemyenntoss say konnvyerrtayng enn
  mayross echoss kay sonn
have happened. They will have become nothing but facts.

enumerados. Pero hay otros para quienes el hecho más insigni-
aynoomayrathoss. payro ay otross para keeaynays ell echo mas
  eenseegnee-
But there are others for whom the smallest event turns

ficante se convierte en experiencia a que le toca al corazón.
feekanntay say konnvyerrtay enn espayreeennthya a kay lay
  toka al korrathong
into an experience that touches the heart.

Y es esto a lo que debemos llamar vida.
ee ess essto a lo kay dayvaymoss llyamar veetha
And that's what we (must) call life.

*   *

El hombre o la mujer que sea feliz dominando su propia vida,
cuyos sentimientos no son destruidos nunca, sino que siempre
son dominados por el cerebro, ha llevado una vida completa.

*

El hombre o la mujer que sea feliz dominando su propia vida,
ell ommbray o la moohayr kay saya fayleeth domeenanndo soo
  proppya veeda
The man or (the) woman who is happy in mastering his own life,

cuyos sentimientos no son destruidos nunca, sino que
kooyoss sennteemyenntoss no sonn desstrooeethoss noonka
  seeno kay
whose feelings are not destroyed at any time but are

siempre son dominados por el cerebro, ha llevado
syemmpray sonn domeenathoss porr ell thayraybro, a lyayvatho
always controlled by the mind, has lived

una vida completa.
oona veetha kommplayta
a full life (has carried a complete life).

Translate into Spanish

Where? Where to? First, it is easier; second, to consider, more important, less important. Much, little. I have a hundred dollars in my pocket. I have much money. I am a rich man. What is the matter with you? A hundred dollars! That is nothing to me. A hundred dollars, that is nothing to me. I have more money than you. Among very rich people, you are still all poor people. I am the richest lady in the world.

The beauty of women, about dresses, qualities of men, quantities of objects. You are more beautiful than the Venus of Milo. You are the most beautiful lady I ever have seen. What a beauty! Beautiful, more beautiful, most beautiful. We men are not alone. There are many women here. My secrets. All you ladies are the most beautiful, one after the other. What do I see? What is the matter? A revolution! What do I hear? It's a long time.

Who? We are great; one is greater than the other one. The greatest man, not in vain. Black cloth, red cloth, the sweet honey. All that is most easy, it is the easiest in the world. Very, very strong; very, very simple; very, very good; very, very bad. I am as happy as you are. As broad as long. As narrow as short. Good, better, best; bad, worse, worst; great, greater, greatest; small, smaller, smallest; much, more, most; little, less, least. I'll see you later! Good bye!

How are you? Thank you, well. I am not very well. Not to be in good health. What is the matter with you? I am suffering from indigestion! I am sick. We are well, we feel well. To be, to have. Of a good man, of a good woman, if I tell you once more. You are an Englishman, you are an American. You are Germans, Spaniards, Frenchmen, we are from America, from France, from Germany, from Bolivia, from Chile. We are all here.

Excuse me! I am not very well, you don't feel very well! The doctor has told me. Pardon me if I interrupt you. I take the liberty, I allow myself. It doesn't matter. That's nothing. No matter at all! It is very disagreeable. The doctor has said, suddenly. I have patience, but what is too much is too much. All right. Take it easy. I have money. My congratulations! I have two eyes and two ears. You too have two ears? Isn't that so?

¡Lea en alta voz!

READ ALOUD

Nada. Somos grandes. Uno es más grande que el otro. El hombre más grande, no en vano. Paño negro, paño rojo, la dulce miel. Todo eso es más facilísimo, es lo más fácil del mundo. Fortísimo, simplísimo, bonísimo, malísimo. Yo soy tan feliz como Vds. Tan ancho como largo; tan estrecho como corto. Bueno, a, mejor, óptimo; malo, peor, pésimo; grande, mayor, maximo; pequeño, menor, minimo; mucho, más, muchisimo; poco, menos, poquísimo. ¡Hasta más ver! ¡Hasta luego!

¿Cómo está Vd.? Bien, gracias. No estoy muy bien. No ser sano. ¿Qué tiene Vd.? Tengo una indigestión. Estoy enfermo. Estamos bien. Ser o estar y tener o haber. De un buen hombre, de una buena mujer, si le digo a Vd. una vez más. Vd. es Inglés, eres Americano. Sois Alemanes, Españoles, Franceses. Somos de America, de Francia, de Alemania, de Bolivia, der Chile. Nosotros todos estamos aquí.

Excuseme o perdone Vd. No estoy muy bien, Vd. no está muy bien. El médico me ha dicho. Dispense Vd. si le interrumpo. Tomo licencias, me permito. ¡No hay de qué! ¡De nada! ¡No, importa! Es muy desagradable. El doctor me ha dicho, de repente. Tengo paciencia, lo que es demasiado, es demasiado. Muy bien. Tenga calmo (a). Tengo dinero. Mis congratulaciones. Tengo dos ojos y dos óidos. Tu tambien tienes dos ojos. ¿No es verdad?

El doctor me ha dicho. He tenido dinero. Reminiscencia es más que nada. Tengo la reminiscencia. He hablado. Vd. ha consultado al médico. Digame ahora en todas partes. La sala de espera, la casa del doctor. ¡Qué lástima! Hay mucha gente. Usted debe estar allí. ¡Ahora continue! En mi reloj son las cuatro de la tarde. Mañana por la mañana he de estar en casa. ¿Cuándo? A las diez de la mañana, si es posible. Hoy es lunes. La semana empieza muy bien. El lunes por la mañana. ¿A cuánto estamos hoy? ¿Qué día del mes es hoy? Espere uno minuto. ayer fué domingo, anteayer fué día de pago. No olvido nunca el día de pago. Anteayer fué sábado, fué el treinta y uno de Octubre; por eso ayer fué domingo el primero de Noviembre; hoy es lunes el dos de noviembre.

¿Cuáles son los días de la semana? Los días de la semana se llaman: lunes, martes, miércoles, jueves, viernes, sabado, domingo. El mes, la semana, el día. El primer mes del año es Enero; el segundo mes del año es Febrero. Los otros meses se llaman: Marzo, Abril, Mayo, Junio, Julio, Agosto, Setiembre, Octubre, Noviembre, Diciembre. El primero de Enero, el dos de Enero, el tres de Mayo, el veinte y uno de Junio, el treinta y uno de Abril. Vd. no puede decirlo porque el mes de Abril tiene solo treinta días. El treinta de Abril es el ultimo día del mes de Abril.

La muchacha más rica de la ciudad. Al mejor médico de la ciudad—¿Cuándo tiene consulta el doctor? ¿Cuándo son las horas de consulta de médico? A las tres y media de la tarde; está ahí hasta las seis menos cuarto. Poco despues de las tres estoy en la sala de espera. Mucha gente está ahí. Son las cuatros menos diez, cuando puedo entrar al cuarto del doctor.

Translate into Spanish

The doctor has told me. I have had money. The memory is better than nothing. I have memories. I have spoken; you have consulted the doctor. Now tell me all about it. The waiting-room, the doctor's house. What a pity! There are many people. You must be there. And now continue, please. According to my watch it is four o'clock in the afternoon. Tomorrow morning I have to be at home. When? At ten o'clock in the morning, if it is possible. Today is Monday. The week begins very well. On a Monday morning. What's the date? What day of the month is today? Wait a minute: yesterday was Sunday, the day before yesterday was pay day. I never forget pay day. The day before yesterday was Saturday, it was the 31st of October; therefore yesterday was Sunday the first of November; and today is Monday the second of November.

¡Haga el favor de repetir!

sin duda	seen dootha	without doubt
¿dónde?	donnday	where?
¿cómo?	komo	how?
¿quién?	kyayng	who?
¿quées eso?	kay ays ayso	what is this?
¿qué hay?	kay aee	what is the matter?
¿para qué sirve esto?	para kay seerrvay aysto	what is it for?
pregunto a una señora	praygoonto a oona sengyora	I ask a lady
la señora me contesta	la sengyora may konntaysta	the lady answers me
el regalo	ell raygalo	the gift
es tarde	ays tarrthay	it is late
la lección	la lekkthyonn	the lesson
¿qué hora es?	kay ora ays	what time is it?
es la una	ays la oona	it is one o'clock
son las cinco	sonn las theengko	it is five o'clock
el paseo	ell passayo	the walk
¡vamos a dar!	vamoss a dar	let us take!

*

esta o aquella persona	essta o akellya perrsona	this or that person
las mismas clases	las meesmas klasays	the same kind
no nos conocemos	no noss konothaymoss	we don't know each other
juntarse	hoontarsay	to get together
al principio	al preentheepyo	in the beginning
tan bien como	tam byayng komo	as good as
¿Cuál es el camino del ayuntamiento?	kval ess ell kameeno dell ayoontamyaynto	What is the way to City Hall?
el ayuntamiento	ell ayoontamyaynto	the City Hall
¿Qué distancia hay?	kay deestanthya aee	How far is it?
¿Adónde quiere Vd. ir?	adonnday kyayray oostayth eer	Where do you want to go?
¿Adónde va Vd.?	adonnday va oostayth	Where do you want to go?
aquí	akee	here

no está lejos de aquí	no essta layhoss thay akee	it is not far from here
está muy cerca	essta mooy therrka	it is very near
¡Vaya Vd. derechito!	vaya oostayth dayretsheeto	Go straight ahead!
¿dónde?	donnday	where?
¿adónde?	adonnday	where to?
fácil	fatheel	easy
más fácil	mas fatheel	easier
más	mas	more
pensar	pennsar	to consider
el mas importante	ell mas eemporrtanntay	the most important
menos	maynoss	less
menos importante	maynoss eemporrtanntay	less important
mucho	mootsho	much
poco	poko	little
tengo mucho dinero	tayngo moocho deenayro	I have much money
soy un hombre rico	soy oon ommbray reeko	I am a rich man
¿Que hay?	kay aee	What is the matter with you?
cien dólares	thyayng dolarays	(a) hundred dollars
eso no es nada para mi	esso no ays natha para mee	that's nothing to me
tengo mas dinero que Vd.	tayngo mas deenayro kay oostayth	I have more money than you
soy mas rico que vosotros todos	soy mas reeko kay vosotross tothoss	I am richer than you all
con la gente muy rica	konn la hayntay mooy reeka	with very rich people
la senora mas rica	la sengyora mas reeka	the richest lady
la hermosura	la errmosoora	the beauty
de las mujeres	de las moohayrays	of women
vestidos	vaysteethoss	dresses
las cualidades de los hombres	las kvaleedadays thay loss ommbrays	the qualities of men
la cuantidad	la kvannteedad	the quantity
no solo	no solo	not only
hermoso, a	errmoso, a	beautiful
Vd. es más hermosa que la Venus de Milo	oostayth ess mas errmosa kay la vaynoos thay meelo	you are more beautiful than the Venus of Milo

la señora más hermosa	la sengyora mas errmosa	*the most beautiful lady*
¡Qué hermosura!	kay errmosoora	*What a beauty!*
nosotros los hombres	nosotross loss ommbrays	*we, the men*
no estamos solos	no esstamoss soloss	*we are not alone!*
mis secretos	mees saykraytoss	*my secrets*
¿Qué veo?	kay vayo	*What do I see?*
¿Qué hay?	kay aee	*What is the matter?*
la revolución	la rayvoloothyong	*the revolution*
¿Qué oigo?	kay oeego	*What do I hear?*
hace mucho tiempo	athay moocho tyaympo	*it's a long time*
simpatico, a	seempateeko, a	*sympathetic*
encantadoro, a	ennkantadoro, a	*charming*
la más encantadora	la mas ennkantadora	*the most charming (fem.)*
la óptima	la oppteema	*the best*
¿quién es?	kyayng ess	*who is?*
antiguo, a	anteegvo, a	*ancient*
nada	natha	*nothing*
somos grandes	somoss grandays	*we are great*
uno es más grande que el otro	oono ess mas granday kay ell otro	*one is greater than the other one*
el hombre más grande	ell ommbray mas granday	*the greatest man*
no en vano	no enn vano	*not in vain*
paño negro	pangyo naygro	*black cloth*
paño rojo	pangyo roho	*red cloth*
la miel	la myayl	*the honey*
la dulce miel	la doolthay myayl	*the sweet honey*
dulce	doolthay	*sweet*
más dulce	mas doolthay	*sweeter*
el más dulce, la más	el mas, la mas doolthay	*the sweetest*
pobre	povray	*poor*
facilísimo	fatheeleeseemo	*most easy*
lo más fácil del mundo	lo mas fatheel dell moondo	*the easiest in the world*
fortísimo	forrteeseemo	*very, very strong*
simplísimo	seempleeseemo	*very, very simple*
bonísimo	boneeseemo	*very, very good*
malísimo	maleeseemo	*very, very bad*
tan—como	tang—komo	*as—as*
estrecho	aystrecho	*narrow*
corto, a	korrto	*short*

¿Qué tal de apetito?
kay tal thay apayteeto
How is your appetite?

estoy con hambre.
esstoy konn ambray
that I am always hungry.

Mi mal es que siempre
mee mal ess kay syemmpray
My trouble (sickness) is

Después del desayuno;
dayspooays dell daysa-yoono
After breakfast;

después de la comida;
dayspooays thay la komeeda
after dinner;

después
desspooays
after

del almuerzo.
dell almooerrtho
lunch.

Lesson Nineteen

But enough philosophy now. Let us get back to earth. *Let us return* volvamos (vollvamoss) to matter-of-fact things! La primavera empieza el veintiuno de marzo (la preemavayra emmpyestha ell vayeentyoono thay martho), *spring begins on the 21st of March;* el verano empieza el veintiuno de junio (ell vayrano emmpyestha ell vayeentyoono thay hoonyo) *summer begins on the 21st of June;* el otoño empieza el veintitres de setiembre (ell otonyo emmpyestha ell vayeenteetress thay settyemmbray) *fall begins on the 23rd of September;* el invierno empieza el veintiuno de diciembre (ell eenvyerrno emmpyestha ell vayeentyoono thay deethyemmbray) *winter begins on the 21st of December.*

As you have seen, como Vd. ha visto (komo oostayth a veesto) *the first* el primero, la primera (ell preemayro, la preemayra) is used in Spanish just as in English. We speak of the *first century,* in Spanish siglo primero (seeglo preemayro); we say *June first,* the Spaniard, el primero de junio (ell preemayro thay hoonyo). But for all other days of the month, for all other centuries, they use the ordinary numbers. For the numbers from 21 to 29 you can write and say, just as you please, either veinte y uno (vayeentay ee oono) or veintiuno (vayeentyoono), but never anything but treinta y uno (trayeentayoono). Occasionally you may see both diecisiete (deeaytheesyaytay) and diez y siete (deeayth ee syaytay) used. But I don't think this should confuse you at all.

Up to and including the *tenth volume of a book* tomo decimo de un libro (tomo daytheemo thay oon leevro)—or the tenth of anything else *we shall use* usaremos (oosaraymoss):

el primero, la primera
(ell preemayro, la preemayra)   *the first*

el segundo, la segunda
(ell saygoondo, a)   *the second*

el, la tercero, a
(ell, la terrthayro, a)   *the third*

el, la cuarto, a
(ell, la kvarto, a)   *the fourth*

el, la quinto, a (keento, a)	the fifth
el, la sexto, a (sexto, a)	the sixth
el, la séptimo, a (ell, la seppteemo, a)	the seventh
el, la octavo, a (okktavo, a)	the eighth
el noveno, a (novayno, a)	the ninth
el, la décimo, a (daytheemo, a)	the tenth

La lección segunda (la lekkthyong saygoonda) *the second lesson.* El capítulo tercero (ell kapeetoolo terrthayro) *the third chapter;* la página novena (la paheena novayna) *the ninth page.*

But after ten: capítulo quince (kapeetoolo keenthay) *the fifteenth chapter;* página ciento tres (paheena thyennto tress) *page 103* or *the 103rd page;* la lección dieciocho diez y ocho (la lekkthyong deeaythyocho) *the 18th lesson.*

These numbers are used also in kings' titles, again up to the tenth. But after ten it is too much even for kings, and then again we make use of the ordinary numbers.

Carlos V (quinto) fué rey de España y emperador de Alemania.
karloss keento fooay ray thay esspangya ee emmpayrathor thay alaymangya
Charles the Fifth was king of Spain and emperor of Germany.
It was a long time ago, hace mucho tiempo (athay moocho tyemmpo) *in the 16th century,* en el siglo XVI (dieciseis) (enn ell seeglo deeaytheesayees).

Felipe II (segundo) fué el fundador del Escorial.
fayleepay saygoondo fooay ell foondathor thell esskoryal
Philip the Second was the founder of the Escorial.

For the Spaniards that is *the eighth wonder of the world,* la octava maravilla del mundo (la okktava maraveelya dell moondo). *In spite of that,* a pesar de oso (a paysar thay esso), *it really is the most wonderful palace,* es el palacio más maravilloso (ess ell palathyo mas maraveellyoso) we can think of, containing (with)

* 99 *

a very well known *collection of paintings*, con una colección de cuadros (konn oona kollekthyong thay kvathross) and a *large library* una biblioteca grande (oona beevleeotayka grannday). *Many Spanish kings are buried there*, muchos reyes españoles están enterrados allí (moochoss rayess esspanyoless esstann ennterrathoss allyee).

El último rey de España fue Alfonso XIII (trece).
ell oolteemo rayy thay esspangya fooay alfonnso traythay
The last king of Spain was Alphonso XIII.

When we mention *Louis XVI* Louis XVI dieciseis (looees deeaytheesayees), then we are in the period of *the French Revolution* la revolución francesa (la rayvoloothyong franthaysa), which began *in the year 1789* en el año mil setecientos ochenta y nueve (enn ell angyo meel saytaythyentoss ochennta ee nooayvay). The greatest historic periods look very different to those who must live through those "good old times." A humorist once said:

No puede Vd. imaginar cuán estupidas eran las gentes
no pooaythay oostayth eemaheenar kvann esstoopeethas ayran las henntays
You can't imagine how stupid the people were

en la Edad Media. No sabían que vivían en la Edad Media.
enn la aydad maythya no saveean kay veeveean enn la aydad maydya
in the Middle Ages; they didn't even know that they lived in the Middle Ages.

They did not notice it. Today it is easy enough for us to say, *it is all the same to me*, me es igual (may ess eegval). And *if it is all the same to you* si le es á Vd. igual (see lay ess a oostayth eegval), we will stop talking history.

Lesson Twenty

Let us turn to a much pleasanter occupation; let us count money, *the more the better* **cuanto más tanto mejor** (kvanto mass tanto mayhor). Even if we do not like millionaires, we would still like to have their money.

mil	(meel)	*1000*
mil uno	(meel oono)	*1001*
mil dos	(meel doss)	*1002*
mil ciento uno	(meel thyennto oono)	*1101*
mil doscientos tres	(meel dossthyenntoss tress)	*1203*
mil ochocientos treinta y seis (meel ochothyenntoss trayeenta ee sayees)		*1836*
dos mil	(doss meel)	*2000*
tres mil	(tress meel)	*3000*
doscientos mil	(dossthyenntoss meel)	*200000*
un millon	(oon meellyong)	*1000000*
un millon quinientos cincuenta mil (oon meellyong keenyenntoss theenkvennta meel)		*1550000*
diez millones	(dyayth meellyoness)	*10000000*

Ahora, puede Vd. contestar la pregunta:
aora pooaythay oostayth konntesstar la praygoonta
And now, can you answer the question:

¿Cuándo nació Vd.?
kvanndo nathyo oostayth
When were you born?

Yo nací el nueve de noviembre de mil ochocientos setenta y ocho.
yo nathee ell nooayvay thay novyemmbray thay meel ochothy-
        enntoss saytennta ee ocho
I was born (the ninth of November) November 9th, 1878.

Es entonces cuándo celebro mi cumpleaños.
ess enntonthays kvando thaylaybro mee koomplayangyoss
That is when I celebrate my birthday.

* 101 *

¿Y cuándo es su cumpleaños? y ¿cuándo es el del padre de Vd.?
ee kvando ess soo koomplayangyoss ee kvando ess ell dell pathray
thay oostayth
And when is your birthday and when is your father's?

El reclamo de un joyero español se lee:
ell rayklamo thay oon hoyayro ayspangyol say layay
The advertisement of a Spanish jeweler (reads itself) says:

Si está Vd. enamorado no olvide que las joyas son el
see essta oostayth ennamoratho no ollveethay kay las hoyas
sonn ell
If you are in love, don't forget that jewels are the

más preciado tesoro de la mujer.
mas praythyatho taysoro thay la mooherr
woman's most precious treasures.
(most precious treasures of the woman).

After counting all day we *finally*, **finalmente** (feenalmenntay),
got tired of all numbers, **estábamos cansados de todos los números**
(esstavamoss kansathoss thay tothoss loss
noomayros). *When we came home*, **cuándo**
regresamos a nuestra casa (kvando ray-
gressamoss a nooesstra kassa), *we wanted*
nothing, **no deseábamos nada más** (no
daysayavamoss natha mass), *but to be*
able to rest, **que descansar** (kay dayskansar), *for a little while*, **un rato** (oon ratto).

¿Cuándo? = *when?*
¿Cuándo viene Vd.?
(kvando vyaynay)
When will you come?
cuando = *when* ...
Cuando viene, voy
(kvando vyaynay voee)
When he comes, I go

Estaba en mi cuarto, cuando nuestro amigo Enrique
esstava enn mee kvarto kvando nooesstro ameego ennreekay
I was in my room when our friend Henry

entró en la casa. ¿Dónde estabas, Juanita, cuando te llamé?
enntro enn la kassa. donnday esstavas hooaneeta kvando tay
llyamay
came into the house. Where were you, Juanita, when I called you?

La muchacha subió y dijo: El Señor Enrique López ha venido
la moochacha soovyo ee theeho: ell sengyor ennreekay lopayth
a vayneetho
The maid has come upstairs and said: Mr. Henry López has come

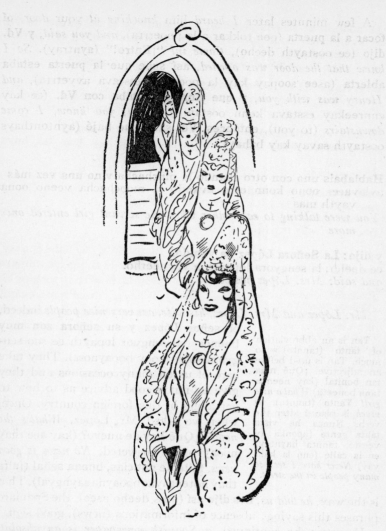

Esta mujer con la mantilla
essta moohayr konn la manteellya
This lady with the shawl

es muy hermosa.
ess mooy errmosa
is very beautiful.

Es la más hermosa de todas.
ess la mas errmosa thay tothas
She is the most beautiful of all.

A few minutes later *I heard* him *knocking at* your *door*, **oí tocar a la puerta** (oee tokkar a la pooerrta), *and you said*, **y Vd. dijo** (ee oostayth deeho), *Come in!* **"¡Entre!"** (ayntray). *So I knew that the door was opened*, **así supe que la puerta estaba abierta** (asee soopay kay la pooerrta esstava avyerrta), *and Henry was with you*, **y que Enrique estaba con Vd.** (ee kay ennreekay esstava konn oostayth). *Then, you know, I came downstairs* (to you), **entonces, Vd. sabe que bajé** (ayntonthays oostayth savay kay bahay).

Hablabais uno con otro cuando la muchacha vino una vez más
avlavaees oono konn otro kvando la moochacha veeno oona
vayth mas
You were talking to each other when the servant girl entered once more

y dijo: La Señora López ha venido.
ee deeho: la sengyora lopayth a vayneetho.
and said: Mrs. López has come.

Mr. López and Mrs. López, his wife, are very nice people indeed, **el señor López y su señora son muy buenos** (ell sengyor lopayth ee soo sengyora sonn mooy booaynoss). They take care of us on many occasions and they give us much good advice as to how to get along in this foreign country. Once, when we asked Mr. López, *What's the news? ¿Qué hay de nuevo?* (kay aee thay nooayvo), he answered, *No news is good news*, **falta de noticias, buena señal** (falta thay noteethyas booayna sayngyal). That

> **Tan** is an abbreviation of **tanto** (tannto) = *so much*. Tan is used before an adjective. **¡Qué niña tan bonita!** (kay neenya tann boneeta) *What a nice girl!* **Tanto** (tannto), *so much* is placed after the verb. **Nunca he visto tanta gente** (noonka ay veesto tannta hayntay) **en la calle** (enn la kallyay) *Never have I seen so many people in the street.*

is the way, *he told us*, **nos dijo así** (noss deeho asee), the Spaniard phrases this saying: absence of informations (news), good sign.

However, he continued, *a Spanish newspaper is an absolute necessity*, **un diario español les hace falta** (oon deearyo esspangyol less athay falta), and he drew one *out of his pocket*, **de su bolsillo** (day soo bollseelyo).

Whatever our new friend thought would *interest us*, **sería interesante para nosotros** (sayreea eentayressantay para nosotross), he showed us *in the newspaper*, **en el diario** (enn ell deearyeo), and though we could not understand every word, we saw many things we had not noticed before. There was *an article*, for instance, **un artículo** (oon arteekoolo), about the fourth of July. I clipped it from the paper and here it is:

~~~~~~~~~~~~~~~~~~~~~~~~~~~~~~~

4 de Julio, 1776

A la luz pálida de una vela, en una casa de piedra gris, en Filadelfia, trabajaba un hombre sobre docenas de cuartillas amarillentas hace 163 años hoy. "Cuando en el transcurso de los acontecimientos humanos se hace necesario para un pueblo disolver los nexos que lo unen a otro y asumir entre las potencias de la tierra, la posición de igualdad, a la cuallas leyes de la naturaleza y la Providencia le dan derecho, el respeto a las opiniones de la raza humana exige a ese pueblo que explique las causas que lo obligan a buscar tal separación . . ."

Así escribía aquel hombre a la luz de una vela en Filadelfia. *"Sostenemos que estas verdades son evidentes... Que todos los hombres han sido creados iguales, que todos han sido dotados por su Creador con ciertos derechos inalienables entre los cuales se cuenta el de vivir en Libertad...*

Aquel hombre se llamaba Thomas Jefferson. El documento que escribía aquella noche estival en Filadelfia, fué leído el 4 de julio de 1776 en la primera reunión del Congreso Continental.

Jefferson era un hombre notable. Alto, esbelto, de frente extraordinariamente ancha; de hombros cuadrados y semblante pálido de asceta. Su profesión era abogado; gozaba fama de ser un gran escritor, y era además, pintor, educador y atleta.

~~~~~~~~~~~~~~~~~~~~~~~~~~~~~~~

Trabajaba un hombre (travahava oon ommbray) *A man was working. So wrote that man,* **así escribía aquel hombre** (asee esskreeveea akell ommbray). *That man was called (called himself) Thomas Jefferson,* **aquel hombre se llamaba Thomas Jefferson** (akell ommbray say lyamava Thomas Jefferson). *The document was read on the 4th of July, 1776, at the first meeting of the Continental Congress,* **el documento fué leído el cuarto de julio de 1776 en la primera reunión del Congreso Continental** (ell dokoomennto fooay layeetho ell kvarto thay hoolyo thay meel seetaythyenntos saytennta sayees enn la preemayra rayoonyong dell konngrayso konnteenayntal). *Jefferson was a remarkable man* **Jefferson era un hombre notable** (Jefferson ayra oon ommbray notavlay). *His profession was practicing law. He enjoyed the reputation (fame) of being a great writer and was, moreover, a painter, educator and athlete.* **Su profesión era abogado; gozaba fama de ser un gran escritor, y era además, pintor, educador y atleta** (soo professyong ayra avogatho; gothava fama thay serr oon grann esskreetor, ee ayra athaymas, peentor, aythookathor ee atlayta).

Translate into Spanish

What are the days of the week? The days of the week are called: Monday, Tuesday, Wednesday, Thursday, Friday, Saturday, Sunday. The month, the week, the day. The first month of the year is January; the second month of the year is February. The other months are called: March, April, May, June, July, August, September, October, November, December. January 1st, January 2nd, May 3rd, June 21st, April 30th. You couldn't say that, for the month of April has only thirty days. The thirtieth of April is the last day of the month of April.

The richest girl in the city. To the best physician in town. What are the doctor's consultation hours? At half past three in the afternoon; he is there until a quarter to six. A short time after three I am in the waiting room. Many people are there. It is ten minutes to four when I can enter the doctor's room. He says to me:

Tell me, what bothers you? Take a seat, sit down! I tell him: I eat very little, my eyes and ears ache; I have a pain in my throat, in my head and in my shoulder. My whole body is not right. I ache in every limb: the breast, the cheek, the legs, the chest, the fingers, the feet, the neck, the hands, the chin, the nose, the forehead.

I have a heart, a liver, nerves. A friend of mine has told me: go to a dentist. I was there: I haven't anything (the matter with me). What do you think of that?

Lesson Twenty-One

If you have been watching the verbs as we went along, you must have noticed that there are two forms to express the past in Spanish. The so-called Imperfect and the Past Definite. There is a very real difference between the two forms. But I remember that I found it difficult to understand the fine difference which exists between the pasts in Latin just as it does in Spanish.

Ayer (ayayr)
yesterday
hoy (oee)
today
mañana (manyana)
tomorrow
mañana por la mañana
(manyana porr la man-
yana)
tomorrow morning

El tiempo que pasó, no vuelve, no viene otra vez (ell tyemmpo kay paso no vooellvay no vyaynay otra vayth). *Time that has passed does not return, does not come again.* An Argentine tango called **"La Sangre de Suburbio"** (sangray thay sooboorrbyo),

Blood of the Suburb, with *words by Ivan Diez*, **letra de Ivan Diez** (laytra thay eevan deeayth), and *music by Hector Palacios,* **música de Hector Palacios** (mooseeka thay ekktor palathyoss), *begins,* **comienza** (kommyenntha):

¡Mi Dios! ¡Qué ganas! de gritar
mee theeoss kay ganas thay greetar
My God! What a joy to proclaim

si tiro a recordar
see teero a raykorrthar
if I draw to remind (if I attempt to recall)

el tiempo que pasó.
ell tyemmpo kay paso
the time that has passed away.

But when an action has taken place over a long period of time in the past, something that was repeated regularly or continually, then in Spanish we use the Imperfect tense.

Era abogado   (ayra avogatho)   *he was a lawyer (he used to be a lawyer).*

Gozaba fama de ser un gran escritor.
gothava fama thay serr oon grann esskreetor
He enjoyed the reputation of being a great writer.

Estaba en mi cuarto, cuando la modista entró, cuando
esstava enn mee kvarto kvando la motheesta enntro, kvando
I was in my room when the dressmaker entered, when

el sastre y la sombrerera vinieron.
ell sastray ee la sommbrayrayra veenyayron.
the tailor and the milliner came.

¿Dónde estaba Vd., cuándo el óptista trajó sus anteojos?
donnday esstava oostayth, kvando ell oppteesta traho soos
antayohoss
Where were you when the optician brought your eyeglasses?

Estaba aquí, cuando yo estuve en casa del relojero.
esstava akee kvando yo esstoovay enn kasa dell raylohayro
He was here when I was at the watchmaker's.

Don't worry too much, **no se preocupe demasiado** (no say
prayokkoopay thaymassyatho), about it, though. The principal
difference is that the **Imperfect** tense points to a more **permanent
action** in the past; the **Definite Past** to a more **temporary** action.

ser (serr)	*to be*		*Imperfect*
soy (soy)	*I am*	era (ayra)	*I was*
fuí (fooee)	*I was*	eras (ayras)	
seré (sayray)	*I shall be*	era (ayra)	
sería (sayreea)	*I should be*	éramos (ayramoss)	
había sido (aveea seetho)		erais (ayraees)	
I had been		eran (ayran)	
habré sido (avray seetho)			
I shall have been			

And in the same way all regular verbs *ending in* -**ar** would be:

Imperfect

estar (esstar) *to be*

estaba (esstava) *I was (in a place) etc.*
estabas (esstavas)
estaba (esstava)
estábamos (esstavamos)
estabais (esstavaees)
estaban (esstavan)

hablar (ablar)   *to speak*

hablaba (avlava)   *I spoke (I used to speak, I was speaking) etc.*
hablabas (avlavas)
hablaba (avlava)
hablábamos (avlavamoss)
hablabais (avlavaees)
hablaban (avlavan)

haber (avayr)   *to have*

había (recibido) (aveea)   *I had, (received) etc.*
habías (aveeas)
había (aveea)
habíamos (aveeamoss)
habíais (aveeaees)
habían (aveean)

tener (taynayr)   *to have*

tenía (dinero) (tayneea)   *I had (money)*
tenías (tayneeas)
tenía (tayneea)
teníamos (tayneeamoss)
teníais (tayneeaees)
tenían (tayneean)

comer (komayr) *to eat*		**vivir** (veeveer) *to live*	
comía (komeea) *I ate*		**vivía** (veeveea) *I lived*	
comías		**vivías**	
comía		**vivía**	
comíamos		**vivíamos**	
comíais		**vivíais**	
comían		**vivían**	

he (ay)	*I have*	**habré** (avray)	*I shall have*
hube (oovay)	*I had*	**habría** (avreea)	*I should have*
tengo (tenngo)	*I have*	**tendré** (tenndray)	*I shall have*
tuve (toovay)	*I had*	**tendría** (tenndreea)	*I should have*

he habido (ay aveetho)   *I have had*
he tenido (ay tayneetho)   *I have had*

había habido (aveea aveetho)   *I had had*
había tenido (aveea tayneetho)   *I had had*

habré habido (avray aveetho)   *I shall have had*
habré tenido (avray tayneetho)   *I shall have had*

hablar	(avlar)	*to speak*. And all regular verbs *ending in* **-ar.**

hablo	(avlo)	*I speak*
hablé	(avlay)	*I spoke*
hablaré	(avlaray)	*I shall speak*
hablaría	(avlareea)	*I should speak*
he hablado	(ay avlatho)	*I have spoken*
hube hablado	(oovay avlatho)	*I had spoken*
habré hablado	(avray avlatho)	*I shall have spoken*

comer	(komayr)	*to eat*. And all regular verbs *ending in* **-er.**

como	(komo)	*I eat*
comí	(komee)	*I ate*

vivir	(veeveer)	*to live*. And all regular verbs *ending in* **-ir.**

vivo	(veevo)	*I live*
viví	(veevee)	*I lived*
viviré	(veeveeray)	*I shall live*
viviría	(veeveereea)	*I should live*
he vivido	(ay veeveetho)	*I have lived*
hube vivido	(oovay veeveetho)	*I had lived*
habré vivido	(avray veeveetho)	*I shall have lived*

La semana	comienza muy bien;	hoy es lunes.
la saymana	komyayntha mooy byayng;	oy ess loonays
The week	*begins very well;*	*today is Monday.*

Lesson Twenty-Two

Usually there is not any difference in Spanish between *I speak* and *I am speaking*. Both are the same, **hablo**. But in the imperfect form we could say that **hablaba** (avlava) corresponds to our *I was speaking*, and **hablé** (avlay) with *I spoke*. The form for *speaking* is **hablando** (avlando), from which we can see that the gerund ending (the participle ending) is **-ando**. This is true of all verbs in **-ar**. And for all verbs in **-er** and **-ir**, the participle ending is **-iendo**. For example, **comiendo** (komyenndo) *eating*, and **viviendo** (veevyenndo) *living*. This form, we repeat, is used to express an action which has some duration.

M o s t adverbs are formed in Spanish by adding the ending **mente** to the feminine forms of the adjectives. **Lento** (lennto), **lenta**, slow; **lentamente** (lenntamayntay), slowly; **hermoso, hermosa** (errmosa) beautiful, **hermosamente** (errmosamenntay) beautifully; **seguro, segura** (saygoora) sure, **seguramente** (saigooramenntay) surely; **probable** (probbablay), **probable, probablemente** (probbablaynenntay) probably;

It was a long lesson, **fué una lección larga** (fooay oona lekthyona larga) *that our friend Henry gave us*, **que nuestro amigo Enrique nos dió** (kay nooesstro ameeho ennreekay noz theeo). *It is not much fun*, **no es muy agradable** (no ess mooy agrathavlay), *but it is absolutely necessary to study the verbs*, **pero es absolutamente necesario estudiar los verbos** (payro ess apsolootamenntay naythaysaryo esstoothyar loz verrboss). *Pardon me*, **perdone Vd.** (perrdonay oostayth), *I am very sorry*, **siento mucho** (syennto moocho) that I must give you this task to accomplish.

¡Vamos a dormir después de esta lección!
vamoss a dorrmeer thesspooez thay essta lekthyong
Let us go to sleep (to bed) after this lesson!

¡Buenas noches, señores y caballeros!
booaynas nochays sengyorays ee kavallyayros
Good night, ladies and gentlemen!

It was a good idea of Henry's to bring us *a Spanish newspaper*, **un diario español** (oon deearyo esspangyol) and we were determined to follow his advice and *read*, **leer** (layerr) *newspapers*, **los diarios** (loz theearyoss) and *periodicals*, **las revistas** (laz rayveestas) regularly *in the future*, **en el futuro** (enn ell footooro).

We said to the doorman, **dijimos al portero** (deeheemoss al porrtayro):

Tráiganos un diario español todos los días por la mañana.
traeeganoss oon deearyo esspangyol tothoss loz theeas porr la mangyana
Bring us a Spanish daily every morning.

¡No lo olvide!
no lo ollveethay
Don't forget it!

Me gusta leer. Nos gusta ver los artículos ilustrados y los anuncios.
may goosta layerr noss goosta verr loss arteekooloss eeloostrathoss ee los anoontheeoss
I like to read. We like to see the illustrated articles and the advertisements.

Para todo lo que desee, lea los clasificados de "La Prensa."
para totho lo kay thaysayay, laya loss klaseefeekathoz thay la prennsa
For anything you want, read the classified ads of The PRESS.

So they said, and we are glad to come across *words we already know very well*, **las palabras que ya conocemos muy bien** (las palavras kay ya konossaymos mooy byayng). *You know already*, **Vd. ya sabe** (oostayth ya savay).

muy (mooy)   *very*
mucho (mootsho)   *much*

Si, señor, lo sé (see sengyor lo say), *Yes, sir, I know it.* I am looking for *a lawyer*, **un abogado** (oon avogatho). *I see*, **veo** (vayo); *you see*, **Vd. ve** (oostayth vay) the heading **Abogados** (avogathoss), *Lawyers*. Let's go to this one *on President Street*, **en la calle del Presidente** (enn la kallyay dell prayseethenntay) *who advertises*, **que dice** (kay theethay):

> **Abogado español que habla inglés**
> avogatho esspangyol kay avla eengless
> *Spanish lawyer who speaks English.*

There is another section. We call it *Help Wanted* and *Positions Wanted*, **oferta de trabajo** (oferrta thay travaho), **solicitúdes de trabajo** (solleetheetoothes thay travaho). Just *let us read*, **leamos** (layamoss) this ad:

* 113 *

> Joven, taquígrafo en inglés y español,
> varios años de práctica, desea colocación
> con firma responsable. Excelentes refer-
> encias. Escriba P. N. 140 "La Prensa."

(hovenn takeegrafo enn eengless ee esspangyol varyoss angyoss
thay prakteeka thaysaya colokathyong konn feerma ressponsavlay
ekkthaylenntess rayfayrennthyas. P. N. 140 la prennsa).

*Young man, stenographer in English and
Spanish, some years of experience, wishes
position with reliable firm. Excellent
references. Write to P. N. 140 The
PRESS.*

Seeing this advertisement, you decide you will help this young man,
viendo esta oferta de trabajo Vd. desea ayudar a este joven
(vyenndo essta oferrta thay travaho oostayth thaysaya a-yoothar
a esstay hovenn). *You will say to your brother,* Vd. dira a su
hermano (oostayth theera a soo errmano): *"Write a postcard or
letter to this young man,* escriba una tarjeta o una carta a este
joven (esskreeva oona tarrhayta o oona karta a esstay hovenn).
Maybe he can get a job with our uncle who is the director of an
importing and exporting firm dealing with South America."
And your brother writes the following letter, y su hermano
escribe la carta siguiente (ee soo errmano esskreevay la karta
seegheeenntay):

Dear Sir:

My uncle is the manager of the Spanish Import
Company. I suggest that you send your application
there. State all details. I shall call my uncle's attention to your advertisement which may, perhaps, be of
some interest to him.

Very truly yours,
John Smith

Estimado señor:

Mi tío es el gerente de la Compañía Española de
Importaciones. Le recomiendo enviarle su solicitud.
Especifique todos los detalles. Llamaré la atención de
mi tío a su anuncio que tal vez pueda interesarle.

Atto. S.S.
John Smith

My dear uncle:

I am sending you herewith an advertisement which appeared in La Prensa. You told me the other day that you are in need of a young man who speaks and writes Spanish fluently. A short time ago I learned to read Spanish papers and my first achievement is to find the right man for you. Isn't that nice of me? But I am always nice. I don't know this young man, but I recommend him to you. Look him over and try to decide whether he is the right one for the job.

Very cordially yours,

Mi querido tío:

Te incluyo un anuncio de La Prensa. Me ijiste el otro día que necesitabas un joven que supiese hablar y escribir el español corrientemente. Desde hace poco tiempo puedo leer los periódicos españoles y ha sido mi suerte encontrar el hombre apropiado para el puesto apropiado. ¿No crees que he tenido suerte? Siempre la tengo. No conozco a este joven. Indaga, y convéncete de que es el joven que necesitas.

Te abraza, tu sobrino,
John Smith

*   *

*

Translate into Spanish

The doctor answers: show me your tongue. It is not coated. I am examined by the doctor. How about your appetite? I eat very little, just two eggs, coffee, bread and butter, some fried fish, jam and marmalade; that is all for breakfast. Then at noon I have my lunch, a very light one too, just to eat a little—soup, two mutton chops, some vegetables, potatoes, a dessert.

Between four and five I just take a cup of tea, toast and cake. At seven o'clock I don't eat much, only my regular dinner of six courses. That is all I eat during the day.

That is not a shame; that is a scandal! You don't work. Don't think of your complaints. You eat too much and you work too little. That's my advice to you. All your life, a prescription, a spoonful every hour. I am sorry to say, you are absolutely healthy! Work is the best medicine!

Lesson Twenty-Three

Though we are modest in our needs, there is still practically no time in our lives when we do not want something which is more or less of a necessity. The child goes to its mother to satisfy these wants and needs.

"Give me a piece of chocolate," he says.
Dame chocolate.
damay chokolatay

Often we would like to be able to say, *Children, here you have* (here is some) *chocolate,* **Niños, aquí tenéis chocolate** (neenyoss akee taynayees chokolatay). But we have no chocolate with us. *So we go to a candy store,* **así vamos a una confitería** (asee vamoss a oona kongfeetayreea) and *the kind aunt,* **la buena tía** (la booayna teea) *asks the employee,* **pregunta a la dependiente** (prayghoonta a la thaypenndyenntay):

¿Tiene Vd. chocolate? (teeaynay oostayth chokolatay). *Have you any chocolate?*

And the sales girl answers,

¿Qué desea Vd.? ¿Qué clase, qué tamaño, qué calidad desea Vd.?
kay thaysaya oostayth kay klasay kay tamangyo kay kaleethath thaysaya oostayth.
What do you want (wish)? What kind? What size? What quality do you want?

Tenemos chocolate para comer crudo.
taynaymoss chokolatay para komerr krootho
We have ordinary chocolate for eating.

Tenemos chocolate para cocinar.
taynaymoss chokolatay para kotheenar
We have chocolate for cooking (for to cook).

Desea una barra de chocolate.
thaysaya oona barra thay chokolatay
You want a bar of chocolate.

Hay también chocolate de vainilla.
aee tammbyayng chokolatay thay vaeeneelya
There is also vanilla chocolate.

Acaso Vd. deseará dulces o confites de chocolate.
akaso oostayth thaysayara thoolthays o kongfeetayz thay
  chokolatay
Perhaps you would like sweets and candies of chocolate.

And now, since you have decided on what you want and wish
to give the order, let us see how the Imperative is used here.

Déme medio kilo (una libra) de dulces y un cuarto de kilo
daymay maydyo keelo (oona leevra) thay thoolthays ee oon
  kvarto thay keelo
Give me half a kilo of chocolates and a quarter of a kilo

de caramelos.
day karamayloss
of caramels.

Las confites de limón y de naranja son muy buenas.
laz konnfeetays thay leemongee thay narangha sonn mooy
  booaynas
The lemon and the orange drops are very good.

You have not forgotten that in Spanish
there are two ways of addressing people,
the familiar and the formal. And, of
course, for both of these forms there is a
singular and a plural.

Some letters is in Spanish **unas cartas** or **algunas
cartas** (oonas karrtas, al-
goonas karrtas). There is
no difference.

The adult says to the adult (formal singular):

Cómprelos Vd.
kommprayloss oostayth
Buy them (m.)

Cómprelas Vd.
kommpraylas oostayth
Buy them (f.)

Cómprelo Vd.
kommpraylo oostayth
Buy it.

Véndame Vd.
venndamay oostayth
Sell me.

Véndamelo Vd.
venndamaylo oostayth
Sell it to me.

Since the occasion arises very often in our daily conversations,
we should also be prepared to address someone with whom we
are familiar, someone to whom we can say **tu** instead of the more
formal **Vd.** For instance:

The child to his mother (familiar singular):

Cómpramelas
kommpramaylas
Buy me them (buy them for me); for instance, las confites de limón.

Cómpramelos
kommpramayloss
Buy me them (buy them for me); for instance, los caramelos.

Cómpramelo
kommpramaylo
Buy it for me (anything).

For this familiar form, the endings are as follows:

For all verbs ending in -ar.

Habla	(avla)	*Speak*
Manda	(manda)	*Send*
Da	(da)	*Give*
Pregunta	(prayghoonta)	*Ask*
Contesta	(konntessta)	*Answer*

For all verbs ending in -er or -ir

Come	(komay)	*Eat*
Vende	(vennday)	*Sell*
Convence	(kombennthay)	*Convince*
Coge	(kohay)	*Catch*
Vive	(veevay)	*Live*
Pide	(peeday)	*Order*
Permite	(perrmeetay)	*Permit*
Recibe	(raytheevay)	*Receive*

But of course, more often you will have to say **Vd.**

Hable Vd.
(avlay oostayth)
Speak

Coma Vd.
(koma oostayth)
Eat

Viva Vd.
(veeva oostayth)
Live

Mande Vd.
(manday oostayth)
Send

Venda Vd.
(vennda oostayth)
Sell etc.

Pida Vd.
(peeda oostayth)
Order etc.

De Vd.
(day oostayth)
Give

One person, familiar

you = **tu**

¡Habla! (avla)	*Speak!*
¡No hables! (no avless)	*Don't speak!*
¡Come! (komay)	*Eat!*
¡No comas! (no komas)	*Don't eat!*
¡Vive! (veevay)	*Live!*
¡No vivas! (no veevas)	*Don't live!*

Many persons, familiar

you = **vosotros**

¡Hablad! (avlath)	*Speak!*
¡No habléis! (no avlays)	*Don't speak!*
¡Vivid! (veeveeth)	*Live!*
¡No viváis! (no veevaees)	*Don't live!*
¡Comed! (kometh)	*Eat!*
¡No comáis! (no komaees)	*Don't eat!*

¡Hablemos!	**¡Comamos!**	**¡Vivamos!**
avlaymoss	komamoss	veevamoss
Let us speak!	*Let us eat!*	*Let us live!*

One person, formal

you = **Vd.** (oostayth)

¡Hable Vd.!	**¡Coma Vd.!**	**¡Viva Vd.!**
avlay oostayth	koma oostayth	veeva oostayth
Speak!	*Eat!*	*Live!*

Many persons, formal

you = **Vds.** (oostaythays)

¡Hablen Vds.!	**¡Coman Vds.!**	**¡Vivan Vds.!**
avlenn oostaythays	koman oostaythays	veevan oostaythays
Speak!	*Eat!*	*Live!*

Don't make a mistake!, **No se equivoque Vd.** (no say aykeevo-kay oostayth). In the familiar form used to a child, to a very good friend or to your relatives you drop the **r** of the verb ending **ar.** For example:

preguntar	**¡Pregunta!**
praygoontar	praygoonta
to ask	*Ask!*

contestar	¡Contesta!
konntesstar	konntessta
to answer	Answer!

In the same way, for verbs ending in **er** and **ir,** the Imperative ending is **e** in both forms.

vender	¡Vende!
venndayr	vennday
to sell	Sell!

escribir	¡Escribe!
esskreeveer	esskreevay
to write	Write!

Lesson Twenty-Four

Let us now consider how we would address several people. To those with whom we are familiar, we would say:

¡Preguntad!	¡Vended!	¡Escribid!
praygoontath	venndeth	esskreeveeth
Ask!	Sell!	Write!

For all other forms of the Imperative, the Spaniard uses a form that we can best translate, perhaps, I may. This form of the Imperative expresses an action as a mere possibility, a supposition or a wish. For example:

that I	may speak	may eat	may live
que (kay) **yo**	hable	coma	viva
tu	-es	-as	-as
el	-e	-a	-a
ella	-e	-a	-a
nosotros	-emos	-amos	-amos
vosotros	-eis	-ais	-ais
ellos	-en	-an	-an
ellas	-en	-an	-an

This same form is also used to express a negative imperative in all cases, whether familiar or not.

And now I think we understand what this really rather confusing Imperative, with which we express a command, is all about.

El primero de enero,
ell preemayro thay aynayro
The first of January,

día de Año Nuevo.
deea thay angyo nooayvo
New Year's Day.

¡Feliz Año Nuevo!
fayleeth angyo nooayvo
Happy New Year!

Mis mas cordiales
mees mas korrthyalays
My most cordial

felicitaciones
fayleetheetathyonays
felicitations (greetings)

para el Año Nuevo.
para el angyo nooayvo
for the New Year!

Don't ask *You may not ask*	**No preguntes** (no praygoontays) **preguntar**
Don't sell *You may not sell*	**No vendas** (no venndas) **vender**
Don't write *You may not write*	**No escribas** (no esskreevas) **escribir**
Let us sell *We may sell*	**Vendamos** (venndamos) **vender**
Let us ask *We may ask*	**Preguntemos** (praygoontaymos) **preguntar**
Let us write *We may write*	**Escribamos** (esskreevamos) **escribir**

And so you will understand why, when I want to say to many boys and girls of a very young age, *Speak!*, I say **¡Hablad!** (avlath).

But *don't speak* is
¡No habléis! (no avlayees) = *You may not speak!* = *Don't speak.*

¡Comed! (kometh) = *Eat!*

¡No comáis! (no komaees) = *You may not eat!* = *Don't eat!*

¡Interrumpid! (eenterroompeeth) = *Interrupt!*

¡No interrumpáis! (no eenterroompaees) = *You may not interrupt!* = *Don't interrupt!*

And to you, **señorita, señora,** or to you, **señor,** returning now to the more formal tone:

Take! = *May your honor take* = **¡Tome Vd.!** (tomay oostayth)

Drink! = *May your honor drink* = **¡Beba Vd.!** (bayva oostayth)

Permit = *May your honor permit* = **¡Permita Vd.!** (perrmeeta oostayth).

To all of you, ladies and gentlemen a **todos Vds., señoras y caballeros** (a tothoss oostaythays sengyoras ee kavalyayross):

Look! = *May your honors look!* = **¡Miren Vds.!** (meerenn oostaythays)
mirar (meerar) = *to look*

* 122 *

Learn! = *May your honors learn!* = **¡Aprendan Vds.!** (aprenndan
oostaythays)
aprender (aprenndayr) =
to learn

Go up(stairs)! = *May your honors go up(stairs)* =
¡Suban Vds.! (soovan oostaythays)
subir (sooveer) = *to go up(stairs)*

Now you must get accustomed to all these forms. But you will
understand them very soon and then you will know why it
sounds so funny to a Spaniard when *a stranger*, **un extranjero**
(oon esstranghayro), **una extranjera** (oona esstranghayra) who
is trying to be very formal, expresses himself or herself in the
familiar way. To a Spaniard this sounds just as bad as when a
gentleman who is introduced to a lady for the first time, says
right away, "Hello, Mary! How do you do, Mary?" In Spanish
there is an expression for that: *He was very familiar with me.*
Me ha tuteado (may a tootayatho) literally: *He said "tú" to me.*

¡No aprenda Vd. demasiado!
no aprennda oostayth thaymasyatho
Don't learn too much!

Translate into Spanish

A healthy mind in a healthy body. What does it mean? Our
body, our mind, our brain, our soul. We eat in order to live. We
don't live in order to eat. Eat in order to live and you may not
live in order to eat. It is the spirit that builds the body. One
eats, one lives, one day after the other. Earn to eat, earn a
livelihood.

I have spoken, to doubt, to eat, to live, to sell, to drink, to
fear, to run, to start, to interrupt, to receive; eaten, lived, sold,
drunk, feared, run, started, interrupted. We have received, you
have run, you have forgotten, they had forgotten. The mother
tongue, these words, these words are understood only by the
mother of the baby. In the eyes of our loving mothers we are all
wonderful children and geniuses.

You are hungry. Let us go to bed. Good night! Sleep well!
Rest well!

¡Lea en alta voz!

¿Digame, que tiene Vd.? ¡Tome Vd. asiento, sientese! Le digo: como muy poco; me duelen los ojos y los óidos; me duele la garganta, la cabeza, la espalda. Todo el cuerpo no está bueno. Me duelen todos los miembros: el seno, el carillo, las piernas, el pecho, los dedos, los pies, el cuello, las manos, la barba, la nariz, la frente.

Tengo un corazon, un higado, nervios. Un amigo mio me ha dicho: vaya Vd. al dentista. Fuí allá: no hay nada. ¿Qué piensa Vd. de eso?

El doctor contesta: enséñeme Vd. la lengua. No está sucia. Soy examinado por le médico: ¿Qué tal de apetito? Yo como muy poco, apenas dos huevos, café, pan y mantequilla, algun pescado frito, jalea y marmelada, eso es todo para el desayuno. Entonces, a mediodía, tomo mi almuerzo muy legero, solamente para comer un poco, sopa, dos chuletas, legumbres, patatas, postre.

Entre las cuatro y las cinco tomo solamente una taza de té, tostadas y torta. A las siete no como mucho, solamente me comida regulare de seis platas. Eso es todo lo que como durante el día. ¿No es una lástima, doctor?

Eso no es lástima, es un escándalo. Vd. no trabaja. ¡No piense en piense su enfermedad! Vd. come demasiado y trabaja muy poco. Este es mi consejo. Toda la vida, una receta, una cuchara cada hora. Sciento decir, Vd. está asolutamente sano (a). El trabajo es la mejor medicina.

Mente sana en cuerpo sano. ¿Qué significa esto? Nuestro cuerpo, nuestro cerebro, nuestra mente, nuestra alma. Comemos para vivir. No vivimos para comer. Come para vivir y no vivas para comer. El éspiritu edifica el cuerpo. Se vive, se come, un día despues del otro. Ganar de comer, ganarse la vida.

He hablado, dudar, comer, vivir, vender, beber, temer, correr, partir, interrumpir, recibir, comido, vivido, vendido, bebido, temido, corrido, partido, interrumpido. Hemos recibido, habéis corrido, hubisteis olvidado, hubieron olvidado. La lengua de la madre, estas palabras. Estas palabras son compredidas por la madre del nene.

Translate into Spanish

Intelligent men and women, in the future. The sun rises and sets every day. We are ignorant and we shall be ignorant. The most important thing on earth. There is nothing as obstinate as a fact. A fortune teller had prophesied to a girl: you will cross a street and enter a house. You will meet a friend in this house. This friend will talk to you. You will return to your home. You will eat. You will receive a very important letter. This letter will decide your fortune.

I shall cross a street, I have crossed the street. I shall enter a house, I have entered a house and I have met a friend. This friend spoke to me. I shall meet a friend who will speak to me. I shall return home. I have returned. I shall eat, I have eaten. I shall receive a letter, I have received a very important letter. This letter, so he said, will decide my fortune. My dear friends, my dear friend. You will understand everything when I shall have told you everything. You will not have forgotten: I have money, I have no money, I shall have money, I shall earn it. My brother earned it a long time ago. Are you happy? I don't know! Do you like to go to a bullfight? We will buy a ticket for a bullfight. The fight will begin at half past four in the afternoon. The doors of the place will be opened two hours earlier. We shall see the picadores. You will see the fighters. The espados who will kill the bulls, and before them the men with the small darts with a bannerol. The audience.

The courageous rule the world (literally: the world is of the courageous ones). It is necessary first to decide what the word courage means. Boldness, truth, I should say. Have courage! Be plucky! To speak Spanish, to read Spanish. I haven't the courage to do it. I can't do it. I don't believe it. We have shown you. But if you were to ask, I would have to answer.

Furnished rooms for rent. Unfurnished rooms to let. It is forbidden. It is forbidden to enter. No admittance! It is requested to close the door. Please close the door! It is requested not to touch. Don't touch, please! You would be wrong.

tan ancho como	tann antsho komo	*as broad as long*
largo	larrgo	
bueno, a	booayno, a	*good*
mejor	mayhor	*better*
óptimo	oppteemo	*best*
malo	malo	*bad*
peor	payor	*worse*
pesimo	payseemo	*worst*
grande	grannday	*great*
mayor	mayor	*greater*
maximo	maxeemo	*the greatest*
pequeño	paykaynyo	*small*
menor	maynor	*smaller*
minimo	meeneemo	*smallest*
mucho	moocho	*much*
más	mas	*more*
muchísimo	mootsheeseemo	*most*
poco	poko	*little*
menos	maynoss	*less*
poquísimo	pokeeseemo	*least*
¡Hasta más ver!	asta mas vayr	*I'll see you later!*
¡Hasta luego!	asta looaygo	*Good bye!*
¿Cómo está Vd.?	komo essta oostayth	*How are you?*
es casi imposible	ess kasee eemposee-vlay	*it is almost impossible*
no estoy muy bien	no esstoy mooy byayng	*I am not very well*
tengo una indigestión	tayngo oona eendeehesstyong	*I am suffering from indigestion*
estoy enfermo	esstoy ennferrmo	*I am sick*
estamos bien	esstamoss byayng	*we are well, we feel well*
Vd. es Inglés	oostayth ess eenglays	*you are an Englishman*
eres Americano	ayrays amayreekano	*you are an American*
el Aleman	ell alayman	*the German*
el Francese	ell frannthaysay	*the Frenchman*
perdone Vd.	perrdonay oostayth	*excuse me*
excuseme	exkoosaymay	*excuse me*

no estoy muy bien	no esstoy mooy byayng	I am not very well
el médico	ell maydeeko	the doctor
el médico me ha dicho	ell maydeeko may a deecho	the doctor has told me
tomo licencias	tomo leethennthyas	I take the liberty
me permito	may payrmeeto	I allow myself
dispense Vd.	deespaynsay oostayth	pardon me
si	see	if
interrumpo	eenterroompo	I interrupt
siempre	syaympray	always
cortes	korrtays	polite
¡no hay de qué!	no aee thay kay	it doesn't matter!
¡no importa!	no eemporrta	no matter at all!
desagradable	daysagrathavlay	disagreeable
el doctor	ell dokktor	the doctor
el doctor me ha dicho	ell dokktor may a deecho	the doctor has said (to me)
la paciencia	la pathyaynthya	the patience
de repente	day raypayntay	suddenly
tengo paciencia	tayngo pathyaynthya	I have patience
demasiado	daymasyatho	too much
lo que es demasiado, es demasiado	lo kay ess daymasyado ess daymasyado	what is too much, is too much
muy bien	mooy byayng	all-right
de nuevo	day nooayvo	now aga n
paciencial	pathyaynthyal	patient
tenga calma	taynga kalma	take it easy!
calmo, a	kalmo, a	quiet
el ojo	ell oho	the eye
el oigo	ell oeego	the ear
mis congratulaciones	mees konngratoolathyonays	my congratulations!
tener	taynayr	to have
haber	avayr	to have
el médico	ell maydeeko	the doctor
he tenido dinero	ay tayneetho deenayro	I have had money
la reminiscencia	la raymeeneesthaynthya	the memory
mas que nada	mas kay natha	better than nothing
he hablado	ay avlatho	I have spoken
Vd. ha contestado	oostayth a konntaystatho	you have consulted
dígame ahora	deegamay aora	tell me now

en todas partes	enn tothas parrtays	*all about it every-where*
la sala	la sala	*the room*
la sala de espera	la sala thay ayspayra	*the waiting room*
la casa del doctor	la casa dell dokktor	*the doctor's house*
¡qué lástima!	kay lasteema	*what a pity!*
hay mucha gente	aee moocha hayntay	*there are many people*
Vd. debe estar allí	oostayth dayvay esstar allyee	*you must be there*
¡por favor!	porr favor	*please!*
en mi reloj son las cuatro	enn mee rayloy sonn las kvatro	*according to my watch it is four o'clock*
de la tarde	day la tarthay	*in the afternoon*
a las diez de la mañana	a las dyayth thay la manyana	*at ten o'clock in the morning*
mañana por la mañana	manyana porr la manyana	*tomorrow morning*
hoy es lunes	oy ess loonays	*today is Monday*
la semana	la saymana	*the week*
la semana empieza	la saymana aympyaytha	*the week begins*
el lunes por la mañana	ell loonays porr la manyana	*on a Monday morning*
¿A cuanto estamos hoy?	a kvanto esstamoss oy	*What's the date?*

Las cartas dicen
las karrtas deethayn
The cards say

que Vd. reciberá
kay oostayth raytheevayra
that you will receive

una carta muy importante.
oona karrta mooy eemporrtantay
a very important letter.

Lesson Twenty-Five

After work is done, we want to rest a little or amuse ourselves, después de trabajar queremos reposar un poco o divertirnos (desspooess day travahar kayraymoss rayposar oon poko o deeverrteernoss). *In the course of time,* however, andando el tiempo (andando ell tyemmpo), we grow accustomed to love *all work, even the most disagreeable,* todo trabajo aun el más desagradable (totho travaho aoon ell mas dessagrathavlay), comforting ourselves with such phrases as: "As the work, so the pay," although I have seldom met anyone who was convinced that he was satisfactorily paid for his work. *"No gains without pains,"* "No hay atajo sin trabajo" (no aee ataho seen travaho), or that other undeniable platitude, *"There is no rose without a thorn,"* "No hay rosa sin espina" (no aee rosa seen esspeena)—are sayings with which all people who work hard are always ready to agree. That is why you see so many people who claim they don't like to win in the sweepstakes. But they gamble just the same and you know how very sad they are if they do win a fortune!

Still, en todo caso, como quiera que sea (enn totho kaso, komo keeayra kay saya) *however you would like it to be,* "God helps those who help themselves" „A quien madruga, Dios le ayuda (a keeyenn mathroogha deeoss lay ayootha), literally, *to whom it arises early, God helps him.* Therefore, *I give you this good advice,* doy un buen consejo (doy oon booenn konnsayho) for what it is worth: "Quien tiene tienda que la atienda" (keeyenn teeaynay tyennda kay la atyennda) *who has a store let him watch it (that he may attend to it)!*

What did you think? ¿Qué pensó Vd.? (kay pennso oostayth). *That the store could be left alone all day?*—¿Que la tienda se quede sola todo el día? (kay la tee-ennda say kayday sola totho ell deea).

It's funny about good advice. I don't blame people for what they do with advice. You see, very often, the only thing that can be done with it; that is, give it right away to somebody else. While I was working in Havana some time ago, on a ten-dollar job, with little money in my pocket, I had to see a doctor and he gave me this advice: "This climate is not good for you. Take the next boat that goes to Spain. That will cost you five dollars— not to go to Spain, but for my advice." I certainly couldn't go to Spain, or anywhere else, for that matter, because I had no money, but later on when my boss was sick, I gave him the advice of that doctor. He was glad to travel abroad and I got a much better job. That made me very healthy, *I can tell you* **ledigo** (lay deegho).

Mucho ruido para nada.
moocho rooeetho para natha
Much ado (noise) about nothing.

It is ironic, *to be serious for a while*, **que sea dicho seriamente** (kay saya deecho sayreeamenntay), that when we are working hard we want to be lazy and when we have nothing to do we would like to work very hard. What we feel, what we want, what we believe, can rarely be stated as a fact; it is only seldom that we can be absolutely certain of anything. **"El hombre propone y Dios dispone"** (ell ommbray proponay ee theeoz theesponay), *"Man proposes and God disposes."*

Again the Spanish language shows us what a difference there is between what really *is* a fact and what only *may be* a fact. A special form is used to express what is possible or probable, and to express a personal feeling. (We have this subjunctive in English too.)

Don't blame me, **no me culpe Vd.** (no may koolpay oostayth). *I am not responsible*, **no soy responsable** (no soy ressponnsablay) *for these difficulties*, **por estas dificultades** (porr esstas deefeekooltathays). I know, *kind though you may be*, **por bueno que sea Vd.** (porr booayno kay saya oostayth) *that you would like*, **desearía darme una bofetada** (daysayareea tharmay oona vofaytatha) *to give me a slap in the face. Don't do it!* **¡no lo haga Vd.!** (no lo agha oostayth).

But to get away from this subjunctive.
You would say:

I want to go to a barber	*or*	*to a hairdresser.*
Quiero ir al barbero	**o**	**al peluquero.**
keeayro eer al barvayro.	o	al paylookayro

Es necesario que vaya Vd. a la barbería o a la peluquería.
ess naythessaryo kay vaya oostayth a la barbayreea o a la
paylookayreea
It is necessary that you go to a barber's or hairdresser's.

Y me río de Vd.
ee may reeo thay oostayth
And I laugh at you.

You have just used the subjunctive again, and even with an
irregular verb.

ir (eer) to go.

voy	(voee)	*I go*	que vaya	(vaya)	*that I may go*
vas	(vas)	*etc.*	vayas		
va	(va)		vaya		
vamos	(vamos)		vayamos		
vais	(vaees)		vayáis		
van	(van)		vayan		

ser (sayr) *to be*, **soy** (soy) *I am*   **estar** (esstar) *to be*, **estoy** *I am*

que sea	(saya) *that I may be*	que esté	(esstay) *that I may be*
seas	(sayas)	estés	(esstay)
sea	(saya)	esté	
seamos	(sayamos)	estemos	
seais	(sayaees)	estéis	
sean	(sayan)	estén	

haber (avayr) *to have*,   **tener** (taynayr) *to have*

he	*I have*	tengo	*I have*
que haya (a-ya) *that I may have*	que tenga	(tennga)
			that I may have
hayas	(a-yas)	tengas	
haya	(a-ya)	tenga	
hayamos	(a-yamos)	tengamos	
hayais	(a-yaees)	tengais	
hayan	(a-yan)	tengan	

With this preparation, *let us look for a hairdresser's shop*,
busquemos una peluquería (booskaymoss oona paylookayreea).
It is possible that we may go to the theatre later on, **es posible que
vayamos al teatro más tarde** (ess poseeblay kay vayamoss al
tayatro mas tarthay). *I am sorry that I didn't tell you before*,
siento que no le haya dicho antes (syennto kay no lay ha-ya
theecho antess).

¿Dónde hay una peluquería?
donnday ai oona paylookayreea
Where is a hairdresser's?

¿Puede Vd. decirme donde hay una cerca de aquí?
pooaythay oostayth thaytheermay donnday aee oona therrka day akee
Can you tell me where there is

un buen peluquero?
oon booyn pailookairoy
a good hairdresser near here?

No creo que la peluquería enfrente de nuestra casa sea buena
no krayo kay la paylookayreea enfrenntay thay nooesstra kasa saya vooayna
I don't think that the hairdresser opposite our house (may be) is good

mas creo que la barbería en la casa de la esquina de la calle próxima
mas krayo kay la varvayreea enn la kasa thay la esskeena thay la kallyay proxeema
but I think that the barber's shop in the corner house of the next street

es muy buena.
ez mooy booayna.
is very good.

Muy bien (mooy byayng) *very well.* Creo que iremos allá (krayo kay eeraymoss allya) *I think we'll go there.* As we enter the hairdresser's, on one side there is the room for gentlemen; the other side is for the ladies. *I hear the barber saying* (Span. say) *to Peter*, oigo al barbero decir a Pedro (oeegho al barvayro thaytheer a paydro):

¡Buenos días, señor! ¡Pronto se le servirá! ¡Tome Vd. asiento!
booaynoz theeas sengyor pronnto say lay serrveera tomay oostayth asyennto
Good morning, sir! You will be served at once! Take a seat!

¡Afeitar! ¿Quiere Vd. afeitarme? Ruégole también que me corte
afayeetar kyayray oostayth afayeetarmay rooaygholay tammbyayng kay may korrtay
Shave! Will you give me a shave? I ask you also to cut

el cabello.
ell kabellyo.
my hair (and cut my hair too).

¿Está buena la navaja?
essta vooayna la navaha
Is the razor all right?

No, hace daño.
no athay dangyo
No, it hurts (it makes hurt).

Duele un poquito.
dooaylay oon pokeeto
It hurts a little bit.

Láveme Vd. la cabeza. Deseo un champú seco.
lavaymay oostayth la kavaytha daysayo oon champoo sayko
Wash my head. I want a dry shampoo.

Corte un poco de aquí.
korrtay oon poko day akee
Cut a little more here.

Quiero arreglarme las uñas.
kyayro arrayglarmay las oongyas
I want a manicure (I want to arrange me the nails).

¿Quiere Vd. polvos?
kyayray oostayth pollvoss
Do you want some powder?

Hágame Vd. la raya al lado derecho, no al lado izquierdo.
agamay oostayth la ra-ya al latho thayrecho, no al latho eethky-
   errtho
Part my hair (make me the line) *on the right side, not on the left
side.*

   Now and then, **de cuando en cuando** (day kvando eng kvando),
we overhear some of the trade expressions in the shop. **Córteme
Vd. el pelo que quede corto por detrás, y no tanto por delante**
(korrtaymay oostayth ell paylo kay kaythay korrto porr thaytras
ee no tanto porr thaylantay), *cut my hair* (*so that it may remain*)
short in the back and not so much in front. We try to pick up *the
soap,* **el jabón** (ell havong), *the towel,* **la toalla** (la toalya), *a hot
towel,* **una toalla cálida** (oona toallya kaleetha), *warm or cold
water,* **agua caliente o fría** (agva kalyenntay o freea); *to lather*
(soap) the face, **dar jabón** (dar havong); *to brush and to comb,*
cepillar y peinar (theppeelyar ee payeenar); *to trim,* **arreglar**
(arrayglar), therefore, *to trim oneself* **arreglarse** (arrayglarsay),
either *the hair,* **el pelo** (ell paylo), or *the beard,* **la barba** (la varva),
or *the mustache,* **el bigote** (ell veeghotay).

* 134 *

In the meantime, our ladies have received just the kind of hairdressing that they wished.

Julia dijo a la peluquera:
hoolya deeho a la paylookayra
Julia said to the hairdresser (a girl):

Primero deseo cortarme las puntas del cabello.
preemayro thaysayo korrtarmay las poontaz thell kabellyo
First I want the ends of my hair cut.

Segundo deme Vd. un champú.
sayghoondo thaymay oostayth oon champoo
Second, give me a shampoo.

Tercero: una ondulación.
terrthayro oona onndoolathyong
Third, a permanent wave.

Cuarto: un masaje facial.
kvarto oon masahay fathyal
Fourth, a facial massage.

When we heard that, we interrupted, **cuando oímos, eso interrumpimos** (kvando oeemoss esso eenterroompeemoss) and asked her:

?Desea Vd. ir al teatro hoy o mañana o más tarde?
daysaya oostayth eer al tayatro oy o mangyana o mas tarthay
Do you want to go to the theater today or tomorrow or later?

That settled the question, and two hours later we were ready to leave the hairdresser's shop. *Julia's curls looked very beautiful,* **los rizos de Julia lucían muy hermosas** (loz reethoz thay hoolya lootheean mooy herrmosas).

Lesson Twenty-Six

Some time ago we saw the bullfights about which we had heard so much. It was a very interesting experience, more exciting for the Spanish and South American people than for us. The bulls and their fighters did all they could, but it certainly was not more interesting to us than any other shows we had seen before. We saw the enthusiasm, but we could not be as fascinated as the Spanish audience. They seemed to know all the bulls and all the bullfighters.

Hace algun tiempo vimos las corridas de toros
athay algoon tyemmpo veemos las korreedaz thay toroz

de que habíamos oído tanto. Fué una experiencia muy
thay kay aveeamoss oeetho tanto fooay oona ekspayryennthya
mooy

interesante (interesantísima), más excitante para la gente española
eentayraysantay (eentayraysanteeseema) mas extheetantay para la henntay espangyola

y de América del Sur que para nosotros. Los toros y sus toreadores
ee thay amayreeka thell soor kay para nosotross. loss toross ee soos torrayathoress

hicieron todo lo que pudieron. Más seguramente no estábamos tan entusiasmados
eethyayron totho lo kay poothyayron. mas saygooramenntay no esstavamoss tann enntoosyazmathos

como en otros espectáculos que habíamos observado antes.
komo enn otross esspekktakooloss kay aveeamoss obserrvatho antess.

Habíamos visto el entusiasmo, pero no nos encantamos tanto
aveeamoss veesto ell enntoosyazmo payro no nos enncantamoss tanto

como el público español. Ellos parecían conocer todos los toros
komo ell poovleeko esspangyol ellyos paraytheean konothayr tothoz loss toross

y a todos los toreros.
ee a tothoz los torayross

* 136 *

Ha matado al toro.
a matatho al toro.
He has killed the bull.

El gran Torero.
ell grann to**rray**ro.
The great Bullfighter.

El mundo es de los audaces.
ell **moon**do ess day loss aooda**thays**
The world belongs to the daring.

There was a long discussion among us, **Hubo una larga discusión entre todos nosotros** (oovo oona larga theeskoosyong enntray tothoss nosotross). Some said that *boxing,* **boxeo** (bokksayo), the noble art of self-defense, and *prize-fighting,* **boxeo** (bokksayo), *are very different,* **son muy diferentes** (sonn mooy theefayrenntess). Others said they could not see that the difference was very great. Julia ended *the dispute,* **la disputa** (la theespoota), by saying, "I don't understand anything about boxing and *boxers,* **los boxeadores** (loz vokksayathoress), nor do I understand anything about bulls or bullfighters. But we can agree, at any rate, that yesterday we all had a very good time at the theatre. *It was wonderful,* **fué maravilloso** (fooay maraveelyoso). *There is no question about that, is there?",* **¡No hay duda! ¿No es verdad?** (no ai thootha no ess verrthath).

And then the conversation turned to yesterday's performance at the theatre. *Peter said,* **Pedro dijo** (paythro theeho):

Os he dicho que vayamos primero al teatro y más tarde también
oss ay theecho kay vayamoss preemayro al tayatro ee mas
    tarrday tambyayng
I told you that we should go to a theatre first and later perhaps

al concierto y a la ópera. Sabía que os gustaría mucho.
al konnthyerrto ee a la opayra saveea kay oz ghoostareea moocho
to a concert or the opera. I knew that you would enjoy yourself very
    much.

Cuando os dije que podríamos ir, ¡cuántas preguntas tuve
kvando oz theehay kay pothreeamoss eer—kvantas pray-
    ghoontas toovay
When I told you we should go, how many questions of yours I had

que contestaros!
kay konntesstaross
to answer!

¿Cuándo empieza? ¿A qué hora empieza?
kvando emmpyaytha a kay ora emmpyaytha
When does it start? What time does it begin?

¿Qué se da? ¿Cuándo se acabará?
kay say tha kvando say akavara
What are they showing? When will it end?

¿Vale la pena de ver la representación?
valay la payna day verr la raypraysenntathyong
Is it worth while to see the performance?

And I have told you, **y os he dicho** (ee oss ay theecho):

No debíais dejar de verlo.
no thayveeaeez thayhar day verrlo
You must not miss (to see) it.

There was a very nice girl with us, **había entre nosotros una muchacha muy amable** (aveea enntray nosotross oona moochacha mooy amavlay). She was wonderful at impersonating a radio-announcer or a radio-reporter for fun. So we asked her to give her impressions of the show as a radio report.

So, she began, **asi ella empezo** (asee ellya emmpaytho):

Esta es la Estación ACD. Su anunciadora es Pepita Caballero.
essta ess la esstathyong ACD soo anoontheeathora ess paypeeta kaballyayro
This is Station ACD (of the Spanish Broadcasting System).
Your announcer is Pepita Caballero.

Le llevamos en este mismo instante al Teatro San Fernando
lay llyayvamoss enn esstay meezmo eenstantay al tayatro sann ferrnando
We bring you now to the St. Ferdinand Theatre

en la calle Colón.
enn la kallyay kolong
on Columbus Street.

Son las nueve y veinte.
sonn laz nooayvay ee vayeentay
It is twenty minutes past nine.

Faltan diez minutos. A las nueve y media empieza el gran estreno
faltan dyayth meenootoss a las nooayvay ee maydya emmpyaytha ell gran esstrayno
We still have ten minutes. At half-past nine will begin the first

de la comedia "La vida es Sueño" en verso y prosa
de la komaydya la veetha ess sooaynyo enn verrso ee prosa
performance of that great comedy "Life is a Dream," in verse and prose,

del poeta más celebrado de España, Calderón de la Barca, que nació
thell poayta mas thelaybratho thesspangya kaldayron day la barka kay nathyo
by Spain's most celebrated poet, Calderon de la Barca, who was born

en 1600 y murió en 1681.
enn *1600* ee mooryo enn *1681*
in 1600 and died in 1681.

Todas las localidades están tomadas, la caja del teatro está cerrada
todaz las lokaleethathess esstan tomathas la kaha thell tayatro essta therratha
Every seat is taken. The house is packed. The box-office is closed.

No hay despacho.
no hay thesspacho
There is no sale.

Those who are unable to get *tickets*, **una entrada, una billete** (oona enntratha, oona beelyaytay), *go, disappointed, to a near by movie*, **desilusionados van al cine proximo** (desseeloosyonathoz van al theenay proxeemo).

The street is crowded, **la calle está llena de gente** (la kallyay essta llyayna thay henntay) full of people; *no automobiles can pass*, **no puede pasar ni un automóvil** (no pooaythay pasar nee oon aootomoveel). *Very slowly, automobiles and coaches approach the entrance of the theatre*, **lentamente los autos y los coches van llegando** (*go arriving*) **a la entrada del teatro** (lenntamenntay loss aootoss ee los kochess vann llyayghando a la enntratha thell tayatro); *the drivers are having a hard time of it*, **los conductores tienen un día muy difícil** (loss konndooktoress tyaynenn oon deea mooy deefeetheel).

We enter the theatre, **entramos en el teatro** (enntramoss enn ell tayatro). There is no use asking *what seat we should take*, **qué localidad tomar** (kay lokaleethath tomar). *There is no choice left*, **no se puede escoger** (no say pooaythay esskoherr). But *where is my seat?* **¿Dónde está mi asiento?** (donnday essta mee asyennto). *Show me your ticket, please*, **per favor, muestreme Vd. su entrada** (perr favor mooesstraymay oostayth soo enntratha).

Lesson Twenty-Seven

We enter the upper balcony, **entramos en el balcón** (enntramoss enn ell balkong), **la segunda grada** (la saygoonda gratha), and can see the waiting audience in *the dress-circle*, **la primera grada** (la preemayra gratha), and in *the boxes, the orchestra and the reserved seats*, **la butaca** (la bootaka). In *the boxes*, **los palcos** (loss palkoss), there are the society people in full dress, *the ladies in (with their) evening gowns*, **las señoras con su vestido de etiqueta** (las sengyoras konn soo vessteedo day ayteekayta), *ornamented with jewels, with the most precious gems*, **adornadas de joyas, con las piedras más preciosas** (athorrnathaz thay hoyas, konn las pyaythras mas praythyossas).

It is difficult to speak to you, because the noise is tremendous, **es difícil hablarle porque el ruido es enorme** (ess theefeetheel avlarlay porrkay ell rooeetho ess aynorrmay). Then *the orchestra begins to play*, **la orquestra empieza a tocar** (la orrkesstra emmpyestha a tokkar). *A singer sings a song*, **una cantante canta una canción** (oona kantantay kanta oona kanthyong). *Do you hear it?* **¿La oyen Vds.?** (la oyenn oostaythays).

It is "La Paloma" (The Dove), **es "La Paloma"** (ess la paloma).

Cuando salí de la Habana,
kvando salee thay la avanna
When I left Havana,

Válgame Dios!
valgamay dyoss
God help me!

Nadie me ha visto salir,
nathyay may a veesto saleer
Nobody saw me leaving,

Sino fuí yo.
seeno fooee yo
No one but myself.

Que una linda Guachinanga
kay oona leenda guacheenanga
That's a pretty damsel.

Allá voy yo
allya voy yo
There I go.

Que se vino tras de mí.
kay say veeno traz day mee
Oh, she came behind me!

Que sí señor.
kay see sengyor
Yes, sir, she did.

Si a tu ventana
see a too venntana
If to your window

Llega una Paloma
lyayga oona paloma
(There) arrives a dove

Trátala con cariño
tratala konn kareenyo
Treat it with kindness

Que es mi persona.
kay ess mee perrsona
For it is myself.

Cuéntale tus amores
quenntalay toos amoress
Tell it of your love,

Bien de mi vida,
byayng day mee veetha
My sweet darling (sweet of my life),

Corónala de flores
koronala day floress
Crown it with flowers

Que es cosa mía
kay ess kosa meea
For it is mine (my thing).

Ah! chinita que sí,
a cheeneeta kay see
Ah, little girl, yes!

Ah! que dame tu amor, ah!
a kay thamay too amor a
Ah! give me your love!

Que vente conmigo chinita,
kay venntay konnmeegho cheeneeta
Come with me, little girl,

Adónde vivo yo.
adonnday veevo yo
To my home (where I live).

Thunderous applause from the audience greets the singer, **calurosos aplausos del público saludan a la cantante** (kaloorosos aplaoososs dell poobleeko saloodan a la kantantay). *Then the curtain rises,* **entonces sube el telón** (enntonthess soobay ell taylong). When the show is over, *the curtain drops* **el telón baja** (ell taylong baha) and *the performance begins on the stage,* **la representación empieza en la escena** (la raypraysenntathyong emmpyestha enn la essthayna).

Un principio magnífico de la temporada de invierno.
oom preentheepyo magneefeeko thay la temmporatha thay
     eenvyerrno
An excellent beginning for the winter season.

We have come to the close of our report, **vamos a terminar nuestro informe** (vamoss a terrmeenar nooesstro eenforrmay). *We hope that you can hear very well* over your radio, **esperamos que Vds. hayán oido muy bien** (esspayramoss kay oostaythays a-yan oeetho mooy byayng). This is the Spanish Broadcasting System, *Station EAQ,* **aquí Madrid Compañía de radio Española. Estación E. A. Q. Madrid España. Madrid saluda a todos los pueblos del mundo** (akee mathreeth kommpanyeea day radyo esspangyola. esstathyong E. A. Q. mathreeth esspangya. mathreeth salootha a tothoss loss pooaybloss thell moondo). The time is now 11:30. *Good night,* **buenas noches** (booaynas nochess).

*   *

*

Translate into Spanish

You will rent. I should speak; you would send; he would sell; we should buy; you would live; they would understand.

This polite way of speaking is very easy. Before you, the other day. I would like to see a bullfight. Would you buy me a ticket now, don't forget. I haven't forgotten. I shall always keep my promise. You too? And my dear, you too? You all, I invite you, all of you will be invited by me. One speaks, one invites. At what time do they go to the bullfight? One doesn't forget. Here is the entrance. Do you prefer to go to horse races? Do you like horse-races better than bullfights? Tickets for a bullfight. Bull courses of Madrid Row of seats 8, sun and shadow, balcony, front seat. Divide and rule. Am I right? Am I wrong? What do you say? Let us say no more about it! I say to myself. I don't say to you. 1939.

Let us return! Spring begins on the 21st of March; summer begins on the 21st of June; fall begins on the 23rd of September; winter begins on the 21st of December. You have seen, June first. The tenth volume of a book; the second lesson; the third chapter; the ninth page! page 103 or the 103rd page; the 18th lesson. Charles V. was king of Spain and emperor of Germany. It was a long time ago, in the 16th century. Philip II. was the founder of the Escorial. The eighth wonder of the world! In spite of that it really is one of the most wonderful palaces, containing a very well known collection of paintings and a large library. Many Spanish kings are buried there. The last king of Spain was Alphonso XIII. The French Revolution, in the year 1789.

You can't imagine how stupid the people in the Middle Ages were. They didn't even know that they lived in the Middle Ages. It is all the same to me. The more the better. And now, can you answer the question: when were you born? I was born the ninth of November 1878. That is when I celebrate my birthday. And when is your birthday and when is your father's? The advertisement of a Spanish jeweler (reads itself) says: If you are in love, don't forget that jewels are most precious treasures, woman's.

We finally got tired of all the numbers. When we came home, we wanted nothing but to be able to rest for a little while. I was

El toca	"La Paloma"	para ella.
ell tokka	la paloma	para ellya
He plays	*"La Paloma"*	*for her.*

* 145 *

in my room when our friend Henry came into the house. Where were you, Juanita, when I called you? The maid came upstairs and said: Mr. Henry López has come. I heard him knocking at the door, and you said: "Come in!" So I knew that the door was opened and Henry was with you. Then, you know, I came downstairs. You were talking to each other, when the servant girl entered once more and said: Mrs. López has come.

¡Lea en alta voz!

READ ALOUD

Crusaré una calle, he cruzado una calle. Entraré en una casa, he entrado en una casa y encontrado un amigo. Este amigo ha hablado conmigo. Encontraré un amigo que hablará conmigo. Volveré a casa. He vuelto. Comeré, he comido. Recibiré una carta, he recibido una carta muy importante. Esta carta, así ha dicho, decidirá mi ventura—. Mis amigos queridos, mi amigo querido, mi querida amiga. Lo comprenderéis todo, si oslo habré dicho todo. Vd. no habrá olvidado: tengo dinero, no tengo dinero, tendré dinero, lo ganaré. Mi hermano lo ha ganado hace mucho tiempo. ¿Está feliz? No lo sé! ¿Quiere Vd. ir a una corrida de toros? Compraremos una entrada para una corrida de toros. La corrida empezará a las cuatro y media en punto de la tarde. Las puertas de la plaza se abrirán dos horas antes. Veremos los picadores. Vds. verán los espadas que matarán los toros. Los banderilleros que trabajan con su banderillas. El publico.

El mundo es de los atrevidos. Es necessario primero pensar, la palabra de coraje. Impudencia, la verdad. Me gustaría decir. ¡Tenga valor! ¡Sea valeroso! De hablar español, de leer español. No tengo valor para hacer lo. No puedo hacerlo. No lo creo. Lo hemos mostrado a Vd. Pero si Vd. preguntaría, debo contestar.

Se alquila habitación amubleada. Se alquila habitación sin amublear. Se prohibe fumar. Se prohibe la entrada. Se suplica cerrar la puerta. Se suplica no tocar. Estaria Vd. en un error. Le tiene razón exactamente como nosotros tenemos rázon. Aquiarás. Hablaría, mandarías, vendería, compraríamos, viviríais, comprenderían.

Lesson Twenty-Eight

Since in these hot countries the days are very warm, even in the winter, we go to bed quite late, como en estos países tropicales los días son muy cálidos, aun en el invierno, nos acostamos bastante tarde (komo enn esstos paeesess tropeekaless loz theeas sonn mooy kaleethoss, aoon enn el eenvyerrno, noss akosstamoz vastantay tarrthay). *Before we rented our room, Mary used to say,* antes de haber alquilado nuestro cuarto, María decía (antess thay averr alkeelatho nooesstro kvarto, mareea daytheea) :

Lo que más me importa es que la cama sea buena.
lo kay mass may eemporrta ess kay la kama saya booayna
The most important thing for me, is that the bed be good.

No me gusta un cuarto con dos camas.
no may goosta oon kvarto konn doss kamas
I don't like a room with two beds.

At that time we had intended to go to bed very early, entonces tuvimos intención de acostarnos muy temprano (enntonthess tooveemoss eentennthyong day akosstarnoss mooy temmprano).

Nuestros cuartos, uno que da a la calle, otro que da al
nooesstross kvartoss oono kay tha a la kallyay otro kay tha al
Our rooms, one looking out on the street, the other on the
patio, son bastante cómodos y muy bien amueblados.   Tienen
patyo sonn bastantay komodoss ee mooy byenn amooaybladoss
   tyaynenn
yard, are pretty large and very well furnished.   They have
una entrada independiente.
oona enntratha eendaypenndyenntay
a separate entrance.

Las ventanas son anchas y altas.
las venntanas sonn anchas ee altas
The windows are broad and high.

When we asked the landlady, cuando preguntamos a la casera (kvando prayghoontamoss a la kasayra), *what is the price?,* ¿Cuánto vale? (kvanto valay), *we could not say,* no podíamos decir (no podeeamoss daytheer) :

El precio es demasiado alto para mí, para nosotros.
ell praythyo ess thaymasyatho alto para mee para nossotross
The price is too high for me, for us.

No me gusta regatear.
no may ghoosta raygatayar
I don't like to haggle (a word used very much, because you are very often obliged to haggle).

En cada cuarto había una mesa grande y una mesa pequeña,
enn katha kvarto aveea oona messa granday ee oona messa paykaynya
In every room there was a large and a small table,

unas sillas, una cómoda, un espejo, un escritorio
oonas seellyas oona komotha oon esspayho oon esskreetoryo
several chairs, a chest of drawers, a mirror and a writing desk.

We were often asked: *Where do you live?* **¿Dónde vive Vd.?** (donnday veevay oostayth). *And we could answer only that we were quite satisfied,* **y nosotros pudimos contestar solamente, que estábamos muy contentos** (ee nossotross pootheemoss konntestar solamenntay kay esstavamoss mooy konntenntoss). *The landlady and the landlord,* **los patrones** (loss patronays), *were always very friendly,* **eran siempre muy amables** (ayran syemmpray mooy amavlays). *Every night they asked us,* **nos preguntaban todas las noches** (noss prayghoontavan tothas las nochays), *When are you getting up?* **¿A qué hora se levanta Vd.?** (a kay ora say layvanta oostayth), *so that they might serve us a very good breakfast,* **para servirnos un almuerzo muy bueno** (para serrveernoss oon almooerrtho mooy booayno). *Usually, in southern countries, people eat very light breakfasts,* **generalmente se come poco en los países del Sur** (haynayralmenntay say komay poko enn loss paeesays dell soor); **se toma un almuerzo frugal** (say toma oon almooerrtho frooghal).

You will see that Spanish **d** is pronounced sometimes like d as in *door*, sometimes like voiced th as in *them*. We do not want to give you too many rules, but follow our pronunciation guide with confidence and try to develop, as soon as possible, a connected speech, without pausing after each word.

But, our landlady said, I know the English and American people very well. Besides, I am old-fashioned and I believe in the old Mexican saying,

"Almuerza bien, come más, cena poco y vivirás mejores?"
almooerrtha byenn komay mas thayna poko ee veeveeras may-
   horayss
Breakfast well, dine better, sup lightly and you will live.

She showed us *the best stores*, **las mejores tiendas** (las may-
horayss tyenndas), *a bakery* **una panadería** (oona panatherreea),
a fruit store, **una frutería** (oona frooterreea), *a shoe store*, **una
zapatería** (oona thapaterreea).

"Quién mucho promete, poco cumple."
kyenng moocho promaytay poko koomplay
"(He) who promises much, fulfils little."

That is a Spanish proverb, **es un proverbio español** (ess oon
proverrbyo esspangyol). But it was the opposite with our landlady. *She didn't promise much, but she did a great deal for us*, **no
prometió mucho, pero ella hizo mucho por nosotros** (no pro-
maytyo moocho payro ellya eetho moocho porr nosotross).

We don't want *to be like the parrot who "says what he knows,
but doesn't know what he says,"* **ser como el perico, que "dice lo
que sabe, pero no sabe, lo que dice"**
(serr komo ell payreeko kay theethay
lo kay savay payro no savay lo kay
theethay). So I think it is time to tell
you something I should have told you
before. But *it doesn't matter*, **no importa**

> Spanish **s** before the
> voiced consonants **b, d, g,
> l, m, n, r** and **v**, is always
> pronounced **z**, like our **z**
> in *zero*. Therefore **mismas**,
> *same*, is pronounced
> **meezmas**.

(no eemporrta). Perhaps you have already noticed it yourself
without being told.

It is certainly not news to you that there is a great difference
between what we like and what we love. If my aunt should
insist that I say to her, *"I like you,"* I would say, in Spanish,
"yo te quiero" (yo tay kyayro). But before I'd say, *"I love you,*
yo te amo" (yo tay amo), I would think it over very carefully
and for a long time. My uncle used to say on such occasions,
Who loves whom? **¿Quién ama a quién?** (kyenng ama a kyenng).
¿Quién quiere a quién?" (kyenn kyayray a kyenng). The answer
to **¿Quién ama?"** (kyenng ama) might be — **yo** (yo) *I*; **tú** (too)
you; **él** (ell) *he*; **ella** (ellya) *she*; **nosotros o nosotras** (nosotross o
nosotras) *we*; **vosotros o vosotras** (vosotross o vosotras) *you*;
ellos o ellas (ellyoss o ellyas) *they*, **Vd.** or **Vds.** (oostayth or
oostaythays) *you*. You might say that in referring to my beloved

aunt *it would not be true,* **no sería verdad** (no sayreea verrthath) to answer, *Everyone,* **cada uno o cada una** (katha oono o katha oona).

But when you answer the question **"¿A quién quiere?"** (a kyenn kyayray) *Whom do you like?* with the one word *"you,"* you must say in Spanish, **"A tí"** (a tee). If you were to say of your *cousin* **el primo** (ell preemo), **la prima** (la preema), *"I like her or I like him," you would say* **"le quiero mucho o la quiero mucho"** (lay kyayro moocho o la kyayro moocho). And if asked once more, *"Whom do you like?"* you'd answer in Spanish: **"A él (a mi primo)** (a ell, a mee preemo) *him, my cousin,* **o a ella (a mi prima)** (o a ellya, a mee preema) *her, my cousin."*

When we wish to be very emphatic — and it does happen sometimes — we say, **"A tí, te amo** (a tee tay amo) *It is you I love."* Do you see the difference?

Used *alone* or *in connection with a preposition,* the pronouns are:

I			you			he		
yo (yo)	*I*		tu (too)	*you*		él (ell)	*he*	
de mí (mee)	*of me*		de tí (tee)	*of you*		de él	*of him*	
á mí	*to me*		á tí	*to you*		á él	*to him*	
á mí	*me*		á tí	*me*		á él	*him*	

she			it			you (formal)		
ella (ellya)	*she*		ello (ellyo)	*it*		Vd.	*you*	
de ella	*of her*		de ello	*of it*		de Vd.	*of you*	
á ella	*to her*		á ello	*to it*		á Vd.	*to you*	
á ella	*her*		á ello	*it*		á Vd.	*you*	

we			you			they (m.)		
nosotros, as	*we*		vosotros, as	*you*		ellos	*they*	
de nosotros, as	*of us*		de vosotros, as	*of you*		de ellos	*of them*	
á nosotros, as	*to us*		á vosotros, as	*to you*		á ellos	*to them*	
á nosotros, as	*us*		á vosotros, as	*you*		á ellos	*them*	

they (f.)			you (formal)			themselves		
ellas	*they*		Vds.	*you*		si	*themselves*	
de ellas	*of them*		de Vds.	*of you*				
á ellas	*to them*		á Vds.	*to you*				
á ellas	*them*		á Vds.	*you*				

One exception: **conmigo** (konnmeegho) = *with me*
contigo (konnteegho) = *with you*
consigo (konnseegho) = *with himself*

Connected with the word that denotes the action, i.e., *the verb*, it becomes:

I			you			he		
yo	(yo)	*I*	tu	(too)	*you*	él	(ell)	*he*
me	(may)	*to me*	te	(tay)	*to you*	le	(lay)	*to him, it*
me		*me*	te		*you*	le		*him, it*

she			it			you (formal)		
ella	(ellya)	*she*	ello	(ellyo)	*it*	Vd.		*you*
le	(lay)	*to her*	lo		*to it*	le	(lay)	*to you*
la	(la)	*her, it*	lo		*it*	le, la		*you (m. and f.)*

we		you		they (m.)	
nosotros	*we*	vosotros	*you*	ellos	*they*
nos (noss)	*to us*	os (oss)	*to you*	les (lays)	*to them*
nos	*us*	os	*you*	los (loss)	*them*

they (f.)		you (formal)			
ellas	*they*	Vds.		*you*	
les	*to them*	les		*to you*	
las	*them*	los, las		*you*	

EL PRIMERO POR LA COLA.
ell preemayro porr la kola
The first at the tail.

El papá: En los últimos exámenes fuiste el vigésimo;
ell papa enn loss oolteemoss eksamaynays fooeestay ell veehayseemo
Daddy: In the last examinations you were the twentieth on the list,

> **es decir, el último**
> ess daytheer ell oolteemo
> *that is (is to say), the last one.*

El hijo: Papá, no tengo yo la culpa de que no haya más
ell eeho papa no tenngo yo la koolpa thaykay no a-ya mass
Son: Daddy, it's not my fault that there weren't any more

> **alumnos en mi escuela**
> aloomnoss enn mee esskooayla
> *pupils in my school (class).*

Combinaciones de los pronombres personales.

kommbeenathyonez thay loss pronommbress perrsonaless
Combinations of the personal pronouns.

me le	*him*	*to me, to myself*
me la	*her, it*	*to me, to myself*
me lo	*it*	*to me, to myself*
me los, les	*them (m.)*	*to me, to myself*
me las	*them (f.)*	*to me, to myself*
nos le	*him*	*to us, to ourselves*
nos la	*her, it (f.)*	*to us, to ourselves*
nos lo	*it (m.)*	*to us, to ourselves*
nos los, les	*them (m.)*	*to us, to ourselves*
nos las	*them (f.)*	*to us, to ourselves*
te le	*him*	*to you, to yourself*
te la	*her, it*	*to you, to yourself*
te lo	*it*	*to you, to yourself*
te los, les	*them (m.)*	*to you, to yourself*
te las	*them (f.)*	*to you, to yourself*
os le	*him*	*to you, to yourselves*
os la	*her, it*	*to you, to yourselves*
os lo	*it*	*to you, to yourselves*
os los, les	*them (m.)*	*to you, to yourselves*
os las	*them (f.)*	*to you, to yourselves*

se le	*him*		
se la	*her, it*	*to him,*	*to himself, herself, itself,*
se lo	*it*	*to her,*	*yourself*
se los, les	*them (m.)*	*to you,*	
se las	*them (f.)*		

se le	*him*		
se la	*her, it*	*to them,*	*to themselves, yourselves*
se lo	*it*	*to you,*	
se los, les	*them (m.)*		
se las	*them (f.)*		

Lesson Twenty-Nine

When we see so many very small words in a foreign language, **viendo tantas palabras tan pequeñas en una lengua extranjera,** (vienndo tantass palavrass tann paykvaynyas enn oona lenngva esstranhayra) *we are always somewhat discouraged,* **nos desilusionamos siempre un poco** (noz thesseeloosyonamoss syemmpray oom poko). But we know that *one learns by studying,* **estudiando se aprende** (esstoothyando say aprennday). *We are afraid,* however, **tenemos miedo** (taynaymoss myaytho), that it will be very hard to remember all these little words and use them correctly.

We feel somewhat like the father whose son always uses foreign words and expressions in order to show off his so-called education, but, unfortunately always uses them incorrectly. *He says to him one day,* **Le dice una vez** (lay theethay oona vayth): *Don't use foreign words; one (we) never knows what they mean,* **no uses** (no use Vd.) **palabras extranjeras; no podemos nunca saber lo que significan** (no oosess palabras estranhayras no pothaymoss noonka saverr lo kay seegneefeekan).

Nothing can be done right in a hurry and our saying, "more haste, less speed" (haste is waste), **poco a poco se va lejos** (poko a poko say va layhoss), literally translated, *little by little one goes far,* is especially applicable to the task of learning a foreign language. At the beginning, learning to read, write and speak a foreign language is a slow process. But the first step is for us to understand how the Spaniard handles his language.

Just a while ago you saw the word **estudiando** (esstoothyando) *studying.* We should be mistaken *if we thought,* **si pensaríamos,** (see pensareeamoss) that this form is always used in Spanish *as we use it in English,* **como lo usamos en inglés** (komo lo oosamoss enn eengless). This form (Gerund or Participle) for regular verbs, has the ending -ando -iendo.

The masculine forms of **bueno, alguno, primero, portrero, malo, ninguno, tercero,** and **uno** lose the ending **o** before a noun: **mal tiempo** (mal tyemmpo), *bad weather* **un buen padre** (oon booayn pathray), *a good father,* but **un tiempo muy malo** (oon tyemmpo mooy malo), *a very bad time,* **un padre muy bueno** (oon pathray mooy booayno), *a very good father;* always **la buena señora** (la booayna sengyora), *the good lady.*

* 153 *

'hablar (avlar)	to speak	hablando (ablando)	speaking
dar (dar)	to give	dando (dando)	giving
estar (esstar)	to be	estando (esstando)	being
comer (komerr)	to eat	comiendo (komyenndo)	eating
ser (serr)	to be	siendo (syenndo)	being
haber (averr)	to have	habiendo (avyenndo)	having
tener (taynerr)	to have	teniendo (tainyenndo)	having
vivir (veeveer)	to live	viviendo (veevyenndo)	living
dudar (doothar)	to doubt	dudando (doothando)	doubting

We are riding in a street car, **estamos paseando en el tranvía** (esstamoss pasayando enn ell trambeea), or *in a cab*, **en coche** (enn kochay), or *in the omnibus*, **en ómnibus** (enn omneevoos). *If we had the money, we would always take a taxicab*, **teniendo el dinero, siempre tomaríamos un taximetro** (taynyenndo ell deenayro syemmpray tomareeamoss oon takseemaytro). *Yes, we would take it*, **si, que lo tomaríamos** (see kay lo tomareeamoss). *Not having it (the money), we take the street car which passes every five minutes*, **no teniéndolo (el dinero), tomamos el tranvía que pasa cada cinco minutos** (no taynyenndolo ell deenayro, tomamoss ell tranveea kay pasa kara theenko meenootoss).

The conductor says at every stop, **el cobrador va diciendo siempre en cada parada** (ell kovrathor va theethyenndo syemmpray enn katha paratha): *Let them off*, **Deje Vd. bajar** (dayhay oostayth bahar), and then, *Please step in*, **Por favor suba Vd.** (porr favor soova oostayth).

¡Cuidado! (kveethatho) *Attention! Watch your step!*

¡Qué movimiento! (kay moveemyennto) *What traffic!*

¡Sentémonos! (senntaymonoss), *let us sit down!*

Translate into Spanish

What's the news? No news is good news. A Spanish newspaper is an absolute necessity. An article in the newspaper. A man worked, so wrote that man. That man was called Thomas Jefferson. The document was read on the 4th of July, 1776, at the first meeting of the Continental Congress. Jefferson was a remarkable man. His profession was practicing law; he enjoyed the reputation of being a great writer and was, moreover, a painter, an educator, and an athlete.

Time that has passed doesn't return, doesn't come again. He was a lawyer. He enjoyed the reputation of being a great writer. I was in my room, when the dressmaker entered, when the tailor and the milliner came. Where were you when the optician brought your eyeglasses? He was here when I was at the watchmaker's. It was a long lesson that our friend Henry gave us. It is not much fun, but it is absolutely necessary to study the verbs. I am very sorry. Let us go to sleep after this lesson. Good night, ladies and gentlemen!

A Spanish newspaper, periodicals, articles. Bring us a Spanish daily every morning. Don't forget it! I like to read, we like to see the illustrated articles and the advertisements. For anything you may want, read the classified ads of **The** PRESS. Words we already know very well. You know already. Yes, sir, I know it. Spanish lawyer who speaks English. Seeing this advertisement you decide you will help this young man.

Give me a piece of chocolate. Children, here you have chocolate! So we go to a candy store. And the kind aunt asks the employee: have you any chocolate? What do you want? What kind? What size? What quality do you want? We have ordinary eatable (for to eat raw) chocolate. We have chocolate for cooking. You want a bar of chocolate? There is also vanilla chocolate. Perhaps you would like sweets and candies of chocolate. Give me half a kilo of chocolates and a quarter of a kilo of candy. The lemon and orange drops are very good. Don't learn too much!

¡Lea en alta voz!

Este modo cortés de hablar es muy fácil. Enfrente de Vd., el otro día. Querría ver una corrida de toros. ¿Compraría Vd. una entrada? ¡no lo olvide! No lo he olvidado. Yo cumpliré siempre mi promesa. ¿Vd. tambien? ¿Y mi querida, tu tambien? Vosotros todos, os convido, vosotros todos seréis convidado por me. Se habla, se convida. ¿A qué hora se visita las corridas de toros? No se olvida. Ahí está la entrada. ¿Prefere Vd. ir a las corridas de caballos? ¿Gusta Vd. más las corridas de caballos que las corridas de toros? Billete para una corrida de toros. Plazas de toros de Madrid. Tendido ocho, sol y sombra, balconcillo, delantera. Divide y gobierna. ¿Tengo razón? ¿Me equivoco? ¿Estoy en un error? ¿Qué dice Vd.? ¡Qué no haya más que decir sobre eso! Me digo a mi mismo. No te digo a ti. Mil novecientos treinta y nueve.

¡Volvamos! La primavera empieza el veintiuno de marzo; el verano empieza el veintiuno de junio; el otoño empieza el veintitres de setiembre; el invierno empieza el veintiuno de diciembre. Ha visto, el primero de junio. Tomo decimo de un libro, la lección segunda; el capitulo tercero; la pagina novena; capitulo quince; pagina ciento tres; la lección dieciocho. Carlos V (quinto) fué rey de España y emperador de Alemania. Hace mucho tiempo, en el siglo XVI (dieciseis): Felipe II (segundo) fué el fundador del Escorial; la octava maravilla del mundo. A pesar de eso es el palacio mas maravilloso con una collección de cuadros y una biblioteca grande. Muchos reyes españoles están enterrados allí. El rey último de España fué Alfonso XIII (trece). La revolución francesa. En el año mil setecientos ochenta y nueve.

No puede Vd. imaginar cuán estupidas eran las gentes en la Edad Media. No sabían que vivían en la Edad Media. Me es igual. Cuánto más tanto mejor. Ahora, puede Vd. contestar la pregunta: ¿Cuándo nació Vd.? Yo nací el nueve de noviembre de mil ochocientos setenta y ocho. Es entonces cuándo celebro mi cumpleaños. ¿Y cuándo es su cumpleaños y cuándo es el del padre de Vd.? El reclamo de un joyero se lee: Si está Vd. enamorado no olvide que las joyas son el más preciado tesoro de la mujer.

¡Haga el favor de repetir!

¿Qué día del mes es hoy?	kay deea thell mess ess oee	What day of the month is today?
espere un minuto	ayspayray oono meenooto	wait a minute
ayer fué domingo	ayayr fooay thomeengo	yesterday was Sunday
anteayer	anteeyayayr	the day before yesterday
el día de pago	ell deea thay pago	the payday
no olvido nunca	no ollveetho noonka	I never forget
sábado	savatho	Saturday
fué el treinta y uno	fooay ell trayeenta ee oono	it was the 31st
el primero de noviembre	ell preemayro the novyembray	the first of November
el dos de noviembre	ell doz thay novyaymbray	the 2nd of November
los días de la semana se llaman	loz theeaz thay la saymana say llyaman	the days of the week are called (call themselves)
lunes	looness	Monday
martes	marrtess	Tuesday
miércoles	myerrkoless	Wednesday
jueves	hooayvess	Thursday
viernes	veeerrness	Friday
sábado	savatho	Saturday
domingo	domeengo	Sunday
el mes	ell mess	the month
el año	ell angyo	the year
el segundo mes	ell saygoondo mess	the second month
los otros meses	los otross messess	the other months
Enero	aynayro	January
Febrero	fayvrayro	February
Marzo	martho	March
Abril	avreel	April
Mayo	mayo	May
Junio	hoonyo	June
Julio	hoolyo	July

Agosto	agosto	*August*
Setiembre	settyemmbray	*September*
Octubre	okktoovray	*October*
Noviembre	novyemmray	*November*
Diciembre	deethyemmbray	*December*
el primero de Enero	ell preemayro thay aynayro	*the 1st of January January 1st*
el dos de Enero	ell doz thay aynayro	*January 2nd*
Vd. no puede thecirlo	oostayth no pooay-thay thaytheerlo	*you couldn't say that*
porque	porrkay	*for, because*
el último día	ell oolteemo theea	*the last day*
estar	esstar	*to be*
ser	sayr	*to be*
la muchacha	la moochacha	*the girl*
la muchacha más rica	la moochacha maz reeka	*the richest girl*
la ciudad	la thyoothath	*the city, the town*
el mejor médico de la ciudad	ell mayhor may-theeko thay la thyoothath	*the best doctor of the city*
¿Cuándo son las horas de consulta del médico?	kvando sonn las oraz thay konn-soolta thell may-theeko	*What are the doctor's consultation hours?*
a las tres y media de la tarde	a las trays ee may-thya thay la tarr-thay	*at half past three in the afternoon*
está ahí	essta aee	*he is here*
hasta las seis menos cuarto	asta las sayees may-noss kvarto	*until a quarter to six*
poco después de las tres	poko thayspooess thay las trays	*a short time after three*
mucha gente está ahí	moocha henntay essta aee	*many people are there*
entrar al cuarto del doctor	enntrar al kvarto thell dokktor	*to enter the doctor's room*
me dice	may theethay	*he says to me*
dígame, qué tiene Vd.	deegamay kay teeay-nay oostayth	*tell me, what do you have? (what troubles you?)*
¡tome Vd. asiento!	tomay oostayth as-yennto	*take a seat!*

siéntese Vd.!	syenntaysay oostayth	*sit down!*
le digo	lay theego	*I tell him*
como muy poco	komo mooy poko	*I eat very little*
me duelen los ojos	may thvaylayn loss ohoss	*my eyes ache*
la garganta	la garganta	*the throat*
la cabeza	la kabaytha	*the head*
la espalda	la ayspalda	*the shoulder*
todo el cuerpo	totho ell kverrpo	*my whole body*
no está bueno	no essta vooayno	*is not right*
todos los miembros	tothoss loss myemmbross	*every limb*
el seno	ell sayno	*the breast, the bosom*
el carillo	ell kareellyo	*the cheek*
las piernas	las pyerrnas	*the legs*
el pecho	ell paycho	*the chest*
los dedos	loz thaythoss	*the fingers*
los pies	loss pyayss	*the feet*
las manos	laz manoss	*the hands*
la barba	la varrva	*the chin*
la nariz	la nareeth	*the nose*
la frente	la frenntay	*the forehead*
el corazón	ell korrathong	*the heart*
el hígado	ell eegatho	*the liver*
los nervios	loz nerrvyoss	*the nerves*
tengo un corazón	tenngo oon korrathong	*I have a heart*
un amigo mío	oon ameego meeo	*a friend of mine*
¿qué piensa Vd. de eso?	kay pyennsa oostayth thay esso	*what do you think of that?*
el doctor contesta	ell dokktor konntessta	*the doctor answers*
la lengua	la lenngva	*the tongue*
no está sucia	no essta soothya	*it is not coated*
soy examinado por el doctor	soee exameenatho porr ell dokktor	*I am examined by the doctor*
¿qué tal de apetito?	kay tal day apayteeto	*how about your appetite?*
yo como muy poco	yo komo mooy poko	*I eat very little*

apenas dos huevos	apaynaz thoss ooay-voss	*just two eggs*
pan y mantequilla	pan ee mantay-keellya	*bread and butter*
algun pescado frito	algoon pesskatho freeto	*some fried fish*
jalea y mermelada	halaya ee mermay-latha	*jam and marmalade*
a mediodía	a maythyotheea	*at noon*
mi almuerzo	mee almooerrtho	*my lunch*
entonces	enntonnthess	*then*
la sopa	la sopa	*the soup*
dos chuletas	doss tshoolaytas	*two mutton chops*
legumbres	laygoombrays	*vegetables*

1000 Words

SPANISH

Section VI · BY ERNST WALLENBERG · Lesson 30-34

Lesson Thirty

Learning these traffic rules is very simple, **el aprender estas reglas del tráfico es muy fácil** (ell aprennderr esstas rayglas thell trafeeko ez mooy fatheel). Here the Spaniard cannot use the participial form, as we do in English, but the Infinitive; he must also use it after prepositions.

Without asking us anything, the conductor gave us the tickets, **sin preguntarnos nada el cobrador nos dió los billetes** (seen prayghoontarnoss natha ell kovrathor nos deeo los beellyaytess). *A lady came to help us*, **una señora vino a ayudarnos** (oona sengyora veeno a a-yootharnoss).

We heard the conductor say, as he went through the car, **oímos** (Imp.) **al cobrador decir al pasar** (oeemoss al kovrathor thaytheer all pasar) : "**¡Me hace Vd. el favor!**" (may athay oostayth ell favor) "*Fares, please!* (Do me the favor)." In Spanish, after verbs of hearing and seeing, you may use either the Participle (saying) or the Infinitive (to say) : **oímos decir al cobrador cuando pasó** (oeemoss thaytheer al kovrathor kvando paso). In English the proper form is, *we heard him saying*—**le oímos decir** (lay oeemoss thaytheer). *We heard him say so*, **le oímos**

Between vowels a, e, i, o, u, y or (w) the consonants b, v, d, g are vibrant; d becomes then English voiced *th* like in *th(em)*, b is nearly English v, g is a *gargled sound*.

decirlo (lay oeemoss thaytheerlo). *I said to Mary,* dije a Maria (deehay a mareea); *I said to her,* le dije (lay deehay):

Pay for the tickets for me, pay for them for me, paga los billetes por mí, págalos por mí (paga loss beellyaytess porr mee pagaloss porr mee), but *give them to me,* dámelos (damayloss), *because I like to occupy myself in reading every bit of printed matter in order to learn Spanish,* porque quiero ocuparme leyendo todos los impresos *(all printed matters)* para aprender el Español (porrkay kyayro okooparmay layyenndo tothoss loss eempraysoss para aprennderr ell esspangyol).

May I advise you (can I give you the advice) to do likewise? ¿puedo darle a Vd. el consejo de hacer lo mismo (pooaytho tharlay a oostayth ell konnsayho thay athayr lo meesmo)? *Mary, do so too,* hazlo también, Maria (athlo tambyenng, mareea), *and you, Mr. Lopez (do so),* y Vd., señor López, hágalo Vd. (ee oostayth sengyor lopayth aghalo oostayth). *All of you (do so)!* ¡Hacedlo! (athethlo), *Let us do so!* ¡Hagámoslo! (aghamosslo). *In so doing we are learning everywhere,* haciéndolo vamos aprendiendo en todas partes *(in all parts),* (athyenndolo vamoss aprennddyenndo enn tothas partess).

El tranvía se para (ell tranveea say para), *the street car stops.*

*

We get off the street car, Nos bajamos del tranvía (noz vahamoss dell trambeea). *There is a man selling papers* (seller of papers), allá está un vendedor de periódicos (allya essta oon vayndaythor thay payryotheekoss). *Buy me the night editions and one of the morning papers. Buy them for me, Mary.* Cómprame todas las ediciones de la noche y de la una de la mañana. Maria, cómpramelos (kommpramay tothas las aytheethyonez thay la nochay ee thay la oona thay la mangyana, mareea, kommpramayloss). *Or, to be more polite, I say, Mr. Lopez, buy them for me, if you please,* cómpremelos Vd., haga el favor, señor López (kommpraymayloss oostayth aga ell favor, sengyor lopayth). *You know better what we are able to read,* Vd. sabe mejor lo que podemos leer (oostayth savay mayhor lo kay podaymoss layayr).

¿Dónde se baja Vd.,
donnday say baha oostayth
Where are you getting off,

señorita?
sengyoreeta
young lady?

¿Está Vd. bien,
essta oostayth byayng
Are you well,

señorita?
sengyoreeta
young lady?

Muy bien.
mooy byayng.
Very well.

(Continued on next page.)

¿Por qué?   Entonces no   le pediré
porr kay   enntonthays no   lay paydeeray
Why?   *Then I shall not* *ask you*

que se quite de mi pie.
kay say keetay day mee pyay
to get off my foot.

I will buy them for you, **se los compro, se los compraré** (say loss kommpro say loss kommpraray).

Now I am going to tell you, ladies and gentlemen, what you have probably noticed, **ahora voy a decirles** (aora voy a thaytheerless), **señoras y caballeros, lo que probablemente Vds. han observado** (sengyorays ee kavallyayross lo kay probablaymenntay oostaythess an obserrvatho), *a long time ago*, **hace mucho tiempo** (athay moocho tyemmpo), *even wi'hout knowing any rule for it*, **sin saber** (Inf., not Part.) **ninguna regla para ello** (seen savayr neengoona raygla para ellyo).

cuyo (kooyo), *whose, of which* points out the owner and is used like an adjective. **El señor** (ell sengyor), **cuyas hijas he visto, es Don Alfonso** (kooyas eehas ay veesto ess donn alfonnso)—*the gentleman whose daughters I have seen is Mr. Alfonso;* **cuyos hijos** (kooyoss eehoss), *whose sons;* **cuyo dinero** (kooyo deenayro) *whose money;* **cuya casa** (kooya kasa), *whose house.*

The pronouns that go with the verbs, e.g., **me, te, le, la, lo, nos, os, les, las, los, se** are usually placed *before the verb.* But they are *connected with the verb, forming one word, in the imperative form,* the *participle* form and the *infinitive* form. When two of these little pronouns are used together, **me, te, nos, os** are placed *before* **le, la, lo, les, las, los.** Therefore it is **me le, te le, me la, te la,** and so on. Or whne connected with the Imperative, the Participle or the Infinitive we say **-mele, -tele,** and so on.

If the pronouns **le, la, les** (indirect object) are used together with **lo, le, la, los, les** (direct objects), we use for the indirect objects **le, la, les,** the word **se** (say). **Le lo** would be impossible for a Spaniard to speak or to hear. It does not sound right to the Spanish ear *although it may seem*, **aunque nos parezca** (aoonkay noss parethka), a little foolish to us. **Se lo he dicho** (say lo ay

deecho), *I (have) told him so, I (have) told her so (it)*. If you
want to emphasize the person you mean, you can say, **se lo
he dicho a él** *(to him)*, **se lo he dicho a ella** *(to her)*, **se lo he
dicho a Vd.**

Let us go to the department store "La Parisienne," **vámos al
almacén "La Parisienne"** (vamoss al almathenn la pareesyenn).
Here we always see the latest models, **allí se ven siempre los últimos
modelos** (allyee say venn syemmpray loss oolteemoss mothay-
loss); literally, they see themselves. *My friend (a lady) recommended it to me,* **mi amiga me lo ha recomendado** (mee ameegha
may lo a raykommenndatho). *You enter (in) the store,* **entra en
la tienda** (enntra enn la tyennda), *to see a dress for me,* **a ver
un vestido para mí** (a verr oon vessteetho para mee). *(Of) what
color (do you want it), madam?* **¿De qué color lo desea Vd.,
señora?** *Coffee-brown* (color), **color café marrón** (kolor kafay
marrong), *the color they are wearing (that is much worn) now,*
del color que se lleva ahora mucho (dell kolor kay say llyayva
aora moocho). *Here are (I bring you) some very fashionable
dresses,* **aquí le traigo a Vd. unos vestidos muy elegantes** (akee
lay traeego a oostayth oonoss vessteethoss mooy aylayghantess).
I'd like you (I ask you) to look at them, **le ruego a Vd. de verlos**
(lay rooaygo a oostayth day verrloss). *What may I do for you?*
¿En qué puedo servirle a Vd.? (enn kay pooaytho serrveerlay
a oostayth).

El marido: ¡Pruébátelos! ¡Anda!
ell mareetho prooayvatayloss annda
The husband: Try them on (to you). Go ahead.

¿Te gusta ése?
tay ghoosta essay
Do you like this one?

A mí no. Yo prefiero los vestidos sencillos.
a mee no yo prayfyayro loss vessteethoss sonntheellyoss
Not for me. I prefer the simple dresses.

Show me some others, please. **¡Hágame el favor de mostrarme
otros!** (agamay ell favor day mostrarmay otross). *These don't
please either my husband or myself,* **esos no nos gustan ni a mi
marido ni a mí** (essoss no noss goostan nee a mee mareetho
nee a mee). *Here I see two very nice silk ones,* **aquí veo dos de
seda muy bonitos** (akee vayo doss day saytha mooy boneetoss).

Why don't you show them to us? ¿Por qué no nos los enseña Vd.?
(porr kay no noss loss ennsayngya oostayth). *I am going to bring them to you,* voy a traérselos (voy a traerrsayloss). *I'll get them for you.*

¡Mira, ese vestido me parece el más bonito! ¿Y a tí?
meera essay vessteetho may paraythay ell mas boneeto ee a tee
Look, this dress looks like (seems to me) the nicest one. Does it to you (and to you)?

A mí también.
a mee tambyenng
To me, too.

Me lo pondré en seguida.
may lo ponndray enn saygeetha
I will put it on (to me) at once.

Voy a probármelo.
voy a provarmaylo
I'll try it on (I go to try me it).

Sí, señora, ciertamente este vestido le sienta a Vd. muy bien.
see sengyora thyerrtamenntay esstay vessteetho lay syennta a oostayth mooy byenng
Yes, madam, this dress certainly suits you very well.

¿Cuanto vale?
koanto valay
How much is it?

El precio era de quinientas pesetas; hoy vamos
ell praythyo ayra thay keenyenntas paysaytas, oy vamoss
The price was 500 pesetas; today we

a dárselo por 250 (doscientas cincuenta) pesetas.
a thársaylo porr dosthyenntas theenquennta paysaytas
will give it to you for 250 pesetas.

Es demasiado (ess thaymasyatho), *it is too much.* Lo tomaré por 175 pesetas (lo tomaray porr 175 paysaytas), *I'll take it for 175 pesetas.* Muy bien, envíemelo a mi casa (mooy vyenn ennvy-aymaylo a mee kasa), *all right, send it (me) to my house.* ¡Adiós! (atheeoss) *good-bye.* ¡Qué Vd. lo pase bien! (kay oostayth lo pasay vyenng) *that you may pass it well (get along very well), good luck to you!*

Lesson Thirty-One

A great Spanish poet, Tomás de Iriarte, **un gran poeta español Tomás de Iriarte** (oon grann poayta esspangyol tomas day Eereeartay), *who died almost 150 years ago,* **que murió hace casi 150 (ciento cincuenta) años** (kay mooryo athay kasee thyennto theenquennta angyos) *once said,* **dijo** (deeho):

Todos somos hijos de Adán y Eva, sino que nos diferencia tothoss somoss eehoss day athann ee ayva seeno kay noss deefayrennthya
We are all sons (children) of Adam and Eve, but what (makes us different) distinguishes us

la lana y la seda.
la lana ee la saytha
is the wool and the silk.

Although Iriarte may have spoken the truth, **aun que Iriarte haya dicho la verdad** (aoon kay eereeartay a-ya deecho la verrdad), *the world is nevertheless full of hatred,* **el mundo de los hombres está lleno de enemistades** (ell moondo day loss ommbress essta llyayno day aynaymeestathess).

It is much to be able to say (seems to be a great deal if one can say), **ya parece mucho, si alguno pudiera decir** (ya paraythay moocho see algoono poodyayra daytheer): *I have a friend of whom I can say that he really is a friend,* **tengo un amigo de quién puedo decir que es un amigo verdadero** (tenngo oon ameegho thay kyenng pooaytho daytheer kay ess oon ameegho verrthathayro). *A friend in need is a friend indeed,* **amigo en la adversidad amigo de realidad** (ameegho enn la adverrseethath ameegho day rayaleethath).

Often, **a menudo** (a maynootho), we don't know how to make friends or to keep them. There is some truth in the Spanish proverb **"Como te ven así te tratan"** (komo tay venn asee tay tratann), *as they see you, so shall they treat you.*

¡Qué lástima!	**¡Cuidado!**	**¡Por dios!**
kay lasteema	queethatho	porr dyoss
What a pity!	*Take care!*	*For goodness (God's) sake!*
	Attention!	

* 167 *

¡Caramba!　　¡Cómo! ¿De veras?
karammba　　komo day vayras
Confound it!　*What! Really?*
Good gracious!

I hear you say, **le óigo a Vd. decir** (lay oeegho a oostayth thaytheer) *I doubt that this is true*, **dudo que eso sea la verdad** (dootho kay ayso saya la verrthath).

Pedro, Vd. continúa, es mi mejor amigo, es mi amigo íntimo (paythro oostayth konnteenooa ess mee mayhor ameegho ess mee ameegho eenteemo). "*Peter*," *you continue, "is my best friend; he is my intimate friend.*" **Haría cuanto pudiese por él** (areea kvanto poodyessay porr ell) *I would do anything for him.* **Y estoy convencido de que él haría cuanto pudiese por mí** (ee esstoy konnvenntheetho thay kay ell areea kvanto poothyessay porr mee) *and I am convinced that he would do what he could for me.*

especial, especialmente (esspaythyalmenntay), *especially.* The English adverbial ending *-ly* is **-mente** (menntay) in Spanish.

"*On the other hand*," *you proceed, "there is a man whose name I won't tell you, but* **I detest him, le detesto** (lay daytessto). *Everybody hates him,* **todo el mundo le aborrece** (totho ell moondo lay avorraythay). *Whenever he is with us, I always wish (that) he would go,* **me alegraría que se fuera** (may alaygrareea kay say fooayra). *I do not like that man,* **ese hombre no me gusta** (essay ommbray no mai ghoosta). *I would never have believed it,* **no lo hubiera creído** (no lo oovyayra krayeetho). *Who would have believed it?* **¿Quién lo hubiera creído?** (kyenn lo oovyayra krayeetho)."

But after all, unlike you, I don't think that the Spanish proverb which says that "to know how to live in this world is the greatest heroism" is correct—**mas al fin y al cabo, no creo que el proverbio español "saber vivir en este mundo es la mejor hazaña" tenga rasón** (mas al feen ee al kavo no krayo kay ell proverrvyo esspangyol saverr veeveer enn esstay moondo ess la mayhor athangya tennga rathong). I

Gran is used instead of **grande** before masculine and feminine nouns: **un gran hombre** (oon grann ommbray), *a great man;* **una gran mujer** (oona grann moohayr), *a great woman.*

rather think that for the man who does know, it is not heroic at all. But don't let us argue *about that*, **acerca de ello** (atherrka day ellyo). *To get away from philosophy*, however, **lejos de la filosofía** (layhoss day la feelosofeea), *let us return a minute to our* *talk on friendship*, **volvemos uno minuto a nuestra conversación acerca de la amistad** (volvaymoss oono meenooto a nooesstra komberrsathyong atherrka thay la ameestath). I am quite sure that nothing is worse than writing a letter to someone and not getting an answer. That can really destroy friendships, acquaintanceships and business or other relationships. How often do we hear people say, "*If only I had answered his letter on time, it would have been much better* **si hubiese contestado su carta, sería mucho mejor** (see oovyessay konntesstatho soo karta sayreea moocho mayhor). *We would have written a letter if we had known that his father was sick*, **hubiésemos escrito una carta, si hubiéramos sabido que su padre estaba enfermo** (oovyessaymoss esskreeto oona karta see oovyerramoss saveetho kay soo pathray esstava ennferrmo)."

It is no mistake in Spanish to use the present form instead of the future. **Mañana escribimos** (manyana esskreeveemoss) *tomorrow we shall write* (In Spanish, they say very often, *tomorrow we write* whereas in English we must say, *tomorrow we shall write.*

Let us go to a stationery store, where there is all the stationery we need, **vamos a una papeleria donde hay todos los útiles de escribir que queremos** (vamoss a oona papaylayreea donnday aee tothoss loss ooteelez thay esskreeveer kay kayraymoss).

Compramos papel de carta, tarjetas, un portaplumas, kommpramoss papell day karta tarhaytas oon portaploomas *We buy (us) writing paper, cards, a penholder,*

las plumas, la tinta, un tintero, el papel secante las ploomas la teenta oon teentayro, ell papell saykantay *pens, ink, an inkstand and blotting paper.*

Hoy lo haremos día de correspondencia oy lo araymoss theea thay korresspondennthya *Today we will make it a day for correspondence.*

Paul tells us that he will travel to Argentina very soon, **Pablo nos dice que viajará para la Argentina muy pronto** (pavlo noz theethay kay veeahara para la arhennteena mooy pronnto). *Mr. Alfonso has given him a good address*, **El Señor Don Alfonso le ha dado una dirección buena** (ell sengyor donnalfonnso lay·a thatho oona theerekthyong booayna), *and he is going to write the following letter*, **y va a escribir la carta siguiente** (ee va a esskreeveer la karta seeghyenntay):

Muy señor mío,

Mi amigo Alfonso Ruiz a quién tuve el gusto de conocer hace mucho tiempo mi dió su dirección.

Tengo la intención de viajar por la Argentina y especialmente de ir a Buenos Aires esto invierno y agradecería cualquiera información que Vd. me diera.

Seré absolutamente extranjero en la Argentina. Quedaré alla cerca de seis meses y querría estar siempre con una familia española, porque es la unica manera posible de aprender bien el español y de conocer las costumbras sociales y comerciales.

Le ruego me dispense si le he causado alguna molestia. Los mejores recuerdos de parte de mi amigo.

Quedo suyo affmo. y. s. s. q. s. m. e.

Pablo Diez

Dear Sir:

My friend, Mr. Alfonso Ruiz, whom I have had the pleasure of knowing for a long time, has given me your address. I intend to travel through Argentina this winter and hope especially to spend some time in Buenos Aires. I should be grateful for any information you could give me.

I shall be an absolute stranger in Argentina. I intend to stay there for about six months and would like to spend the whole time in the home of a Spanish family, because that is the only possible way to learn Spanish well and to come to know the social and commercial customs.

I wish to apologize if I have caused you any inconvenience. Best regards from my friend.

Very sincerely yours,
Pablo Diez

affmo. y. s. s. q. s. m. e. =
afectísimo y seguro servidor que su mano estrecha
afekkteeseemo ee saygooro serrveethor kay soo mano esstraycha
very affectionate and constant servant who your hand clasps.

Lesson Thirty-Two

Pablo puts this letter *in an envelope*, **en un sobre** (enn oon sobray) and writes *the address*, **la dirección** (la theerekkthyong). He will send it *by airmail*, **por avión** (porr avyong).

```
Argentina

              Señor Antonio Gomez

                   Calle de Victoria, 24

Por Avión          Buenos Aires
```

If we were writing to a lady, we wouldn't forget that it is polite to address a letter to **Señora Doña Teresa Gomez.** **Si escribiríamos a una señora, no olvidaríamos que es cortes el dirigir una carta a Señora Doña Teresa Gomez** (see esskreeveereeamoss a oona sengyora no ollveethareeamoss kay ess korrtess ell deereeheer oona karta a sengyora dongya tayraysa gomayth).

Todos nosotros escribimos también unas cartas, unas tarjetas
tothoss nosotross esskreeveemoss tamvyenng oonas kartas, oonas tarhaytas
We (all) are also writing some letters, some cards,

y unas tarjetas ilustradas.
ee oonas tarhaytas eeloostrathas
and some picture postcards.

¿Dónde está la próxima oficina de correos?
donnday essta la proxeema ofeetheena thay korrayoss
Where is the nearest post-office?

What is *"care of?"* **"En casa de"** (in the house of) enn kassa thay

¿Cuanto es el porte para países extranjeros?
kvanto ess ell portay para paeesess esstranhayross
How much is the postage to foreign countries?

You would mail, **Vd. echaría al correo** (oostayth aychareea all korrayo) (you would turn to the post) *a registered letter,* **una**

* 171 *

carta certificada (oona karta therrteefeekatha) directly *at the window of the post office,* **en la ventanilla de la oficina de correos** (enn la venntaneellya thay la ofeetheena thay korrayoss). Of course, before you mail it you must be sure that it is marked *"Registered,"* in Spanish, **"Certificada"** (therrteefeekatha) and *you write it on the envelope,* **lo escribirá en el sobre así** (lo esskreeveera enn ell sovray asee).

25 céntimos por cada 20 gramos.
25 thennteemoss porr katha 20 gramoss
25 centimos for every 20 grams (28 gramos = 1 ounce).

El dinero se envía por una libranza de correos.
ell deenayro say ennveea porr oona leevrantha thay korrayoss
Money can be sent as a money order (an order of post).

If you want to send a letter to *"General Delivery"* it is: **en lista de correos** (enn leesta thay korrayoss). *There you would ask,* **allá preguntaría Vd.** (allya prayghoontareea oostayth). *Is there a letter for me?* **¿Hay carta para mí?** (aee karta para mee). *"Registered"* when *you'll write it on the envelope,* **lo escribirá en el sobre así** (lo esskreeveera enn ell sovray asee), **"certificado"** (therrteefeekatho).

Of course you can send a telegram to any point in the world, **Por supuesto puede enviar un telegrama a cualquiér punto del mundo** (porr soopooessto pooaythay ennveear oon taylaygrama a kvalkyerr poonto thell moondo).

By the way, all words ending in -ama are masculine, although otherwise the ending -a is almost always feminine. Only a few words are exceptions. For example: **el día** (ell deea), *the day is masculine;* but **el agua** (ell agva) is feminine. The masculine article is used because it sounds better to the Spanish ear. This

The verb *to do* as it is used in English as an auxiliary verb for questions and negations doesn't exist in Spanish.

attempt to make everything "sound well" Spanish often proves very difficult for the English speaking tongue. But we will soon get accustomed to it, and anyway it will not be the only mistake we will make in the strange idiom. Don't ever be afraid, for even when we say to a stranger, *"You speak English very well,"* **Vd. habla inglés muy bien** (oostayth avla eengless mooy byenn), and we mean it, be sure, he still makes many mistakes, anyhow.

El vendedor de leche está allá.
ell vayndaydor day laychay essta allya.
The milkman is there.

La leche está	**muy fresca**	**y rica.**
la laychay essta	mooy frayska	ee reeka.
The milk is	*very fresh*	*and good (rich).*

No, señoras, no	**pueden recibirla**	**más fresca.**
no sengyoras no	pooaydayn raytheebeerla	mas frayska
No, ladies,	*you could not get*	*it fresher.*

¿No,	**es**	**verdad?**
no	ess	vayrdad
Is	*that*	*so?*

Los sellos se venden también en los estancos.
loss sellyoss say venndenn tambyenn enn loss esstankoss
Yes, sir, stamps are also sold in the "estancos," tobacco stores
owned by the state, which has a monopoly on the whole
tobacco industry. (There is no monopoly in Mexico and
South America).

Hay un buzón en todos los estancos.
aee oon boothong enn tothoss loss esstankoss
There is a letter box in all monopoly stores (in all tobacco stores).

Translate into Spanish

After work is done, we want to rest a little or amuse ourselves.
In the course of time we grow accustomed to love all work, even
the most disagreeable. No gains without pains. There is no rose
without a thorn. God helps those who help themselves. I give
you this good advice. What did you think? I can tell you. Much
ado (noise) about nothing. To be serious. Man proposes and
God disposes. I want to go to a barber or to a hairdresser.
I laugh at you. Let us look for a hairdresser's shop. It is possible
that we may go to the theater later on. I am sorry that I didn't
tell you before. Where is a hairdresser's? Can you tell me where
there is a good hairdresser near here? I don't think that the
hairdresser opposite our house is good, but I think that the
barber's shop in the corner house of the next street is very good.

Very well. I think we'll go there. I hear the barber saying to
Peter: Good morning, sir! You will be served at once. Take a
seat! Will you give me a shave? I ask also to cut my hair. Is
the razor all right? It hurts a little bit. Wash my head! I want
a dry shampoo. Cut a little more here! I want a manicure. Do
you want some powder? Part my hair on the right side, not on
the left side. Now and then. Cut my hair (so that it may remain)
short in the back, and not so much in front.

Lesson Thirty-Three

¿Quiere Vd. fumar un puro?
kyayray oostayth foomar oom pooro
Would you like to smoke a cigar? (**El cigarro** (ell theegarro) is
the cigar; but in Spain they usually say **un puro** *a pure one*).

¿O prefiere Vd. los cigarillos?
o prayfyayray oostayth loss theegareellyoss
Or do you prefer cigarettes?

Yo no fumo, pero mi primo fuma en pipa, si su madre,
yo no foomo payro mee preemo fooma em peepa see soo mathray
I don't smoke, but my cousin smokes a pipe, if his mother,

mi tía, no lo ve. No le gusta el olor del tabaco ni de los
mee teea no lo vay, no lay goosta ell olor thell tavakko nee thay
loss
my aunt, doesn't see him. She doesn't like the smell of cigars or

cigarillos ni de la pipa. Como quiera que sea, cuando mi tía
theegareellyoss nee thay la peepa, komo kyayra kay saya kvando
mee teea
cigarettes or pipes. However, when my aunt

**volvió de la Habana, les trajo a mi tío y a mi primo una caja
de los**
vollvyo thai la avanna less traho a mee teeo ee a mee preemo
oona kaha thay loss
*returned from Havana, she brought my uncle and my cousin a
box of*

mejores cigarros importados para regalarles y ella está muy
mayhoress theegarross eemportathoss para raygalarless ee ellya
essta mooy
the finest imported cigars as a present, and she is very

**orgullosa de haber pasado los aduaneros (el registro) sin pagar
los derechos.**
orrgoollyosa thay avorr pasatho loss advanayross (ell rayheestro)
seen pagar loss dayraychoss
*proud that she was able to pass the customs officers without paying
any duty.*

Es cómico que aun a la gente más rica le gusta un poco el contrabando

ess komeeko kay aoon a la henntay mas reeka lay goosta oom poko ell konntravando

It's funny that even the richest people like to do a little smuggling.

The dialogue *at the border*, **en la frontera** (enn la fronntayra) is, for most people, somewhat exciting, especially *when the baggage is inspected* **cuando se registran los equipajes** (kvando say rayheestran loss aykeepahess).

¿Tiene Vd. algo que declarar?
tyaynay oostayth algo kay thayklarar
Have you anything to declare?

¡No tengo nada que declarar!
no tenngo natha kay thayklarar
I have nothing to declare.

¿Trae Vd. cigarros?
traay oostayth theegarross
Have you (do you bring) any cigars?

Hay solamente efectos usados.
aee solamenntay ayfekktoss oosathoss
There are only used goods.

¡Abra Vd. su baúl por favor!
abra oostayth soo baool porr favor
Open your trunk, please.

Unos de mi uso particular.
oonoz thay mee ooso parteekoolar
Some (things) for my personal use.

Qué alegres están todos cuando el aduanero dice:
kay alaygress esstan tothoss kvando ell advanayro theethay
How glad everyone is when the customs officer says:

¡Puede Vd. cerrar el baúl!
pooaythay oostayth therrar ell vaool
You may close the trunk.

Hasta eso se ha terminado (asta esso say a terrmeenatho). *Even that is finished.* **Entramos en la ciudad** (enntramoss enn la theeoothath) *we enter the city. We can go uptown,* **arriba de la**

ciudad (arreeva thay la theeoothath), *downtown,* **abajo de la ciudad** (avaho thay la theeoothath), *just as we please* **como Vd. gusta** (komo oostayth ghoosta).

(Be) Welcome! **¡Sea Vd. bienvenido!** (saya oostayth byennvay-neektho).
Enjoy yourself! **¡Qué goce mucho!** (kay gothay moocho).
Have a good time! **¡Qué se divierta!** (kay say deevyerrta).

* * *

    In this city we want to stay only for a short time, **en esta ciudad queremos estar solamente poco tiempo** (enn essta theeoothath kayraymoss esstar solamenntay poko tyemmpo). *Our first impression is that the weather is fine,* **nuestra primera impresión es que hace buen tiempo** (nooesstra preemayra eempressyong ess kay athay booenn tyemmpo). *And we don't care what it will be tomorrow,* **y no nos importa qué tiempo hará mañana** (ee no noss eemporrta kay tyempoara mangyana). *Perhaps the weather will be bad tomorrow,* **quizá hará mal tiempo mañana** (keetha ara mal tyemmpo mangyana). *It rains* **llueve** (llyooayvay); *it will rain* **lloverá** (llyovayra). Then, at least, we will be able to say *it was good weather* (the weather was good), **hizó buen tiempo** (eetho vooenn tyemmpo), and years from now we will remember the good weather we had on our arrival. How often we say *many years ago* **hace muchos años** (athay moochoss angyoss).

    The sun is shining, **hace sol** (athay sol), and tonight we may expect something that is a really wonderful sight in these southern districts, for *the moon will be shining,* **hará luna** (ara loona).

Lesson Thirty-Four

We may compare *the weather,* **el tiempo** (ell **tyemmpo**), the weather and the time with *life,* **la vida** (la **veetha**) and with language, which really reproduces life. We learn all the rules of a language, but we cannot overlook the fact that there are many irregularities which cannot be explained or anticipated. We have to take them just as they are.

Now here's something about adverbs. Take the adverbs, *certainly,* **ciertamente** (**thyerrtamenntay**), *surely,* **seguramente** (**sayghooramenntay**), *absolutely,* **absolu-tamente** (**absolootamenntay**). You will notice that in English, -ly is added to the adjective to form the adverb. In Spanish the adverb is produced by attaching

> Between vowels a, e, i, o, u, y or *between a vowel and* r, the vibrants d is th like in *th(em)*, b is like almost v.

-mente to the feminine noun. An example of this is the Spanish word, **seguramente** (**sayghooramenntay**). The noun **la mente** (la **menntay**) is *the mind,* or *sense;* therefore, **seguramente** is *in a sure sense, in a sure way.*

But as soon as we are asked if all words ending in -mente are adverbs, *we must say, no,* **debemos decir que no** (**dayvaymoss daytheer kay no**). *You could not say yes,* **No puede decir que sí** (no **pooaythay daytheer kay see**).

When we know that *where?* is **¿dónde?** it is easy to see that where to? is **¿á dónde?** And from where? is **¿de dónde?** *Why don't you answer?* **¿Por qué no responde Vd.?** (porr kay no **ressponday oostayth**). *Because I don't know what to say* **porque no sé qué decir** (**porrkay** no say kay **daytheer**).

¿por qué? (porr kay)	*why?*	**para** (para)	*for*
porque (porrkay)	*because*	**por** (porr)	*by*

Answer at once, **responda Vd. en seguida** (**ressponda oostayth enn saygheetha**). *Always be polite,* **sea siempre cortés** (**saya syemmpray korrtess**), **tenga Vd. la bondad** (**tennga oostayth la vondath**), *please be so kind (have the goodness).*

¿Quizá le molesto?
keetha lay molessto
Perhaps I am disturbing you?

¿Á quién tengo el honor de hablar?
a kyenng tenngo ell onor day avlar
With whom have I the honor of speaking?

¿quién? (kyenn) *who?*   **¿qué?** *what?*
¿de quién? *whose?*   **¿cuál?** *which one?*
¿a quién? *whom, to whom?*

Haga Vd. el favor de presentarme al caballero.
aga oostayth ell favor day praysenntarmay al kavallyayro
Please introduce me to the gentleman.

Permítame Vd. que le presente a la Señora.
perrmeetamay oostayth kay lay praysenntay a la sengyora
Permit me to introduce you to the lady.

Doña Elvira   **¡Mucho gusto en conocerla!**
donnya ellveera   moocho goosto enn konotherrla
Elvira.   *I'm happy to know you.*

Tome Vd. mi tarjeta.   **¡Es Vd. muy amable!**
tomay oostayth mee tarhayta   ess oostayth mooy amavlay
Here is (take) *my card.*   *It is very kind of you* (you are
                very kind).

Es siempre mejor el ser muy cortés.
ess syemmpray mayhor ell serr mooy korrtess
It is always best to be (the be) *very polite.*

At once, **en seguida** (enn saygeetha), *now* **ahora** (aora), *you
will answer* **Vd. contestará o Vd. responderá** (oostayth konntess-
tara o oostayth rayspon dayra).

UNA VISTA SIGNIFICANTE.
oona veesta seegneefeekanntay
A significant view.

Diga Vd. al señor que está Pérez.
deega oostayth al sengyor kay essta payrayth
Tell the boss that it is Perez.

El señor no recibe.
ell sengyor no retheevay
The boss isn't receiving.

A mi me es igual: con tal que dé . . .
a mee may ess eegval konn tal kay thay
That's all right with me: those who give . . .

(The question is not whether the boss receives,
but whether he gives.)

¿DÓNDE? (DONNDAY) *WHERE?*

¡aquí! (akee)	*here!*	detrás (daytras)	*behind*
¡ahí! (aee)	*there!*	dentro (denntro)	*within*
¡allá! (allya)	*there*	fuera (fooayra)	*outside*
delante (daylantay)	*before*	lejos (layhoss)	*far*

cerca (therrka)   *near*
adelante (adaylantay)   *forward* (also, come in)
atrás (atras)   *backward*
debajo (daybako)   *beneath*

*

¿CUÁNTO? ¿CUÁNTA?   ¿CUÁNTOS? ¿CUÁNTAS?
(KVANNTO, KVANNTA)   (KVANNTOSS, KVANNTAS)
HOW MUCH?   *HOW MANY?*

mucho (moocho)	*much*	bastante (bastantay)	*enough*
poco (poko)	*little*	algo (allgo)	*something*
demasiado (daymasyado)		casi (casi)	*almost*
too much			

(**basta** (bassta)   *that is enough*)

*

¿CÓMO? (KOMO) *HOW?*

bien (byenng)	*well*
mal (mall)	*badly*
despacio (desspathyo)	*slowly*
así así (asee, asee)	*so so*
de veras (day vayras)	*truly*
de burla (day boorla)	*for fun*
claro (klaro)	*clearly*
alto (allto)	*aloud*
de ningún modo (day neengoon motho)	*in no way*
nada de eso (natha thay esso)	*not at all*

*   *

*

Mucho siento,	señorita
moocho syaynto	sengyoreeta
Very sorry,	*young lady,*

que lleguemos demasiado tarde.
kay llyaigaymoss daymasyado tarday
we came too late.

Es una verguénza
ess oona vayrgenntha
It is a shame

que el vapor	no espere	a una señorita como Vd.
kay ell vapor	no esspayray	aoona sengyoreeta komooostayth
that the steamer	*did not wait*	*for a lady like you.*

¡Lea en alta voz!

Finalmente estábamos cansados de todos los numeros. Cuando regresamos a nuestra casa no deseábamos nada más que descansar un poco de tiempo. Estaba en mi cuarto, cuando nuestro amigo Enrique entró en la casa. ¿Dónde estabas, Juanita, cuando te llamé? La muchacha subió y dijo: Señor Enrique López ha venido. Oí tocar a la puerta y Vd. dijo: "¡Entré!" Asi supe que la puerta estaba abierta y que Enrique estaba con Vd. Entonces, Vd. sabe, que bajé. Hablabais uno con otro cuando la muchacha viene una vez más y dijo: Señora López ha venida.

¿Qué hay de nuevo? Falta de noticias, buena señal. Un diario español les hace falta. Un articulo en el diario. Trabajaba un hombre, así escribia aquel hombre. Aquel hombre se llamaba Thomas Jefferson. El documento fué leído el cuarto de julio de 1776 en la primera reunión del Congreso Continental. Jefferson era un hombre notable. Su profesión era abogado; gozaba fama de ser un gran escritor, y era además, pintor, educador y atleta.

Muy bien. Creo que iremos allá. Oigo al barbero decir a Pedro: ¡Buenos días, señor! ¡Pronto se le servira! ¡Tome Vd. asiento! ¿Quiere Vd. afeitarme? ¿Ruégole también que me corte el cabello? ¿Está buena la navaja? Duele un poquito. Laveme Vd. la cabeza. Deseo un champú seco. Corte un poco de aquí. Quiero arreglarme las uñas. ¿Quiere Vd. polvos? Hagame Vd. la raya al lado derecho, no al lado izquierdo. De cuando en cuando. Corteme Vd. el pelo que quede corto por detrás, y no tanto por delante.

Julia dijo a la peruquera: Primero deseo cortarme las puntas de cabello. Segundo deme Vd. un shampú. Tercero una ondulación. Cuartero un masaje facial. ¿Desea Vd. ir al teatro hoy o mañana o más tarde? Habia una discusión larga entre nosotros todos. Os he dicho que vayamos primero al teatro y más tarde también al concierto y a la ópera. Supe que os gustaria mucho. Cuando os dije que podríamos ir—¡cuantas preguntas tuve que contestaros! ¿Cuándo empieza? ¿A qué hora empieza? ¿Qué se da? ¿Cuándo se acabara? ¿Vale la pena de ver la representación?

VERBOS IRREGULARES

ANDAR. Andar (andar), *to go.* Ando, andas, anda, andamos, andáis, andan, *I go, you go, etc.* Imperf.: andaba (andava), andavas, andava, andávamos, andavais, andavan and Pret. Perf.: anduve (andoovay), anduviste (andooveestay), anduvo, anduvimos, anduviste, anduvieron (andoovyayron), *I went, I was going.* Fut. I: andaré, andarás, andará, andaremos, andaréis, andarán (andaran), *I shall go, you will go, etc.* Cond. I.: andaría, andarías, andaría, andaríamos, andaríais, andarían (andareean), *I should go, you would go etc.* Pres. de Subj.: que ande, que andes, que ande, que andemos, que andéis, que anden, *that I may go.* Imperf. de Subj.: que anduviese (kay andoovyaysay), que anduvieses, que anduviese, que anduviésemos, que anduvieseis, que anduviesen, *that I might go.* Fut. I de Subj. si anduviere (see andoovyayray), si anduvieres, si anduviere, si anduviéremos, si anduviereis, si anduvieren, *if I should go, if you would go, etc.* Cond. I de Subj. si anduviera (see andoovyayra), si anduvieras, si anduviera, si anduviéramos, si anduvierais, si anduvieran, *if I should go, if you would go etc.* Imperat. ¡Anda!, *go!* ¡Ande Vd.!, *go* (formal) ¡Andemos!, *let us go.* ¡Anden Vds.!, *go!* (to many persons) Gerund.: andando, *going.* Part. Pas.: andado, *gone.*

DAR. (dar), *to give.* Pres. de Indic. doy (doy), das, da, damos, dais, dan, *I give etc.* Imperf. daba (dava), dabas, daba etc., *I gave, etc.* Pret. Perf. di (dee), diste (deestay), dió (deeo), dimos (deemoss), disteis (deestayees), dieron (deeayron), *I gave, I was giving, etc.* Fut. I. daré, darás, dará etc., *I shall give,* Cond. I. daría, darías, daría etc., *I should give, etc.* Pres. de Subj. que dé, que des, que dé, que demos, que deis, que den, *that I may give etc.* Imperf. de Subj. que diese (kay deeaysay), que dieses, que diese, etc., *that I might give etc.* Fut. I de Subj. si diere (see deeayray), si dieres, si diere etc., *if I shall give etc.* Cond. I de Subj. si diera (see deeayra), si diera, si diera etc., *if I should give.* Imperat. ¡Da!, *give!* (familiar)—¡Dé Vd.!, *give!* (formal) ¡Demos!, *let us give!,* ¡Dad!, *give!,* ¡Den Vds.!, *give* (formal to many persons). Gerund. dando (danndo), *giving.* Part. pas. dado, *given.*

SABER. Saber (sabayr), *to know.* Pres. de Indic. sé (say), sabes (sabays), sabe, sabemos (sabaymoss), sabéis, saben, *I know etc.* Imperf. sabía, sabías, sabía etc. and Pret. Perf. supe (soopay), supiste (soopeestay), supo (soopo), supimos (soopeemoss), supisteis (soopeestayees), supieron (soopeeayronn), *I knew, I was knowing.* Fut. I. sabré, sabrás, sabrá etc., *I shall know etc.*—Cond. I. sabría, sabrías, sabría etc., *I should know etc.* Pres. de Subj. que sepa (kay saypa), que sepas, que sepa, que sepamos, que sepáis, que sepan, *that I may know etc.* Pres. de Imperf. que supiese (kay soopyaysay), que supieses, que supiese etc., *that I might know etc.* Fut. I. de Subj. si supiere (see soopyayray), si supieres, si supiere etc., *if I should know etc.* Cond. I de Subj. si supiera (see soopyayra), si supieras, si supiera etc., *if I should know etc.* Imperat. ¡sabe!, *know!* ¡Sepa Vd.!, *know* (formal), ¡Sepamos!, *let us know!*, ¡Sabed!, *know!* ¡Sepan Vds.!, *know* (formal to many persons). Gerund.: sabiendo (sabyenndo), *knowing.* Part. pas sabido (saveedo), *known.*

HACER. hacer (athayr), *to do.* Pres. de Indic. hago (ago), haces (athays), hace, hacemos, hacéis, hacen. *I do etc.* Imperf. hacía, hacías, hacía etc., and Pret. perf. hice (eethay, hiciste (eetheestay), hizo (eetho), hicimos (eetheemoss), hicisteis (eetheestayees), hicieron (eethyayron), *I did, I was doing etc.* Fut. I. haré, harás, hará, haremos haréis, harán (aran), *I shall do etc.* Cond. I. haría (areea), harías, haría etc., *I should do etc.* Pres. de Subj. que haga (kay aga), que hagas, que haga, que hagamos (agamoss), que hagáis, que hagan (agan), *that I may do etc.* Imperf. de Subj. que hiciese (kay eethaysay), que hicieses, que hiciese, que hicésemos (eethyaysaymoss), que hicieseis, que hiciesen, *that I might do etc.* Fut. I. de Subj. si hiciera (see eethyayra), si hicieras, si hiciera etc., *if I shall do etc.* Cond. I. de Subj. si hiciera (see eethyayra), si hicieras, si hiciera etc., *if I should do etc.* Imperat. ¡Haz! (ath), *do* (familiar), ¡Haga Vd.! (aga oostayth), *do* (formal)! ¡Hagamos! (agamoss), *let us do!* ¡Haced! (athayd), *do* (familiar to several persons). ¡Hagan Vds.! (agan oostaythays) *do* (formal to several persons). Gerund. haciendo (athyenndo), *doing.* Part. pas. hecho (aicho), *done.*

CAER. Caer (kaerr), *to fall.* Pres. de Indic. caigo (kaeego), caes (kaays), cae, caemos (kaaymoss), caéis, caen, *I fall, I am falling.* Imperf. caía (kaeea), caías, caía, caíamos, caíais, caían and Pret. perf. caí (kaee), caíste, cayó (kayo), caímos, caísteis, cayeron (kayayronn), *I fell, I was falling.* Fut. I. caeré (kaayray), caerás, caerá etc., *I shall fall etc.* Cond. I. caería, caerías, caería etc., *I should fall etc.* Pres. de Subj. que caiga (kay kaeega), que caigas, que caiga, que caigamos, que caigáis, que caigan, *that I may fall etc.* Imperf. de Subj. que cayese (kayaysay), que cayeses, que cayese, que cayésemos, que cayeseis, que cayesen, *that I might fall etc.* Fut. I. de Subj. si cayere (kayayray), si cayeres, si cayere, si cayéremos, si cayereis, si cayeren, *if I shall fall.* Cond. I. de Subj. si cayera (see kayayra), si cayeras, si cayera, si cayéramos, si cayerais, si cayeran, *if I should fall etc.* Imper. ¡Cae! (kaay). ¡Caiga Vd.! (kaeega oostayth), *fall* (formal to one person). ¡Caigamos! (kaeegamoss), *let us fall!* ¡Caed! (kaayd), *fall* (familiar to several persons). ¡Caigan Vds.! (kaeegan oostaythays), *fall* (formal to several persons). Gerund.: cayendo (kayayndo), *falling.* Part. pas. caído (kaeedo), *fallen.*

PODER. Poder (podayr), *to be able.* Pres. de Indic.: puedo (pooaydo), puedes, puede, podemos (podaymoss), podéis, pueden, *I am able etc.* Imperf. podía (podeea), podías, podía etc. and Pret. perf. pude (pooday), pudiste, pudo, pudimos (poodeemoss), pudisteis, pudieron (poodyayronn), *I was able etc.* Fut. I. podré (podray), podrás, podrá etc., *I shall be able etc.* Cond. I. podría, podrías, podrías etc., *I should be able etc.* Pres. de Subj. que pueda (kay pooayda), que puedas, que pueda, que podamos (podamoss), que podáis, que puedan, *that I may be able etc.* Imperf. de Subj. que pudiese (poodyaysay), que pudieses, que pudiese etc., *that I might be able etc.* Fut. I. de Subj. si pudiere (poodyayray), si pudieres, si pudiere etc., *if I shall be able etc.* Cond. I. de Subj. si pudiera (see poodyayra), si pudieras, si pudiera, *if I should be able etc.* Imperat. ¡Puede! (pooayday), *be able* (formal to one person). ¡Pueda Vd.! (pooayda Vd.), *be able* (formal). ¡Podamos! (podamoss), *let us be able!* ¡Poded! (podayd), *be able* (familiar to several persons). ¡Puedan Vds.! (pooaydan oostaythays), *be able* (formal to several persons). Gerund. pudiendo (poodyayndo), *being able.* Part. pas. podido (podeedo), *having been able.*

¡Lea en alta voz!

El tiempo que paso, no vuelve, no viene otra vez. Era abogado. Gozaba fama de ser un gran escritor. Estaba en mi cuarto cuando la modista entró, cuando el sastre y la sombrerera vinieron. ¿Dónde estaba Vd., cuando el óptico trajó sus anteojos? Estaba ahí, cuando yo estuve en casa del relojero. Fué una lección larga que nuestro amigo Enrique nos habia dado. No es muy agradable, pero es absolutamente necessario estudiar los verbos. Sciento mucho. ¡Vamos a dormir después de esta lección! ¡Buenas noches, senores y caballeros!

Un diario español, las revistas; Tráiganos un diario español todos los días por la mañana. ¡No lo olvida! Me gusta leer, nos gusta ver los articulos ilustrados y los reclamos. Para todo lo que desee, lea los clasificados de "La Prensa." Las palabras que conocemos muy bien. Vd. ya sabe. Si, señor, lo sé. Abogado español que habla inglés. Viendo esta oferta de trabajo Vd. desea ayudar este joven.

Dame chocolate! Niños, aqui tenéis chocolate! Así vamos a una confiteria. La buena tía pregunta a la dependiente: ¿Tiene Vd. chocolate? ¿Qué desea Vd.? ¿Qué clase, qué tamano, qué calidad desea Vd.? Tenemos chocolate para comer crudo. Tenemos chocolate par cocinar. Desea una barra de chocolate. Hay también chocolate de vainilla. Acaso Vd. deseara dulces o confites de chocolate. Deme medio kilo (una libra) de dulces y un cuarto de kilo de caramelos. Las gotas de limon y de naranja son muy buenas. ¡No aprenda Vd. demasiado!

Después de trabajar queremos tener nuestro reposo o divertirnos. Andando el tiempo, todo trabajo aun el más desagreadable. No hay atajo sin trabajo. No hay rosas sin espinas. A quien madruga, Dios le ayuda. Doy un buen consejo. ¿Qué ha pensado Vd.? Le digo. Mucho ruido para nada. Que sea dicho seriamente. El hombre propone y Dios dispone. Quiero ir al barbero o al peluquero. Me río de Vd. Buscamos una peluquería. Es posible que vayamos al teatro mas tarde. Sciento que no lo haya dicho más temprano. ¿Dónde está una peluquería? ¿Puede

Vd. decirme o recomendarme donde hay cerca de aquí un buen peluquero? No creo que la peluquería enfrente de nuestra casa sea buena, mas creo que la barbería en la casa de la esquina de la calle proxima es muy buena.

Translate into Spanish

Julia said to the hairdresser: First I want the ends of my hair cut. Second, Give me a shampoo. Third, a permanent wave. Fourth, a face massage. Do you want to go to the theater today or tomorrow or still later? There was a long discussion among us. I told you that we should go to a theater first, and later perhaps to a concert or the opera. I knew that you would enjoy yourself very much. When I told you we should go, how many of your questions I had to answer. When does it start? What time does it begin? What are they showing? When will it end? Is it worth while to see the performance?

You must not miss (to see) it. There was a very nice girl with us. Presently she began: this is station ACD. Your announcer is Pepita Caballero. We bring you now to the St. Ferdinand Theater. It is twenty minutes past nine. We still have ten minutes. At half past nine the first performance of that great comedy, "Life is a Dream", in rhyme and prose by Spain's most celebrated poet Calderon de la Barca, who was born in 1600 and died in 1681, will begin. Every seat is taken. The house is packed. The box-office is closed. There is no sale.

¡Haga el favor de repetir!

patatas	patatas	*potatoes*
postres	postrays	*dessert*
entre	enntray	*between*
tomo solamente una taza de té	tomo solamenntay oona tatha thay tay	*I just take a cup of tea*
la torta	la torrta	*the cake*
tostadas	tosstathas	*toast*
mi comida regular	mee komeetha ray-goolar	*my regular dinner*
durante el día	doorantay ell deea	*during the day*
la lástima	la lasteema	*the shame, the pity*
es un escándalo	ess oon esskanndalo	*it is a scandal*
Vd. no trabaja	oostath no travaha	*you don't work*
no piense en su enfermedad	no pyennsay enn soo ennferrmethath	*don't think of your complaints*
tanto como	tannto como	*as much as*
Vd. trabaja muy poco	oostayth travaha mooy poko	*you work too little*
toda la vida	totha la veetha	*all his life*
una receta	oona raythayta	*a prescription*
siento decir	syennto thaytheer	*I am sorry to say*
Vd. es absolutamente sano	oostayth ess absolootamenntay sano	*you are absolutely healthy*
el consejo	ell consayho	*the advice*
hace dos mil años	athay thoz meel angyoss	*two thousand years ago (it makes two thousand years)*
¿Qué significa esto?	kay seegneefeeka essto	*What does it mean?*
nuestro cuerpo	nooesstro kverrpo	*our body*
nuestra mente	nooesstra menntay	*our mind*

* 188 *

comemos para vivir	komaymoss para veeveer	we eat in order to live
no vivimos para comer	no veeveemoss para komayr	we don't live in order to eat
nuestro cerebro	nooesstro thay-rayvro	our brain
nuestra alma	nooesstra alma	our soul
olvidar	ollveethar	to forget
el espíritu	ell esspeereetoo	the spirit
edificar	aytheefeekar	to build
se come	say komay	one eats
se vive	say veevay	one lives
un día después de otro	oon deea thesspooess thell otro	one day after the other
ganar de comer	ganar thay komayr	earn a livelihood
ganarse la vida	ganarsay la veetha	earn a livelihood
dudar	doothar	to doubt
comer	komayr	to eat
pagar	pagar	to pay
ganar	ganar	to gain, to earn
trabajar	travahar	to work
vender	venndayr	to sell
beber	bayvair	to drink
temer	taymayr	to fear
correr	korrayr	to run
partir	parteer	to start
interrumpir	eenterroompeer	to interrupt
recibir	raytheeveer	to receive
decir	daytheer	to say
el niño	ell neengyo	the child
la lengua de su madre	la lenngva thay soo mathray	the mother language
la palabra	la palavra	the word
estas palabras son comprendidas	esstas palavras sonn kommprenndee-thas	these words are understood
el nene	ell naynay	the baby
la madre del nene	la mathray thell naynay	the mother of the baby
cuentos largos	kvenntoss largoss	long stories

la palabra (de) mama	la palavra thay mama	*the word mamma*
en los ojos de nuestra madre amada	enn loss ohoss thay nooesstra mathray amatha	*in the eyes of our loved mother*
maravilloso, a	maraveellyoso, a	*wonderful, marvelous*
nuestra grandezza	nooesstra grandaytha	*our greatness*
más tarde	mas tarthay	*later on*
sentencias	senntennthyas	*sentences*
el oro	ell oro	*the gold*
Vd. tiene hambre	oostayth teeaynay ammbray	*you are hungry*
¡vamos a dormir!	vamoss a thorrmeer	*let us go to bed*
¡Buenas noches!	booaynas nochays	*Good night!*
¡Qué duerma bien!	kay dooerrma byayng	*Sleep well!*
¡Qué descanse!	kay desskansay	*Rest well!*
descansar	desskansar	*to rest*
inteligente	eentelleehenntay	*intelligent*
hombres inteligentes	ommbrays eentelleehenntays	*intelligent people*
en el futuro	enn ell footooro	*in the distant future*
el sol sale	ell sol salay	*the sun rises*
el sol se pone	ell sol say ponay	*the sun sets*
todos los días	tothoz loz theeas	*every day*
la naturaleza	la natooralaytha	*the nature*
ignoramos e ignoraremos	eegnoramoss ay eegnoraraymoss	*we are ignorant and we shall be ignorant*
la cosa más importante	la kosa mas eempoortantay	*the most important thing*
es inclinado	ess eenkleenatho	*he is inclined*
decidores de la buena ventura	daytheethorayz thay la vooayna venntoora	*fortune-tellers, tellers of the good fortune*
terco, a	terrko	*obstinate*
el futuro	ell footooro	*the future*
la ventura	la venntoora	*the fortune*

la ocasión	la okkasyong	*the occasion*
la calle	la kallyay	*the street*
unos días más tarde	oonoss theeas mas tharthay	*a few days later*
cruzaré una calle	krootharay oona kallyay	*I shall cross a street*
he cruzado una calle	ay kroothatho oona callyay	*I have crossed a street*
entraré en una casa	enntraray enn oona kasa	*I shall enter a house*
encontraré un amigo	ennkonntraray oon ameego	*I shall meet a friend*
volveré a casa	vollyayray a kasa	*I shall return home*
he vuelto	ay vooellto	*I have returned*
una carta muy importante	oona karta mooy eemporrtantay	*a very important letter*
mis amigos queridos	mees ameegoss kayreethoss	*my dear friends*
mi amigo querido	mee ameego kay reetho	*my dear friend*
lo comprenderéis todo	lo kommprennday-rayees totho	*you will understand everything*
Vd. no habrá olvidado	oostayth no avra oll-veethatho	*you will not have forgotten*
tengo dinero	tayngo theenayro	*I have money*
no tengo dinero	no tayngo theenayro	*I have no money*
tendré dinero	tayndray theenayro	*I shall have money*
lo ganaré	lo ganaray	*I shall earn it*
¿Está feliz?	aysta fayleeth	*Are you happy?*
¡No lo sé!	no lo say	*I don't know*
¿Quiere Vd. ir?	kyayray oostayth eer	*Do you like to go?*
el toro	ell toro	*the bull*
la entrada	la enntratha	*the ticket*
una corrida de toros	oona korreetha thay toross	*a bullfight*
una entrada para una corrida de toros	oona enntratha para oona korreetha thay toross	*a ticket for a bullfight*
en punto	enn poonto	*punctual*

la corrida empezará	la korreetha aympaythara	*the bullfight will begin*
un viejo proverbio	oon veeayho provayrvyo	*an old proverb*
viejo, a	veeayho, a	*old*
actuar	akktooar	*to act*
es necesario	ayz naythaysaryo	*it is necessary*
la palabra	la palavra	*the word*
el coraje	ell korrahay	*the courage*
la palabra (de) coraje	la palavra (thay) korrahay	*the word courage*
atrevido, a	atrayveetho, a	*courageous*
¡Tenga valor!	taynga valor	*Have courage!*
¡Sea valeroso!	saya valayroso	*Be plucky!*
hablar español	avlar esspañyol	*to speak Spanish*
no diga	no theega	*don't say!*
la ocasión	la okkasyong	*the occasion*
leer	layayr	*to read*
para hacerlo	para athayrlo	*to do it*
no puedo hacerlo	no pooaytho athayrlo	*I can't do it*
no lo creo	no lo krayo	*I don't believe it*
le hemos mostrado	lay aymoz mosstrado	*we have shown you*
debo contestar	daybo konntaystar	*I would have to answer*
ciertamente	thyerrtamenntay	*certainly*
se habla español	say avla ayspangyol	*Spanish is spoken*

(Caption on Top of Next Page.)

Mente sana en cuerpo sano; pero no es
mayntay sana enn kverrpo sano; payro no ess
A healthy mind *in a healthy body;* *but it is*

siempre igual.
syemmpray eegval
not always the same.

Lesson Thirty-Five

¿Está Vd. cansado, Alfonso? Y tu también, Juanita, ¿estás cansada?
essta oostayth kansatho alfonso ee too tambyenng hooaneeta esstas kansatha
Are you tired, Alphonso? And you, Juanita, are you tired, too?

¡Vámonos al hotel! Queremos quedarnos solamente unos días
vamonoss al otell kayraymoss kaytharnoss solamenntay oonoz theeas
Let us go to the hotel. We will stay only a few days

en esta ciudad antes de regresar a casa.
enn essta theeoothath antayz thay raygraysar a kasa
in this city before we go home.

Gastaremos el último dinero que tenemos.
gastaraymoss ell oolteemo theenayro kay taynaymoss
We shall spend the last money we have.

Es un hotel de primera clase.
ess oon otell day preemayra klassay
It is a first-class hotel.

Los viajantes se alojan en una fonda.
loz veeahantays say alohan enn oona fonnda
The traveling salesmen stop at (reside themselves in) a simple hotel.

El gerente del hotel (ell hayrenntay thell otell), *the manager of the hotel* **nos recibe** (noz raytheevay) *receives us,* **y la conversación usual comienza** (ee la konnverrsathyong oosooal kommyenntha) *and the usual conversation begins.*

¿Puede Vd. darnos tres cuartos pequeños?
pooaythay oostayth tharnoss trays kvartos paykaynyos
Can you give us three small rooms?

Sí, señor, tenemos tres no occupados.
see sengyor taynaymoss tress no okkooopathoss
Yes sir, we have three free ones.

¿Cuánto cuesta esto cuarto por una noche o a la semana?
kvanto kvessta essto kvarto porr oona nochay o a la saymana
How much is this room by the day (for one night) or by the week?

¿No tiene Vd. un cuarto más barato?
no tyaynay oostayth oon kvarto mas barato
Don't you have a cheaper one?

¿Cuanto tiempo piensa Vd. estar aquí?
kvanto tyemmpo pyennsa oostayth esstar akee
How long do you plan to stay (stop) here?

Como una semana.
komo oona saymana
About a week.

¿No puede Vd. rebajar nada del precio?
no pooayday oostayth raybahar natha thell praythyo
Can't you make it any cheaper?

Bueno, nos quedaremos en los cuartos
booayno noss kaydaraymoss enn loss kvartoss
Well, we'll take the rooms.

¿Á qué hora se come?
a kay ora say komay
When are the meals served? (At what hour does one eat?)

¿Desea Vd. algo más, señor?
daysaya oostayth algo mas sengyor
Do you want anything else, sir?

¡Llámeme Vd. a las ocho de la mañana!
llyamaymay oostayth a las ocho thay la mangyana
Call me tomorrow morning at eight o'clock.

Muy bien. ¿Qué deserían Vds. señoras y caballeros, para
mooy byenng kay daysayreean oostaythays sengyoras ee kavallyayross, para
Very well. What would you, ladies and gentlemen, like for

el desayuno?
ell daysa-yoono
breakfast?

Café con leche, mantequilla, huevos fritos o estrellados,
kaffay konn laychay mantaykeellya ooayvoss freetoss o
esstrellyathoss
Coffee with milk, butter, fried eggs,

huevos revueltos, panecillos, conserva y mermelada.
ooayvoss rayvooelltoss, panaytheellyos, konnserrva ee merr-
maylatha.
scrambled eggs, rolls, jam and marmalade.

RAZONAMIENTO.
rathonnamyennto
Reasoning.

En una escuela rural pregunta el cura a uno de los examinados:
enn oona esskooayla rooral prayghoonta ell koora a oono de loss
eksameenathoss
In a country school, the curate asked one of the students:

Dime, hijo mío: ¿está Dios en todas partes?
deemay eeho meeo essta deeoss enn tothas partays
Tell me, my son, is God everywhere?

Si, señor.
see sengyor
Yes, Sir.

Entonces, ¿también está en el corral de tu casa?
enntonnthays tammbyenng essta enn ell corral de too kasa
Then he is also in the yard of your house?

No, señor.
no sengyor
No, sir!

¿Y por qué dices que no está?
ee porr kay theethays kay no essta
And why do you say that he is not?

Porque mi casa no tiene corral.
porrkay mee kasa no teeaynay korral
Because my home has no yard.

* 196 *

Lesson Thirty-Six

Our friend Paul, Don Paul or Señor Paul Diez, wrote a letter to Argentina two weeks ago, **nuestro amigo Pablo, Don Pablo o el Señor Pablo Diez, escribio una carta a La Argentina hace dos semanas** (nooesstro ameegho pavlo donn pavlo o sengyor pavlo deeayth aveea esskreeveeo oona karta a la arhennteena athay thoss saymanas). *Today the answer was received,* **hoy fué recibida la respuesta** (oy fooay raytheeveetha la rayspooessta) **o se recibió la respuesta hoy** (say raytheeveeo la rayspooessta oy).

Pablo ha abierto la carta; ha visto en seguida que
pavlo a avyerrto la karrta a veesto enn saygeetha kay
Paul (has) opened the letter; he saw at once that

la carta viene de La Argentina. La ha puesto en su bolsillo
la karrta vyaynay thay la arhennteena la a pooessto enn soo
    bollseellyo
the letter came from Argentina. He put it in his pocket

para mostrarnosla.
para mosstrarnossla
to show it to us.

Now we call once more to your attention the very important fact —a fact which is, indeed, not so easy to understand, at first, for one who does not speak a Romance language. Spanish, like many other Romance languages, is spoken in so-called "connected" speech. That means that the Spaniards, in speaking their language, contract one word with the following word. They do not separate one word from the other as we do in English. Even when we speak English very quickly we do not contract two words into almost one. This liaison, interrupted only by breathing pauses or by any kind of punctuation such as a comma, colon, question-mark, etc., has a great influence on the pronunciation. Take, for instance, the word **tan,** pronounced tang, meaning: *so;* **tan bueno,** so good, is pronounced tambooayno. We avoid demonstrating this time and again by making a connection sign (M) between pronunciation-guide words, because it would annoy you to see such a repetition always again. But don't wonder when you see that word endings are different in the pronunciation guide. It is not inconsistent at all, but it shows you how you have to connect the words with each other. The th in a liaison is always the voiced th, as in *them.* In the same manner, Spanish **d,** between words is pronounced almost like voiced th as in them.

You see, there are some verbs that have an irregular participle. You remember the regular ones: **hablado** (avlado) *spoken*; **comido** (komeetho) *eaten*; **vivido** (veeveetho) *lived*. But we have to take particular note of such verbs as these:

abrir	**abierto**	**cubrir**	**cubierto**
avreer	avyerrto	koovreer	koovyerrto
to open	*opened*	*to cover*	*covered*
escribir	**escrito**	**hacer**	**hecho**
esskreeveer	esskreeto	athayr	echo
to write	*written*	*to do*	*done*
decir	**dicho**	**freír**	**frito**
daytheer	deecho	frayeer	freeto
to say	*said*	*to fry*	*fried*
imprimir	**impreso**	**morir**	**muerto**
eempreemeer	eemprayso	moreer	mooerrto
to print	*printed*	*to die*	*died*
resolver	**resuelto**	**ver**	**visto**
raysollvayr	raysooellto	vayr	veesto
to solve	*solved*	*to see*	*seen*
poner	**puesto**	**volver**	**vuelto**
ponayr	pooessto	volvayr	vooellto
to put	*put*	*to turn*	*turned.*

There are other verbs which have two forms of this participle, a regular one and an irregular one. When you read, you will find the irregular forms used, but in conversation the regular form is preferred.

Generally a person who is leaving says: Quede **Vd. con Dios** (kayday oostayth konn deeoss) *stay with God.* The one who is staying: **Vaya Vd. con Dios** (vaya oostayth konn deeoss) or **Dios le acompaña** (deeoss lay akommpanya), *May God go with you!* or *May God accompany you!*

You will often see the word **cocido** (kotheetho) which is the name of one of the best Spanish dishes, **cocido de garbanzos, patatas, una verdura, carne de vaca, tocino** (cotheetho thay garvanthoss, patatas, oona verrthoora, karnay thay vaka, totheeno) *of chick peas, potatoes, a vegetable, beef bacon.*

✴

Ahora queremos leer aquella carta.
aora kayraymoss layerr akellya karrta
Now we want to read that letter.

Muy señor mío,

Acúsole gustoso recibo de su carta; los amigos de mis amigos son mis amigos.

Es verdad, que quiero, hacer todo lo que pueda para ayudarle a Vd.

Pienso que será mejor si le digo a Vd. todo lo que quiere saber después de llegar aquí.

Me gustaría mucho esperar su llegada. Será mi mayor placer el mostrarle a Vd. nuestro magnífico país.

Me tiene Vd. siempre a sus órdenes.

Suyo

Antonio Gomez

Dear Sir:

I acknowledge with pleasure the receipt of your letter; friends of my friends are my friends.

I really wish to do all that I can (Subj.) to help you.

I think that it will be best if I (shall) tell you all (what) you want to know after you arrive here.

I would like very much to see you upon your arrival. It will be my greatest pleasure to show you our wonderful country.

(Have me always to your order) I am always at your disposal.

Very sincerely yours,

Antonio Gomez

A short time later, Paul received a postcard from his good friend, Henry (Enrique), with whom he had communicated in the meantime about his correspondence.

Querido amigo,

Agradecí muchísimo tu amable carta. Hubiera querido escribirte en seguida, pero me fué imposible por estar en cama con un fuerte resfriado.

Ya, gracias a Dios, estoy mejor. En casa todos siguen bien. Mucha alegría tuvimos al saber de tu viaje a Buenos Aires que estará muy bien preparado y que será seguramente un viaje feliz.

No dejes de mandarnos de vez en cuando alguna tarjeta postal diciéndonos como te va el viaje.

Afectuosos recuerdos de todos, especialmente de mi esposa.

Tuyo afmo.,
Enrique

Dear Friend:

Thank you very much for your kind letter. I would have written you at once (I would have liked to write to you), but it was impossible because I had to stay (Spanish by to stay) in bed with a bad cold.

Now, thank goodness (thanks to God), I am better. All at home are well. We were very pleased to learn of your forthcoming trip to Buenos Aires, for which no doubt you will be very well prepared and which will surely be a happy experience.

Don't forget (omit) to send a post-card from time to time telling us how the trip progresses.

Cordial regards from all and especially from my wife.

Sincerely yours,

Henry

* 200 *

Lesson Thirty-Seven

Very soon our friend Paul will leave us. But we shall not part from each other without a farewell dinner which Paul will give.

"I invite you all," he said, "and I promise you that we shall have a very good time. No low spirits will be allowed! Why should there be any? We'll see each other again."

Muy pronto nuestro amigo Pablo nos dejará, pero no nos
mooy pronto nooesstro ameegho pablo noss dayhara payro no noss

despediremos sin un convito que Pablo nos dará.
desspaydeeraymoss seen oon kombeeto kay pablo noz thara

Yo os invito a todos vosotros, así ha dicho, y os prometo
yo oss eembeeto a tothoz vosotross asee a theecho ee oss promayto

que nos divertiremos mucho. Nada de melancolía; ¡de ningún modo!
kay noss deeverrteeraymoss moocho natha thay maylankoleea thay neengoon motho

¿Por qué? Porque nos veremos de nuevo.
porr kay porrkay noss vayraymoss day nooayvo.

*

Nadie sabe tan bien como Pablo el dar una fiesta y así lo hizo
nathyay savay tam byenn komo pavlo ell dar oona fyessta ee asee lo eetho
Nobody knows better than Paul how to arrange a party, and so he prepared this one

a la española.
a la esspangyola.
in Spanish style.

Al día siguiente todos vimos la tarjeta de invitación que Pablo
al deea seegyenntay tothoz veemoss la tarhayta thay eembeetathyong kay pablo
The next day all of us looked on an invitation card which Paul

había puesto sobre las mesas en todos los cuartos.
aveea pooessto sobray las messas enn todoz loss quartoss
had placed on the tables in all the rooms.

The next day every one of us found an invitation card from Paul on the table in his room.

> Pablo Diez
>
> Solicita el placer de su compañía
> en una fiestecita de despedida el 9 de
> diciembre de 1945 a las 7 P.M.
>
> **R.S.V.P.**

*Mr. Pablo Diez requests the pleasure of
your company at a farewell dinner party on
December 9, 1945, at 7 o'clock. R.S.V.P.*

*

*Attached to this invitation were two printed sheets, a leaflet about
the hotel and the bill of fare. On a separate piece of paper, each of
us was expected to put down his own choice of a six-course dinner.
"Eat what and as much as you like," that was Paul's slogan,
and he added (continuing), "Bring all your happiness with you."*

Junto con la invitación había dos impresos: una hoja del hotel
y el menú del mismo. Sobre un pedazo de papel cada uno de
nosotros deberíamos escribir nuestras selecciones de una
comida de seis platos. Coman lo que deseen y cuanto puedan,
ése era el lema de Pablo, continuando: Traed toda vuestra
felicidad.

And here are the two *enclosures*, **anexos** (anayxoss).

EL PARAÍSO DE LAS MONTAÑAS

Tenemos el gusto de comunicar a Vd. que a cinco millas de aquí le ofrecemos una finca de recreo donde puede Vd. pasar su tiempo libre aspirando aire puro, buen sol y una alimentación sana y excelente.

EL PARAÍSO está situado en la cima de una montaña, a una elevación de más de mil pies. Desde allí se recrea la vista con un panorama sin igual.

Visite EL PARAÍSO y se convencerá que es difícil encontrar un lugar más sano y pintoresco para pasar unas deliciosas vacaciones. Precios especiales para toda la temporada.

The Paradise of the Mountains

It is our pleasure to inform you that, five miles from here, we can offer you a recreation resort where you may pass your leisure time in an atmosphere of fresh air, warm sun and healthful and excellent food.

The Paradise is situated on the top of a mountain, at a height of more than one thousand feet. From there you can enjoy a view which has no equal.

Pay a visit to the Paradise and you will be convinced that it would be difficult to find a healthier and more picturesque place to spend a delightful vacation.

Special rates arranged by the season.

And here is the *second enclosure*, **anexo segundo** (anayxo saygoondo)

PARA VENIR A EL PARAÍSO

Si viene Vd. por auto, tome la carretera occidental y siga la misma hasta que pase un campo de golf que queda a mano derecha. Un poco más adelante encontrará un letrero que dice "a la Playa." Aqui coja Vd. a la izquierda y siga esa carretera sin doblar en ninguna dirección. Cuando termine la carretera de asfalto siga un poco más adelante y tome la primera que dobla hacia la derecha, hasta ver el letrero EL PARAÍSO.

Si viene Vd. por tren, por autobús o por vapor, llegada a la estación de Santa María llámenos por teléfono y nosotros iremos inmediatamente por Vd. a la estación.

Quedamos de Vd. muy atentamente,

EL PARAÍSO.

How to get to the Paradise

If you go by automobile, take the western highway and follow it straight along until you pass a golf course which is on the right. A little farther on you will come upon a sign which says, to La Playa (the beach). Here, turn to the left and follow this highway without turning (in Spanish without to turn) in any direction. When the paved road ends, go on a little further and take the first turning to the right, until you see (in Spanish until to see) the sign "The Paradise."

If you go by train, by bus or by boat, call us up by telephone when you arrive at the station Santa Maria, and we will go immediately to pick you up at the station.

We remain very sincerely,

THE PARADISE.

And then there was *the menu*—**la carta, el menú** (la karrta, ell mainoo)—*of the restaurant in "The Paradise"*—**del restaurant "El Paraiso"** (dell raistaoorang ell paradeeso).

EL PARAÍSO		The Paradise	

CERVECERÍA Y RESTAURANT

Restaurant Bar

ENTREMESES

Hors d'oeuvres

Variado "El Paraíso"	Mantequilla	Paradise Variety	Butter
Ensalada italiana	Arenques	Italian salad	Herrings
Ensalada de patatas	Sardines an aceite	Potato salad	Sardines in oil
Aceitunas	Anchoas	Olives	Anchovies
Fiambres variados		Assorted cold cuts	

SOPAS

Soups

Consommé	Puré	Consommé or broth	Purée
Al cuarto de hora	De legumbres	In a quarter of an hour (ready to eat)	Vegetable (soup)
De ajo con huevos	De rabo de buey	With (of) garlic and (with) eggs	Oxtail (soup)

PLATOS DEL DÍA

Daily Specials

Cocido española	Spanish dish (made of boiled beef and vegetables)
Garbanzos "El Paraíso"	Chick-peas à la Paradise
Calamares en tortilla	Calamares omelette
Pescadillos fritos	Fried small fish

HUEVOS

Eggs

Fritos	Fried
Fritos con tomate	Fried with tomatoes
Fritos con patatas	Fried with potatoes
Revueltos con tomate	Scrambled with tomatoes
Fritos con jamón	Fried with ham
Al plato	(on one side)
Tortilla española	Spanish omelette
Tortilla con esparragos	Omelette with asparagus

PESCADOS

Fish

Langostines	Shrimp
Langosta con mayonesa	Lobster with mayonnaise
Langosta o vinagreta	Lobster with vinegar sauce
Lenguado	Sole
Salmonetes	Red mullets
Calemares	Calamares
Bacalao con tomate	Codfish with tomato
Merluza frita o rebozada	Fried hake or breaded hake
Pescadilla	Little fish
Turbot	Turbot
Almejas marinera	Saltwater clams

LANGOSTA AMERICANA (sobre pedido)

American Style Lobster (to order)

ENTRADAS Y ASADOS

Bifteck con patatas fritas
Solomillo con patatas fritas
Entrecot
Chuleta de ternera
Chuleta de cordero
Rosbif a la inglesa
Contra de ternera asada
Filetes de ternera
Escalop vienés
Cordero lechal asado
Sesos fritos
Lengua de vaca

AVES

Pollo asado—racion
Perdiz escabechada

VERDURAS Y LEGUMBRES

Guisantes con mantequilla
Judías verdes
Patatas fritas
Patatas salteadas
Espinacas
Esparragos
Alcachofas
Chucrute

ENSALADAS

De Lechuga
De Lechuga con tomate
De escabeche y pimiento

MERMELADAS

Guinda
Fresa
Frambuesa
Melocoton
Giruela
Albaricoque
Flan
Tortilla confiture

QUESOS

Gruyer
  (grooyerr)   racion o media
Bola   racion o media

Roquefor
  (rokayforr)   racion o media
Nata (nata)   racion o media

Entrees and Roasts

Beefsteak with fried potatoes
Filet mignon with fried potatoes
Veal
Cutlet
Lamb chops
Roastbeef, English style
Roast veal
Roast veal filet
Wiener Schnitzel
Roast spring lamb
Fried brains
Ox tongue (in Spanish, cow's tongue)

Fowl

Roast chicken—portion
Pickled partridge

Vegetables

Peas with butter
String beans
Fried potatoes
Hash browned potatoes
Spinach
Asparagus
Artichokes
Sauerkraut

Salads

Lettuce
Lettuce and tomato
Pickles and pimiento (pepper)

Marmalades

Cherry
Strawberry
Raspberry
Peach
Prune
Apricot
Creamtart
Sweet omelette

Cheeses

Swiss   portion or half portion
Bola cheese portion or
  (Spanish) half portion
Roquefort   portion or
            half portion
Cream cheese portion or
  (Spanish) half portion

MARISCOS	Shellfish
Langostinos	Shrimp
Langosta	Lobster
Ostras y Almejas	Oysters and clams
Quisquillas	Assorted small crabs and fish

Translate into Spanish

The street is crowded, no automobiles can pass, very slowly automobiles and coaches approach the entrance of the theater. The drivers are having a hard time of it. We enter the theater. What seat should we take? There is no choice left. Where is my seat? Show me your ticket, please. We enter the upper balcony. The ladies in evening gowns ornamented with jewels, with the most precious gems. It is difficult to speak to you, because the noise of the chattering people is tremendous. The orchestra begins to play. A singer sings a song. Do you hear it? La Paloma Thunderous applause from the audience greets the singer. Then the curtain rises. The performance begins on the stage. The curtain drops. An excellent beginning for the winter season. We have come to the close of our report. We hope that you can hear very well over your radio. This is the Spanish Broadcasting System Station.

Since in these hot countries the days are very warm, even in the winter, we go to bed quite late. Before we had rented our rooms, Maria used to say: the most important thing for me, is that the bed be good. I don't like a room with two beds. At that time we had intended to go to bed very early. Our rooms—one looks out on the street, the other on the yard—are pretty large and furnished very well. They have a separate entrance. The windows are broad and high. When we asked the landlady "what is the price?" we could not say: the price is too much for us. I don't like to haggle. In every room there was a large and a small table, several chairs, a chest of drawers, a mirror and a writing desk.

Where do you live? And we could answer only that we were very much satisfied. The landlady and the landlord were always very nice. Every night they asked us, "When do you get up?" so that they could serve us a very good breakfast on time. Usually in southern countries, people eat only very light breakfasts.

Recommendación cumplida.
raykommenndathyonn koompleetha
Full recommendation.

Buenos dias, portero
booaynoss deeas porrtayro
Good morning, porter!

Buenos dias.
booaynoss deeas
Good morning!

¿Como va de salud?
komo va thay salood
How do you feel?

Perfectamente.
perrfekktamenntay
Perfect.

¿Y la portera?
ee la porrtayra
And your wife (and the portress)?

Buena, gracias.
booayna grathyas
Well, thank you.

¿Hace mucho tiempo que esta Vd. casado?
athay moocho tyemmpo kay essta oostayth kasatho
Have you been married a long time?

Diez años. Pero ¿a que viene tanta pregunta?
dyayth angyoss. payro a kay vyaynay tanta prayghoonta
Ten years. But why do you ask so many questions?

A nada. Pero como al entrar he visto ese cartel que dice:
a natha. payro komo al enntrar ay veesto essay kartayl kay deethay
Oh, no reason. But when I entered I saw a notice which said:

Nadie pase sin hablar al portero . . .
nathyay pasay seen avlar al porrtayro
No admittance without speaking to the porter . . .

¡Lea en alta voz!

No, debíais dejar de verlo. Había entre nosotros una muchacha muy amable. Ahora ella empezó: esa es la Stación ACD. Su annuncadora es Pepita Caballero. Le llevamos en este mismo instante al Teatro San Fernando. Son las nueve y veinte. Faltan diez minutos a las nueve y media la gran primera representación de la comedia "La Vida es Sueño" en verso y prosa de poeta más celebrado de España, Calderon de la Barca, que nació en 1600 y murio en 1681, empeza. Todas las localidades están tomadas, la caja del teatro está cerrada. No hay despacho.

Pedro dijo: os he dicho que vayamos primero al teatro y más tarde también al concierto y a la ópera. Supe que os gustaría mucho. Cuando os dije que podríamos ir—¡cuantas preguntas tuve que contestaros! ¿Cuándo empieza? ¿A qué hora empieza? ¿Qué se da? ¿Cuándo se acabara? ¿Vale la pena la representación?

La calle esta llena de gente, no puede pasar ni un automóvil, lentamente los autos y los coches van llegando a la entrada del teatro. Los conductores tienen un día muy dificil. Entramos al teatro. ¿Qué localidad tomaremos? No se puede escoger. ¿Dónde está mi asiento? Per favor, muestreme Vd. su entrada. Entramos el balcón. Las señoras con su vestidos de etiqueta adornadas con las joyas, con las piedras más preciosas. Es dificil hablerle a Vds. porque el ruido es enorme. La orquesta empieza a tocar.

Vd. tiene hambre. ¡Vamos a dormir! ¡Buenas noches! ¡Qué duerma bien! ¡Qué descanse!

Hombres y mujeres inteligentes, en el futuro. El sole sale y se pone todos los días. Ignoramos e ignoraremos. La cosa más importante del mundo. No haya nada tan terco come un hecho. Una decidora de la buena ventura hubo profetizado a una muchacha: Vd. cruzará una calle y entrará en una casa. Vd. encontrará en esta casa un amigo. Este amigo hablará con Vd. Volverá a casa. Vd. comerá. Vd. recibirá una carte muy importante. Esta carta decidera su ventura.

Hay cinco sentidos,
ay theenko saynteedoss
There are five senses,

el tacto, la vista, el olfato, el gusto, el óido,
ell takto, la veesta, ell ollfato, ell goosto, ell oeedo
touch, sight, smell, taste and hearing,

y tú, mi madre, tienes todos los cinco
ee too mee madray tyaynays todoss loss theenko
and you, mother, have all five of them,

pero no adivinarías lo
payro no adeeveenareeas lo
but still you couldn't guess

que tengo en mi mano.
kay tayngo enn mee mano
what I have in my hand.

Translate into Spanish

Breakfast well, dine better, sup lightly and you will live. He who promises much, keeps little. She didn't promise much, but she did a great deal for us. We don't want to be like the parrot who says what he knows but doesn't know what he says. Who loves whom? I like her or I like him. Whom do you like, him, my cousin?

When we see so many small words of a foreign language, we always are somewhat discouraged. We are afraid. He tells him once: don't use foreign words, one never knows what they mean. As we use it in English. We are riding in a street car, in a cab. If we had the money, we would always take a taxicab. Yes, we would take it. Not having it, we are taking the street car which passes every five minutes.

The conductor is always saying at every stop: let them off. Please, step in! Watch your step! What traffic! Let us sit down! Learning these traffic rules is very simple. Without asking us anything, the conductor gave us the tickets. A lady helps us. We heard the conductor saying when he went through the car: fares please! We heard him say so!

I said to Mary, I said to her: pay for the tickets for me, pay for them for me. Give them to me, because I like to occupy myself in reading every bit of printed matter in order to learn Spanish. May I advise you to do likewise? Mary, do so too! And you do so, Mr. López! You all do so! Let us do so! In so doing we are learning everywhere.

VERBOS IRREGULARES

PONER. Poner (ponayr), *to put.* Pres. de Indic. **pongo** (ponngo), **pones** (ponays), **pone, ponemos, ponéis, ponen,** *I put* or *I am putting etc.* Imperf. **ponía, ponías, ponía** etc. and Pret. Perf. **puse, pusiste, puso** (pooso), **pusimos, pusisteis, pusieron** (poosyayron), *I put, I was putting etc.* Fut. I. **pondré** (ponndray), **pondrás** (pondras), **pondrá** etc., *I shall put etc.* Cond. I. **pondría, pondrías, pondría** etc., *I should put etc.* Pres. de Subj. **que ponga** (kay ponnga), **que pongas, que ponga, que pongamos, que pongáis, que pongan,** *that I may put etc.* Imperf. de Subj. **que pusiese** (kay poosyaysay), **que pusieses, que pusiese** etc., *that I might put etc.* Fut. I. de Subj. **si pusiere** (see poosyayray), **si pusieres, si pusiere** etc., *if I shall put etc.* Cond. I. de Subj. **si pusiera, si pusieras, si pusiera** etc., *if I should put etc.* Imperat. **¡Pon!** (ponn), *put!* (familiar to one person). **¡Ponga Vd.!** (ponnga oostayth), *put!* (formal). **¡Pongamos!** (ponngamoss), *let us put!* **¡Poned!** (ponayd), *put!* (familiar, to several persons). **¡Pongan Vds.!** (ponngan oostaythays), *put* (formal, to several persons). Gerund. **poniendo** (ponyayndo), *putting.* Part. pas. **puesto** (pooaysto), *put.*

QUERER. Querer (kayrayr), *to want, to wish, to like.* Pres. de Indic. **quiero** (kayayro), **quieres, quiere, queremos** (kayraymoss), **queréis, quieren** (kyayrayn), *I want, wish, like etc.* Imp. **quería, querías, quería** etc., *I wanted, wished, liked etc.* and Pret. perf. **quise** (keesay), **quisiste** (keeseestay), **quiso** (keeso), **quisimos, quisisteis, quisieron** (keesyayronn), *I wanted, wished, liked etc.* Fut. I. **querré, querrás, querrá** (kerra), *I shall want, wish, like etc.* Cond. I. **querría** (kerreea), **querrías, querría** etc., *I should want, wish, like etc.* Pres. de Subj. **que quiera** (kyayra), **que quieras, que quiera, que queramos, que queráis, que quieran,** *that I may want, wish, like etc.* Imperf. de Subj. **que quisiese** (keesyaysay), **que quisieses, que quisiese** etc., *that I might want, wish, like etc.* Fut. I. de Subj. **si quisiere** (keesyayray), **que quisieres, que quisiere** etc., *if I should want, wish, like etc.* Cond. I. de Subj. **si quisiera** (keesyayra), **si quisieras, si quisiera** etc., *if I should want, wish, like etc.* Imperat. **¡Quiere!** (kyayray), *want, wish, like!* (familiar to one person). ¡**Quiera Vd.!** (kyayra oostayth), *want* (formal to one person). ¡**Queramos!** (kayramoss), *let us want, wish, like!* ¡**Quered!** (kayrayd), *want, wish, like* (familiar to several persons). ¡**Quieran Vds.!** (kyayran oostaythays), *want, wish, like* (formal to several persons)! Gerund. **queriendo** (kayryayndo), *wanting, wishing, liking.* Part. pas. **querido** (kayreedo), *wanted, wished, liked.*

TRAER. **Traer** (traayr), *to bring.* Pres. de Indic. **traigo** (traeego), **traes** (traays), **trae, traemos, traéis, traen,** *I bring, I am bringing.* Imperf. **traía, traías, traía** (traeea) etc. and Pret. perf. **traje** (trahay), **trajiste** (traheestay), **trajo, trajimos** (trayeemoss), **trajisteis, trajeron**—*I was bringing, I brought etc.* Fut. I. **traeré, traerás, traerá** etc., *I shall bring etc.* Cond. I. **traería, traerías, traería** etc., *I should bring etc.* Pres. de Subj. **que traiga** (traeega), **que traigas, que traiga, que traigamos, que traigáis, que traigan,** *that I may bring etc.* Imperf. de Subj. **que trajese** (kay trahaysay), **que trajeses, que trajese** etc., *that I might bring etc.* Fut. I. de Subj. **si trajere** (see trahayray), **si trajeres, si trajere** etc., *if I shall bring etc.* Cond. I. de Subj. **si trajera** (see trahayra), **si trajeras, si trajera** etc., *if I should bring etc.* Imperat. ¡**Trae!** (traay), *bring* (familiar to one person). ¡**Traiga Vd.!** (traeega oostayth), *bring* (formal to one person). ¡**Traigamos!** (traeegamoss), *let us bring!* ¡**Traed!** (traayd), *bring* (familiar to several persons). ¡**Traigan Vds.!** (traeegan oostaythays), *bring* (formal to several persons). Gerund. **trayendo** (trayayndo), *bringing.* Part. pas. **traido** (traeedo), *brought.*

VALER. **Valer** (valayr), *to be valuable.* Pres. de Indic. **valgo** (valgo), **vales** (valays), **vale, valemos, valéis, valen,** *I am valuable etc.* Imperf. **valía** (valeea), **valías, valía** etc. and Pret. perf. **valí** (valee), **valiste** (valeestay), **valió** (valyo), **valimos** (valeemoss), **valisteis** (valeestayees), **valieron** (valyayronn), *I was valuable etc.* Fut. I. **valdré** (valdray), **valdrás, valdrá** etc., *I shall be valuable etc.* Cond. I. **valdría** (valdreea), **valdrías, valdría** etc., *I should be valuable etc.* Pres. de Subj. **que valga** (valga), **que valgas, que valga** etc., *that I may be valuable etc.* Imperf. de Subj. **que valiese** (kay valyaysay), **que valieses, que valiese** etc., *that I might be valuable etc.* Fut. I. de Subj. **si valiere** (valyayray), **si valieres, si valiere** etc., *if I shall be valuable etc.*

Cond. I. de Subj. **si valiera** (see valyayra) **si valieras, si valiera** etc., *if I should be valuable etc.* Imperf. **¡Vale!** (valay), *be valuable* (familiar to one person). **¡Valga Vd.!** (valga oostayth), *be valuable* (formal to one person). **¡Valgamos!** (valgamoss), *let us be valuable!* **¡Valed!** (valayd), *be valuable* (familiar to several persons). **¡Valgan Vds.!** (valgan oostaythays) *be valuable* (formal to several persons). Gerund. **valiendo** (valyayndo), *being valuable.* Part. pas. **valido** (valeetho), *having been valuable.*

VER. **Ver** (vayr), *to see, to look.* Pres. de Indic. **veo** (vayo), **ves** (vays), **ve, vemos, véis, ven,** *I see, I am seeing etc.* Imperf. **veía** (vayeea), **veías, veía** etc. and Pret. perf. **vi** (vee), **viste, vió** (veeo), **vimos, visteis, vieron,** *I saw, I was seeing etc.* Fut. I. **veré** (vayray), **verás, verá** etc., *I shall see etc.* Cond. I. **vería** (vayreea), **verías, vería** etc., *I should see etc.* Pres. de Subj. **que vea** (vaya), **que veas, que vea, que veamos, que veáis, que vean,** *that I may see etc.* Imperf. de Subj. **que viese, que vieses, que viese** etc., *that I might see etc.* Fut. I. de Subj. **si viere** (vyayray), **si vieres, si viere** etc., *if I shall see etc.* Cond. I. de Subj. **si viera, si vieras, si viera** etc., *if I should see etc.* Imperat. **¡Ve!** (vay), *see* (familiar to one person). **¡Vea Vd.!** (vaya oostayth), *see* (formal to one person). **¡Veamos!** (vayamoss), *let us see!* **¡Ved!** (vayd), **see** (familiar to several persons). **¡Vean Vds.!** (vayan oostaythays), *see* (formal to several persons). Gerund. **viendo** (vyayndo), *seeing.* Part. pas. **visto** (veesto), *seen.*

DECIR. **decir** (daytheer), *to say.* Pres. de Indic. **digo** (deego), **dices** (deethays), **dice, decimos** (daytheemoss), **decís** (daythees), **dicen** (deethayn), *I say, I am saying etc.* Imperf. **decía** (daytheea), **decías, decía** etc. and Pret. perf. **dije** (deehay), **dijiste, dijo** (deeho), **dijimos, dijisteis, dijeron,** *I was saying, I said, etc.* Fut. I. **diré, dirás, dirá** etc., *I shall say etc.* Cond. I. **diría** (deereea), **dirías, diría** etc., *I should say etc.* Pres. de Subj. **que diga, que digas, que diga** etc., *that I may say etc.* Imperf. de Subj. **que dijese** (kay deehaysay), **que dijeses, que dijese, que dijésemos** (kay deehaysaymoss), **que dijeseis, que dijesen** (kay deehaysayn), *that I might say etc.* Fut. I. de Subj. **si dijere** (see deehayray), **si dijeres** (deehayrays), **si dijere, si dijéremos** (deehayraymoss), **si dijereis, si dijeren,** *if I shall say etc.* Cond.

UN "QUID PRO QUO"
oon keed pro ko
A "What for whom"

¿Quién ha colgado ahí, tan alto, el termómetro?
kyenng a kollgatho aee tann alto ell terrmomaytro
Who hung the thermometer so high?

Yo.
yo
I.

¿Y por qué?
ee porr kay
Why?

Porque ayer dijiste que estaba bajo.
porrkay a-yerr deeheestay kay esstava baho
Because yesterday you said that it was low.

I. de Subj. si dijera (deehayra), si dijeras, si dijera, si dijéramos, si dijerais, si dijeran, *if I should say etc.* Imperat. ¡Di! (dee), *say* (familiar to one person). ¡Diga Vd.! (deega oostayth), *say* (formal to one person). ¡Digamos! (deegamoss), *let us say!* ¡Decid! (daytheeth), *say* (familiar to several persons). ¡Digan Vds.! (deegan oostaythays), *say* (formal to several persons). Gerund. diciendo (deethyayndo), *saying*. Part. pas. dicho (deetsho), *said.*

¡Lea en alta voz!

Una cantante canta una canción. ¿La oyen Vds? La Paloma.
Aplausos frenéticos del público saludan a la cantante. Entonces
el telón sube. La representación empieza en la escena. El telón
baja. Un principio magnífico de la temporada de invierno. Vamos
a terminar nuestro informe. Esperamos que hayáis oido bien.
Aquí Madrid Compañia de radio Española.

Como en estos países tropicales los días son muy cálidos, aun
en invierno, nos accostamos bastante tarde. Antes de haber
alquilado nuestro cuarto, Maria decia: lo que más me importa
esque la cama sea buena. No me gusta un cuarto con dos camas.
Entonces tuvimos intención de accostarnos muy temprano.
Nuestros cuartos, uno, que da a la calle, otro que da al patio,
son bastante cómodos y muy bien amueblados. Tienen una
entrada independiente. Las ventanas son anchas y altas. Cuando
preguntamos a la casera ¿Cuánto vale? no podiamos decir: el
precio es demasiado alto para mí, para nos. No me gusta regatear.
En cado cuarto había una mesa grande y una mesa pequeña,
unas sillas, una cómoda, un espejo, un escritorio.

¿Dónde vive Vd? Y nos pudimos contestar solamente, que
estábamos muy contentos. Los patrones eran siempre muy
amables. Nos preguntaban todas las noches: ¿A qué hora se
levanta Vd?, para servirnos un almuerzo muy bueno. Generaí-
mente se come poco en los países del Sur. Almuerza bien, come
más, cena poco y vivirás. Quien mucho promete, poco cumple.
No prometio mucho, pero ella hizo mucho por nosotros. Ser
como el perico, que dice lo que sabe, pero no sabe, lo que dice.
¿Quién quiere a quién? La quiero mucho o la quiero mucho.

Viendo tantas palabras muy pequeñas de una lengua extranjera, nos desilusionamos siempre un poco. Estudiando se aprende.
Tenemos miedo. Le dice una vez: no uses palabras extranjeras,
no puedes nunca saber lo que significan. Como lo usamos en
inglés. Estamos paseando en el tranvía, en coche. Teniendo el
dinero, siempre tomaríamos un taxímetro. Sí, lo tomaríamos.
No teniendolo tomamos el tranvía que pasa cada cinco minutos.

El cobrador va diciendo siempre en cada parada: ¡Deje los

bajar! ¡Por favor suba Vd! ¡Cuidado! ¡Qué movimiento! ¡Sentámonos! El aprender estas reglas de movimiento es fácil. Sin preguntarnos nada el cobrador nos dió los billetes. Una dama vino a ayudarnos. Oíamos al cobrador diciendo cuando paso "¡Me hace Vd. el favor!" Le oíamos decirlo.

Dije a Maria, la dije: paga los billetes por mí, págalos por mí. Dámelos, porque quiero ocuparme leyendo todos los impresos para aprender el Español. ¿Puedo darle a Vd. el consejo de hacer lo mismo? ¡Maria, hazlo también! ¡Y Vd. señor López, hágalo Vd! ¡Hagámoslo! Haciéndolo vamos aprendiendo en todas partes.

El tranvía se para. Nos bajamos de tranvía. Allá está un vendedor de periódicos. Cómprame todas las ediciones de la noche y de la una de la mañana, Maria, comprámelos. Comprémelos Vd., haga el favor, señor López. Vd. sabe mejor lo que podemos leer.

Se los compro, se los compraré. Ahora voy a decir les, señoras y caballeros, lo que probablemente Vds. han observado hace much tiempo sin saber ninguna regla para ello. Se lo he dicho.

Vámonos al almacén "La Parisienne." Allí se ven siempre los ultimos modelos. Mi amiga me lo ha recomendado. Entran en la tienda. A ver un vestido para mí. ¿De qué color lo desea Vd., señora? ¡Color café marrón! Del color que se lleva ahora mucho. Aquí le traígo a Vd. unos vestidos muy elegantes. Le ruego a Vd. de verlos. ¿En qué puedo servirle a Vd?

El marido: ¡Pruébatelos! ¡Anda! ¿Te gusta ese? A mí no. Yo prefiero los vestidos sencillos. ¡Hágame el favor de mostrame otros! Esos no nos gustan ni a mi marido ni a mí. Ahí veo dos de seda muy bonitos. ¿Por qué no nos los enseña Vd? Voy a traerselos.

¡Mira, ese vestido me parece el mas bonito! ¿Y a tí? A mí también. Me lo pondré en seguida. Voy a probarmelo. Sí, señora, ciertamente este vestido le sienta a Vd. muy bien. ¿Cuanto vale? El precio era quinientas pesetas, hoy vamos a darselo por doscientas cincuenta pesetas. Es demasiado. Lo tomaré por 175 pesetas. Muy bien, envíemelo a mi casa. ¡Adíos! ¡Qué Vd. lo pase bien!

Translate into Spanish

The street car stops! We get off the street car. There is a man selling papers. Buy me the night editions and one of the morning papers, buy them for me, Mary! Mr. López, buy them for me, if you please! You know better what we are able to read.

I shall buy them for you. Now I am going to tell you, ladies and gentlemen, what you probably have already noticed a long time ago even without knowing any rule for it. I (have) told him so, I (have) told her so (it).

Let us go to the department store, "La Parisienne." Here we always see the latest models. My friend recommended it to me. You enter the store. To see a dress for me. What color do you want madame? Coffee-brown. The color that is so much worn now. Here are some very fashionable dresses. I ask you to look at them. What can I do for you?

The husband: try them on (to you). Go ahead! Do you like this one? Not for me. I prefer the simple dresses. Show me others, if you please! These don't please us, neither my husband nor me. Here I see two very nice silk ones. Why don't you show them to us? I am going to bring them to you. I'll get them for you.

Look, this dress seems to me the nicest one! And to you? To me too. I shall put it on (to me) at once. I'll try it on (I go to try me it). Yes, madame, surely this dress suits you very well. How much is it? The price was 500 pesetas. Today we will give it to you for 250 pesetas. It is too much. I'll take it for 175 pesetas. All right, send it (me) to my house! Good bye! Good luck to you!

A great Spanish poet, Tomas de Iriarte, who died almost 150 years ago, once said: We all are sons of Adam and Eve, but what makes us different is the wool and the silk. Although what Iriarte said may be true, the world is, nevertheless, full of hatred. It seems to be a great deal, if one can only say: I have a friend of whom I can say that he really is a friend. A friend in need, a friend indeed. As they see you, so shall they treat you. I hear you say: I doubt that this is true.

Peter is my best friend, he is my intimate friend. I would do anything for him. And I am convinced that he would do what he could for me. I detest him; he is hated by everyone; I always wish he would go. I do not like that man; I would never have believed it. Who would have believed it?

But, after all, I don't believe that the Spanish proverb which says that "to know how to live in this world is the greatest heroism" is correct. About that. If only I had answered his letter on time, it would have been much better. We would have written a letter, if we had known that his father was sick.

Let us go to a stationery store, where we get all the stationery we need. We buy writing paper, cards, a penholder, pens, ink, an inkstand and blotting paper. Today we will make it a day for correspondence.

¡Haga el favor de repetir!

se alquila habitación amueblada	say alkeela aveetathyong amooayvlatha	*furnished room for rent*
se alquila habitación sin amueblar	say alkeela aveetathyong seen amooayblar	*unfurnished rooms to let (without furnishing)*
se prohibe fumar	say proeevay foomar	*it is forbidden to smoke*
se prohibe la entrada	say proeevay la enntratha	*it is forbidden to enter, no admittance!*
se suplica cerrar la puerta	say soopleeka therrar la pooerrta	*it is requested to close the door, please close the door!*
se suplica no tocar	say soopleeka no tokkar	*it is requested not to touch, don't touch please!*
estaría Vd. en un error	aystareea oostayth enn oon error	*you would be wrong*
tienen razón	teeaynenn rathong	*they are right*
nosotros tenemos razón	nosotross taynaymoss rathong	*we are right*
hablaría	avlareea	*I should speak*
mandarías	manndareeas	*you would send*
vendería	venndayreea	*he would sell*
compraríamos	kommprareeamoss	*we should buy*
viviríais	veeveereeaees	*you would live*
comprenderían	kommprenndayreean	*they would understand*
este modo cortés	esstay motho korrtays	*this polite way*
es muy fácil	ayz mooy fatheel	*it is very easy*
sin duda	seen dootha	*without doubt*
enfrente de Vd.	ennfrenntay day oostayth	*before you*
el otro día	ell otro theea	*the other day*
querría ver	kerreea vayr	*I would like to see*
la corrida	la korreetha	*the bull fight*
no lo he olvidado	no lo ay ollveethatho	*I haven't forgotten*
yo cumpliré mi promesa	yo koompleeray mee promaisa	*I shall keep my promise*

vosotros todos seréis convidados por me	vosotross tothoss sayrayees konnveethathos porr may	*you will be invited by me*
¿a qué hora?	a kay ora	*at what time?*
no se olvida	no say ollveeda	*one doesn't forget*
la corrida de caballos	la korreetha thay kaballyoss	*the horse race*
¿Le gusta a Vd. más?	le goosta a oostayth mas	*do you like better*
billete para una corrida de toros	beellyaytay para oona korreetha day toross	*ticket for a bull-baiting*
sol y sombra	sol ee sommbra	*sun and shadow*
delantera	daylanntayra	*front seat*
¿Tengo razón?	tayngo rathong	*Am I right?*
¿Me equivoco?	may aykeevoko	*Am I wrong?*
mil novecientos treinta y nueve	meel novaythyenntoss trayeenta ee nooayvay	*1939*
los buenos tiempos de antaño	loz booaynoss tyaympoz thay anntangyo	*the good old times*
estaríamos en un error	aystareeamoss enn oon error	*we would be wrong*
no podemos olvidar	no podaymoss ollveethar	*we cannot forget*
al mismo tiempo	al meezmo tyaympo	*in the same time*
alguna vez y al mismo tiempo	algoona vayth ee al meesmo tyaympo	*at one and the same time*
en alguna parte	enn algoona partay	*in some part*
las bendiciones de la paz	laz venaydeethyonayz thay la path	*the blessings of peace*
con respecto	konn rayspaykto	*with regard*
debemos decir	daybaymoz thaytheer	*we must say, we must realize*
casi todo el mondo	kasee totho ell moondo	*almost everyone*
buenos días	booaynoz theeas	*good days*
buenas horas	booaynas oras	*good hours*
no importa cuán	no eemporrta quann	*no matter how*
¡volvamos!	vollvamoss	*let us return!*
La primavera empieza	la preemavayra aympyaytha	*Spring begins*
el verano empieza el veintiuno de junio	ell vayrano emmpyaytha ell vayeentyoono day hoongyo	*summer begins on the 21st of June*

ha visto	a veesto	*you have seen*
el primero de Junio	ell preemayro thay hoongyo	*June first*
la lección segunda	la lekkthyonng saygoonda	*the second lesson*
el capítulo tercero	ell kapeetoolo tayrthayro	*the third chapter*
la página novena	la paheena novayna	*the ninth page*
capítulo quince	kapeetoolo keenthay	*the fifteenth chapter*
Carlos V (quinto)	karloss keento	*Charles V or Charles the Fifth*
rey de España	rayee thay esspangya	*king of Spain*
el emperador	ell aympayrathor	*the emperor*
emperador de Alemaña	aympayrathor thay Alaymangya	*emperor of Germany*
el fundador	ell foondathor	*the founder*
el fundador del Escorial	ell foondathor thell ayskoryal	*the founder of the Escorial*
la octava maravilla del mundo	la okktava maraveellya dell moondo	*the eighth wonder of the world*
a pesar de eso	a paysar thay ayso	*in spite of that*
el palacio	ell palathyo	*the palace*
la colección	la kollekthyonn	*the collection*
la colección de cuadros	la kollekthyonn day quathross	*the collection of paintings*
la biblioteca	la beevleeotayka	*the library*
la biblioteca grande	la beevleeotayka granday	*the large library*
el rey último	ell rayy oolteemo	*the last king*
Louis XVI (dieciséis)	looees dyaytheesayees	*Louis XVIth (Louis XVI)*
la revolución francesa	la rayvoloothyong franthaysa	*the French Revolution*
no puede imaginar	no pooaythay eemaheenar	*you cannot imagine*
la Edad Media	la aythath maythya	*the Middle Ages*
me es igual	may ays eegval	*it is all the same to me*
¿Cuándo nació Vd.?	qvando nathyo oostayth	*When were you born?*
Yo nací el nueve de noviembre	yo nathee ell nooayvay thay novyemmbray	*I was born the ninth of November*
es entonces cuando	ays enntonthays kvando	*that is when*
mi cumpleaños	mee koomplayangyoss	*my birthday*

¿Cuándo es su cumpleaños?	kvando ays soo koomplayangyoss	*When is your birthday?*
el reclamo	ell rayklamo	*the advertisement*
el joyero	ell hoyayro	*the jeweler*
si está Vd. enamorado	see aysta ennamorado	*if you are in love*
el más preciado tesoro	ell mas praithyado taysoro	*the most precious treasure*
estábamos cansados	aystabamoss kansadoss	*we were tired*
no deseábamos nada más	no daysayavamoz natha mas	*we wanted nothing but*
un poco de tiempo	oon poko thay tyaympo	*a little while*
estaba en mi cuarto	aystava enn mee kvarto	*it was in my room*
oí tocar a la puerta	oee tokkar a la pooerrta	*I heard him knocking at the door*
¡Entre!	ayntray	*Come in!*
abierto, a	avyerrto, a	*open*
con Vd.	konn oostayth	*with you*
entonces	ayntonthays	*then*
¿Qué hay de nuevo?	kay ay day nooayvo	*what's the news?*
en el diario	enn ell deearyo	*in the newspaper*
un hombre notable	oon ommbray notablay	*a remarkable man*
la profesión	la profaysyong	*the profession*
el escritor	ell ayskreetor	*the writer*
el pintor	ell peentor	*the painter*
el educador	ell aythookathor	*the educator*
el atleta	ell atlayta	*the athlete*
además	athaymas	*moreover*
el tiempo que pasó	ell tyaympo kay paso	*time that has passed*
no vuelve otra vez	no vooaylvay otra vayth	*doesn't return*
letra de Ivan Díez	laytra daí eevan deeaíth	*words by Ivan Díez*
la música	la mooseeka	*the music*
¡Dios mío!	dyoss meeo	*My God! (my goodness!)*
era abogado	eyra avogado	*he was a lawyer*
la modista	la motheesta	*the dressmaker*
el sastre	ell sastray	*the tailor*
la sombrerera	la sommbrayrayra	*the milliner*
el óptico	ell oppteeko	*the optician*
los anteojos	loss antayohoss	*the eyeglasses*
el relojero	ell raylohayro	*the watchmaker*

(Caption on Top of Next Page.)

Cuando un burro trajo las frutas	y una
kvando oon boorro traho las frootas	ee oona
If a donkey carries the fruit	*and a*

muchacha simpática	va a comprar los melones,
moochacha seempateeka	va a kommprar los maylonays
pretty girl	*comes to buy melons,*

le digo que es una buena profesión
lay deego kay ess oona booayna profaysyong
I tell her it is a fine job

el ser	un vendedor de frutas.
ell sayr	oon vayndaydor day frootas.
to be	*a fruit-vendor.*

Lesson Thirty-Eight

We are all looking forward to spending an evening with Paul.
We are sure his dinner will turn out to be one of the nicest we
have ever had. We shall make it a *"Spanish night," "*noche
española*"* (nochay esspangyola). It is agreed among us that no
word of English will be spoken. Of course, the subjects of our
talk will be limited to Paul's invitation, the pamphlet on "El
Paraíso" and the bill of fare.

So we will study hard during the few days we have left before
the party. We don't want to have to say later on, "*If I had only
known a few more words, I might have expressed myself much
better,*" "Si hubiese sabido unas palabras más, me habría ex-
presado mucho mejor" (see oobyaysay saveetho oonas palavras
mas may avreea expraysatho moocho mayhor).

Si yo hubiera or hubiese (oobyayra, oobyaysay)   *if I had*

si yo hubiera	or hubiese	*if I had*
si tú hubieras	or hubieses	*if you had*
si él ella hubiera Vd.	or hubiese	*if he, she, you had*

si nosotros hubiéramos	or	hubiésemos	*if we had*
si vosotros hubiérais	or	hubiéseis	*if you had*
si ellos			
ellas hubieran	or	hubiesen	*if they, you had*
Vds.			

*

si yo	fuera	or	fuese	*if I were, etc.*
si tú	fueras	or	fueses	
si él				
ella	fuera	or	fuese	
Vd.				
si nosotros	fuéramos	or	fuésemos	
si vosotros	fuérais	or	fuéseis	
si ellos				
ellas	fueran	or	fuesen	
Vds.				

*

si yo	estuviera	or	estuviese	*if I were, etc.*
si tú	estuvieras	or	estuvieses	
si él				
ella	estuviera	or	estuviese	
Vd.				
si vosotros	estuviéramos	or	estuviésemos	
si vosotros	estuviérais	or	estuviéseis	
si ellos				
ellas	estuvieran	or	estuviesen	
Vds.				

*

si yo	tuviera	or	tuviese	*if I had, etc.*
si tú	tuvieras	or	tuvieses	
si él				
ella	tuviera	or	tuviese	
Vd.				
si nosotros	tuviéramos	or	tuviésemos	
si vosotros	tuviérais	or	tuviéseis	
si ellos				
ellas	tuvieran	or	tuviesen	
Vds.				

Si hubiese tenido dinero, hoy sería un hombre muy rico (or **estaría rico**) *If I had had money, I would have been a rich man.* (*I would be rich*). But let us say good-bye to the "if" people! They are always talking about the things they could have done if . . . And there was always a reason why they could not do them.

*

It is seldom that anything is handed to us on a platter. Usually we must try very hard to get it, and the best way to try is by working, sometimes by working very hard. Sad though it may be, if we wish to speak correctly, we must work hard to learn the irregular verbs (see pages 183, 184, 185, 241, 242, 243).

Usually before he enters a room, the Spaniard says: ¿Se puede pasar? or ¿Hay permiso?—*May I (one) pass? Is it permitted?* (*May I come in?*)

Don't blame me, **no me culpe** (no may koolpay), for these two classes of Spanish verbs. There is even another class of half-regular verbs. I had a teacher once who said to one of the students, "As far back as the time of ancient Rome many different classes of verbs were invented. What good did they do you? You, my dear boy, were too lazy to learn the regular verbs; you are too lazy to learn irregular ones, and you will even be too *lazy*, **perezoso** (payraythoso) to learn the half-regulars." This *youth*, **joven** (hovayn) later on became one of the best Spanish commercial interpreters.

Let us begin, **comencemos** (komennthaymoss), with the verb, *to begin,* **comenzar** (komennthar), which is one of those *half-regular verbs* of which we spoke. It is just a little irregular and even then in only a few forms.

comienzo komyenntho	*I begin*		**comience** komyennthay	*I may begin*
comienzas	*you begin*		**comiences**	*you may begin*
comienza	*he begins*		**comience**	*he may begin*
comienzan	*they begin*		**comiencen**	*they may begin*

¡comienza!	*you (fam.) (sing.) begin!*
¡comience Vd.!	*you (sing.) begin!*
¡comiencen Vds.!	*you (pl.) begin!*

All other forms are regular, e.g., **comenzamos** (komenntha-moss) we begin; **comenzáis** (komennthaees) *you begin.* Don't be disturbed by the change of **z** to **c**. It is done only to keep the same pronunciation, for **c** preceding ˜**e** and **i** = th and **z** preceding **a, o, u** = th. *Z is seldom followed by* **e** *or* **i**.

The only irregularity is the inserted **i** in the forms first listed and that is inserted in many verbs when there is an **e** in the *syllable before the verb-ending*.

Take, *for instance*, **por ejemplo** (porr ayhemmplo), *to guess right* **acertar** (atherrtar). *I guess right* **acierto** (athyerrto); *guess right* **¡acierte Vd.!** (athyerrtay oostayth). *To awake* is **despertar** (dessperrtar). **Vd. despierta** (oostayth thesspyerrta) *you awake; that he or she may awake*, **que despierte** (thesspyerrtay). To *freeze*, **helar** (aylar); *they freeze*, **hielan** (eeaylan). *To deny*, **negar** (naygar); *you deny*, **niegas** (nyaygas, familiar form). *To think*, **pensar** (paynsar); *I think*,

In a restaurant, people very often ask for a kind of buttered toast, **tostadas**, with their coffee, or half-toasted rolls **media tostada**.

Los garbanzos (chickpeas) are a national dish, which is served almost every day.

pienso (pyennso). *To sit*, **sentar** (senntar); *sit down*, **siéntese Vd.** (syenntaysay oostayth). And so on. It is the same with **errar** (errar) *to err*, only the irregular forms are written **yerro** (yerro) *I err*; **¡No yerre Vd.!** (no yerray oostayth) *don't err!* **¿No yerra Vd.?** (no yerra oostayth) *don't you err?*

Did you understand? **¿Ha entendido Vd.?** (a enntenndeetho oostayth). *I understand*, **entiendo** (enntyenndo); *I may understand*, **entienda** (enntyennda); **¡Qué me entienda Vd.!** (kay may enntyennda oostayth). *Understand me! Don't lose your patience!* **¡No pierda Vd. la paciencia!** (no pyerrda oostayth la pathyennthya). *To understand*, **entender** (enntennderr); *to lose* **perder** (perrderr). *I have lost the key to my room*, **he perdido la llave de mi cuarto** (ay perrtheetho la llyavay thay mee kvarto). *I lose almost everything (all things)*, **yo pierdo casi todas las cosas** (yo pyerrtho kasee tothas las cosas).

Some verbs which have an **o** in the same forms as are mentioned above, in the *syllable before the ending*, use a **ue** instead of this **o**. *To extract, to ask*, is **rogar** (rogar); *I ask*, **ruego**, but **rogamos** (roghamoss) *we ask*; **ruegue** (rooaygay) *I may ask*; **¡Ruegue Vd.!** (rooaygay oostayth) *Ask!;* **ruegan** (rooayghan) *they ask.* You see, in order to keep the **g** hard, as in the word **gift**, a **u** is inserted before the **e**. If that weren't done, it would be pronounced incorrectly, for, as you know, **ge** and **gi** are pronounced **hay** and **hee**.

To agree, **accordar** (akkorrthar) has an **o** in the syllable before the ending; therefore it is **acuerdo** (akverrtho) *I agree. Do you agree?* **¿Acuerda Vd.?** (akverrtha oostayth).

To lie down, **acostar** (akosstar); *we go to bed*, **nos acostamos** (nossakosstamoss) regular; *go to bed!* **¡Acuéstese!** (akvesstaysay). *To eat breakfast*, **almorzar** (almorrthar); *they may eat breakfast*, **qué almuercen** (almooerrthenn); *we eat breakfast*, **almorzamos** (almorrthamoss); *I eat breakfast*, **almuerzo** (almooerrtho).

To count, **contar** (konntar); **cuento** (kvennto) *I count*; *Count!* **¡cuenta!** (kvennta). *Count to 33!* **¡Cuente Vd. hasta treinta y tres** (kvenntay oostayth asta trayeenta ee tress). *To cost* **costar** (kostar); *how much is it?* **¿Cuanto cuesta?** (kvanto kvessta); *it costs*, **cuesta** (kvessta).

To meet, **encontrar** (ennkonntrar); *I meet*, **encuentro** (ennkvenntro); *I have met, I met*, **he encontrado** (ay ennkonntratho). *To show*, **mostrar** (mosstrar); *show me the museum!* **¡Muestreme el museo!** (mooesstraymay ell moosayo); *we shall show her the pictures*, **le mostraremos los cuadros** (lay mosstraraymoss loss kvathross). *To dream*, **soñar** (songyar); **sueño** (sooayngyo) *I dream*; *we dream*, **soñamos** (songyamoss); *I would dream*, **soñaría** (songyareea).

To return, **volver** (vollverr); *I return*, **vuelvo** (vooellvo); **vuelvan** (vooellvan) *they may return*; *I returned*, **volví** (vollvee); *return at once!* **¡Vuelva Vd. en seguida!** (vooellva oostayth enn saygheetha); *we return*, **volvemos** (vollvaymoss); *let us return!* **¡Volvamos!** (vollvamoss); *if I should return home I would meet you*, **si volviese a casa le encontraría a Vd.** (see vollvyaysay a kasa lay ennkonntrareea a oostayth).

To hurt, ache, pair **doler** (dolerr); *it hurts me*, **me duele** (may dooaylay). *To rain*, **llover** (llyoverr); *it rains*, **llueve** (llyooayvay). *To move*, **mover** (moverr); *everything is (all things are) moving;* **to as las cosas se mueven** (tothas las kosas say mooayvenn). *Move a little!* **¡Muévase un poco!** (mooayvasay oon poko).

To play, **jugar** (hooghar); *I play*, **juego** (hooaygho); *the children are playing*, **los niños juegan** (loss neengyoss hooayghan); *we may play as long as we feel young*, **juguemos mientras nos sinta-**

Soy demasiado vieja para jugar con la bola,
soy daymasyado vyayha para hoogar konn la bola
I am too old to play ball,

especialmente
esspaythyalmenntay
especially

(Continued on Top of Next Page.)

* 231 *

con un muchacho tan pequeño   come tú.
konn oon moochacho tan paykayngyo   komay too.
with a little boy   *like you.*

Es imposible. Debes entender.
ess eemposeeblay, daybays entayndayr
No, it is no use.   You must see that.

---

mos jóvenes (hooghaymoss myenntras noss seentamoss hovaynays).

The same thing happens also with verbs ending in **-entir, -erir** and **-ertir**. *To feel,* **sentir** (sennteer); **siento** (syennto) *I feel, I am sorry. To amuse,* **divertir** (deeverrteer); *I amuse myself,* **me divierto** (may deevyerrto); *enjoy yourself!* **¡Diviértase¡** (deevyerrtasay). The regular form is **sentimos** (sennteemoss) *we feel;* **sentís** (senntees) *you feel* (plur. fam.). But, **sintamos** (seentamoss) *we may feel;* **sintáis** (seentaees) *you may feel;* **sientan** (syenntan) *they may feel;* **sienten** (syenntenn) *they feel.*

I know perfectly well that it will be a long time before you master all the irregularities in the Spanish language. But I had to show them to you, because if you didn't know that they existed, you would never know from what words these irregular

Our *jazz-band* is called **banda.**
The given name preceded by **Don** is used more often in Spanish than the last name.

forms are derived, and in that case you would not know how to locate them in the dictionary. Now, if you see in a paper the words **siento,** or **recuerdo,** you will know that they come from **sentir** *to feel* and **recordar** *to remind.* We needn't say anything right now about the completely irregular verbs, for those are listed in a special section.

Lesson Thirty-Nine

Prepared as well as we are, we go to the farewell dinner. The time has passed quickly. Today is the ninth of December, the day on which Mr. Paul Diez requested the pleasure of our company.

Bien preparados como estamos, vamos a la fiesta de desperdida. El tiempo pasa rapidamente. Hoy es el nueve de Deiciembre cuando Don Pablo Diez nos invito.

All of us, the ladies, the gentlemen, the girls and the boys, carried flowers, red roses, blue violets, yellow tulips, dahlias of different kinds and colors, lilies, carnations and orchids. The dinner table was decorated with bunches of daisies and, as a symbol, forget-me-nots.

Todos nosotros, las señoras, los señores, las muchachas y los muchachos, llevamos flores, rosas rojas, violetas azules, tulipanes, amarillos, dalias de varias clases y colores, lirios, claveles, orquídeas. La mesa estaba decorada con muchas margaritas y como símbolo con no-me-olvides.

Era una noche deliciosa. Al hablar solo español cometimos muchos
ayra oona nochay dayleethyosa al avlar esspangyol komaytee-
moss moochoss
It was a delightful evening. In trying to speak only Spanish, we certainly made many

errores. Algunos fueron corregidos por nuestros amigos
erroress. algoonoss fooayron korrayheethoss porr nooesstross
ameeghoss
Mistakes. Some of them were corrected by our Spanish friends

españoles que estaban con nosotros. Sin embargo nos entendimos
esspangyoless kay esstavan konn nosotross. seen emmbargho
noss enntenndeemoss
who were with us. However, we understood each other.

bien. Y luego nos paseamos por el jardin. Allí sobre una terraza
byaing ee looaygho noss pasayamoss porr ell hartheen allyee
sobray oona terratha
And later on we walked through the garden. There, on a terrace

al aire libre vimos una bailarina española con su pareja
al aeeray leevray veemoss oona vaeelareena aispanyola konn
    soo paraiho
in the fresh air, we watched a Spanish dancer and her partner

y vimos los maravillosos bailes de la tarantella y el bolero y
ee veemoss loss maraveellyososs baeeless day la tarantaylya ee
    ell bolayro ee
and we saw the wonderful dances, the tarantella and the bolero, and

luego un tango moderno y una rumba. No habíamos visto nunca
looaygho oon tango moderrno ee oona roomba. no aveeamoz
    veesto noonka
then a modern tango and a rumba. We had never seen dancing

bailar así, contanto encanto y gracia. Entonces comenzamos
baeelar asee kontanto ennkanto ee grathya. enntonnthess
    komennthamoss
like that before, with so much charm and grace. Then we started

a bailar nosotros también. En realidad era delicioso.
a baeelar nosotross tambyenng. enn rayaleethath ayra thaylee-
    thyoso
to dance ourselves. It was really very enjoyable.

Le diré que era muy tarde o mejor dicho era ya muy temprano.
lay theeray kay ayra mooy tarthay o mayhor theecho ayra ya
    mooy temmprano
*I'll tell you; it was very late, or, to be correct, it was already very
early in the morning.*

We took leave of each other and promised to meet again. This
opportunity to learn the Spanish language will be of lasting value
to us and will always give us pleasure, enjoyment and practical
advantages.

*   *

*

We have come to the end. I know that it has been quite impossible, within the limits I had to observe, to give you a complete
and perfect picture of the Spanish language. This is not a system,
not a "method." There is no patent medicine for getting to know
a language in one dose. What I have attempted to do has been
to teach with a smile and, at the same time, in earnest. If you
have smiled at times, then I am sure you will not be too severe

a judge if there were some things which you would have liked to know and I did not tell you.

I should be satisfied, therefore, if I have succeeded in my simple intention to give you an introduction to the Spanish idiom without overtaxing your energy and patience. And I know that your interest has been rewarded by the knowledge of something that is worthwhile and which will give you ever-renewed pleasure.

Translate into Spanish

Paul tells us that he will travel very soon to Argentina. Mr. Alfonso has given him a good address, and he is going to write the following letter. If we were writing to a lady, we wouldn't forget that it is polite to address the letter to Mrs. Dona Teresa Gomez.

We are all also writing some letters, some cards and some picture-postcards. Where is the nearest post office? How much is the postage to foreign countries? 25 centimos for every 20 grams. Money can be sent as a money order. There you would ask: is there a letter for me? You write it on the envelope. At the window of the post office. Certainly you can send a telegram to any point in the world.

Stamps are also sold in the "estancos" (tobacco stores). There is a letter box in all monopoly stores. Do you like to smoke a cigar? Or do you prefer cigarettes? I don't smoke, but my cousin smokes a pipe if his mother, my aunt, doesn't see him. She doesn't like the smell of cigars or cigarettes or pipes. However, when my aunt returned from Havana, she brought for my uncle and my cousin a box of the finest imported cigars as a present and she is very proud that she was able to pass the custom officers without paying any duty. It is a funny thing that even the richest people like to do a little smuggling and to be a little of a smuggler.

Have you anything to declare? I have nothing to declare. Open your trunk, please! Have you any cigars? Some for my personal use. There are only used goods. How glad everyone is when the custom officer says: you can close the trunk!

In this city we want to stay only for a short time. Our first impression is that the weather is fine, and we don't care what it will be tomorrow. Perhaps tomorrow the weather will be bad. it rains, it will rain. It was good weather. Many years ago. The sun is shining. The moon will be shining. We must say no. It is the same in Spanish and in English. Answer at once! Have the kindness of being polite!

Perhaps I am disturbing you? With whom have I the honor of speaking? Please introduce me to this gentleman. Permit me to introduce you to Mrs. Elvira. Very glad to meet you! Here is my card. It is very nice of you. It is always best to be very polite.

Are you tired, Alphonso? And you, Juanita, are you tired too? Let us go to the hotel! We will stay only a few days in this city before we go home. We shall spend the last money we have. It is a first class hotel. The traveling salesmen reside in a simple hotel. The manager of the hotel receives us and the usual conversation begins. Can you give us three small rooms? Yes, sir, we have three free ones. What is the price? How much is this room by the day or by the week? No cheaper one? How long do you plan to stay here? About a week. Can't you make it any cheaper? Well, we will take the rooms. When are the meals served? Do you want anything else, sir? Call me tomorrow morning at eight o'clock! Very well, ladies and gentlemen, what would you, like for breakfast? Coffee with milk, butter, fried eggs, scrambled eggs, rolls and horns, jam and marmalade.

Our friend Paul wrote a letter to Argentina two weeks ago. Today the answer was received. Paul opened the letter; he saw at once that the letter came from Argentina. He put it in his pocket to show to us. Now we shall read that letter.

¡Lea en alta voz!

Un gran poeta español, Tomasi de Iriarte, que murió hace casi ciento cincuenta años dijo: Todos somos hijos de Adán y Eva, sino que nos diferencia la lana y la seda. Aun que Iriarte haya dicho la verdad, el mundo de los hombres está lleno de enemistades. Ya parece mucho, si alguno pudiera decir: tengo un amigo de quién puedo decir que es un amigo verdadero. Amigo en la adversidad amigo de realidad. "Como te ven asi te tratan." Le oígo a Vd. decir: dudo que eso sea la verdad.

Piedro es mi mejor amigo, es mi amigo intimo. Haría cuanto pudiese por él. Y estoy conveincido de que el haría cuanto pudiese por mí. Le detesto. Todo el mundo le aborrece. Me alegraría que se fuera. Ese hombre no me gusta. No lo hubiera creído. ¿Quién lo hubiera creído?

Mas al fin y al cabo, no creo que el proverbio español "Saber vivir en este mundo es la mejor hazaña" tenga razón. Acerca de ello. Si hubiese contestado su carta, sería mucho mejor. Hubiesemos escrito una carta, si hubieramos sabido que su padre estaba enfermo.

Vamos a un papelero donde hay todos los útiles de escritorio que queremos. Compramos papel de carta, tarjetas, un portaplumas, las plumas, la tinta, un tintero, el papel secante. Hoy lo haremos el día de correspondencia.

Pablo nos dijo que viajerá por la Argentina lo más pronto posible. Señor Alfonso le ha dado una dirección buena y va a escribir la carta siguiente. Si escribiríamos a una señora, no olvidaríamos que es cortés de dirigir una carta a la señora Doña Teresa Gomez.

Nosotros todos escribimos también unas cartas, unas tarjetas y unas tarjetas ilustradas. ¿Dónde está la proxima oficina de correos? ¿Cuánto es el porte para países extranjeros? 25 centimos por cada 20 gramos. Dinero se envia por una libranza de correos. Allá Vd. preguntaría: ¿hay carta para mí? Lo escribirá en el sobre. En la ventanilla de la oficina de correos. Seguramente puede enviar un telegrama a cualquién punto del mundo.

Los sellos se venden también en los estancos. Hay un buzón en todos los estancos. ¿Quiere Vd. fumar un puro? ¿O prefiere Vd. los cigarillos? Yo no fumo, pero mi primo fuma en pipa, si su madre, mi tía, no lo ve. No le gusta el olor del tobacco ni de los cigarillos ni de la pipa. Como quiera que sea, cuando mi tía volvió de la Habana, trajo a mi tío y a mi primo una caja de los mejores cigarros impotados para regalarles y ella está muy orgullosa de pasar los aduaneros sin pagar los derechos. Es cómico que aun la gente más rica quiere un poco el contrabando y de ser un pequeño contrabandista.

¿Tiene Vd. algo que declarar? ¡No tengo nada que declarar! ¡Abra Vd. su baúl! ¿Trae Vd. cigarros? Unos de mi uso particular. Hay solamente efectos usados. ¡Qué alegres están todos cuando el aduanero dice: ¡Puede Vd. cerrar el baúl!

En esta ciudad queremos estar solamente poco tiempo. Nuestra primera impresión es que el tiempo es bueno, y no nos importa como será mañana. Quiza hará mal tiempo mañana. Llueve, lloverá. Hizo buen tiempo. Hace muchos años. Hace sol. Hará luna. Debemos decir que no. Es lo mismo en español que en inglés. Responda Vd. en seguida. Sea siempre cortés.

¿Quiza le molesto? ¿A quién tengo el honor de hablar? Haga Vd. el favor de presentarme al caballero. Permítame Vd. que le presente a la Señora Doña Elvira. ¡Mucho gusto en conocerla! Tome Vd. mi tarjeta. ¡Es Vd. muy amable! Es siempre mejor el ser muy cortés.

¿Está Vd. cansado, Alfonso? Y tu también, Juanita, estas cansada? ¡Vámonos al hotel! Queremos quedarnos solamente unos días en esta ciudad antes regressar a casa. Gastaremos el último dinero que tenemos. Es un hotel de primera clase. Los viajantes se alojan en una fonda. El gerente del hotel nos recibe y la conversación usual comienza. ¿Puede Vd. darnos tres cuartos pequeños? Sí, señor, tenemos tres no occupados. ¿Cuánto cuesta esto cuarto por una noche o a la semana? No tiene Vd. un cuarto más barato? ¿Cuanto tiempo piensa Vd. estar aquí? Como una semana. ¿No puede Vd. rebajar nada del precio? Bueno, nos quedaremos en los cuartos. ¿A que hora se come? ¿Desea Vd. algo más, señor? ¡Llámeme Vd. a las ocho de la mañana! Muy bien. Que deserían Vds., señoras y caballeros, para el desayuno? Café con leche, mantequilla, huevos fritos o estrellados, huevos revueltos.

Nuestro amigo Pablo había escrito una carta a La Argentina hace dos semanas. Hoy fué recibida la respuesta. Pablo ha abierto la carta; ha visto en seguida que la carta viene de La Argentina. La ha puesto en su bolsillo para mostrarnos. Ahora queremos leer aquella carta.

¡ASI SE COMPRA!

¿Cuanto valen esas camisetas?
kvanto valenn essas kameesaytas
How much are (worth) these short shirts (with wide sleeves)?

Un duro—
oon dooro
One duro (Spanish copper coin)

¿Y estos calcetines?
ee esstoss kalthayteenays
And these socks?

Lo mismo.
lo meesmo
The same (price).

Bueno, pues me llevo las camisetas.
booayno pooess may lyayvo las kameesaytas
Good, then I'(ll) take (I carry away) the short shirts.

Venga el duro.
vennga ell dooro
Come on, the Duro (with the money)

No, hombre, para eso le dejo a Vd. los calcetines.
no ommbray para esso lay dayho a oostayth loss kalthayteenays
No, sir (man), for that I am leaving (to) you the socks

Es que no me los ha pagado Vd.
ess kay no may loss a pagatho oostayth
But you have not paid me for them.

Es que tampoco me los llevo.
ess kay tammpoko may loss lyayvo.
I didn't take them either, did I?

* 240 *

VERBOS IRREGULARES

DORMIR. **Dormir** (dorrmeer), *to sleep.* Pres. de Indic. **duermo** (dooerrmo), **duermes, duerme, dormimos** (dorrmeemoss), **dormís** (dorrmees), **duermen** (dooerrmayn), *I sleep, I am sleeping etc.* Imperf. **dormía** (dorrmeea), **dormías, dormía** etc. and Pret. perf. **dormí** (dorrmee), **dormiste** (dorrmeestay), **durmió** (doormyo), **dormimos** (dorrmeemoss), **dormisteis, durmieron** (doorrmyayron), *I was sleeping, I slept etc.* Fut. I. **dormiré** (dorrmeeray), **dormirás, dormirá** etc., *I shall sleep etc.* Cond. I. **dormiría** (dorrmeereea), **dormirías, dormiría** etc., *I should sleep etc.* Pres. de Subj. que **duerma** (kay dooerrma), que **duermas,** que **duerma,** que **durmamos** (kay doorrmamoss), que **durmáis,** que **duerman,** *that I may sleep etc.* Imperf. de Subj. que **durmiese** (kay doorrmaysay), que **durmieses,** que **durmiese** etc., *that I might sleep etc.* Fut. I. de Subj. si **durmiere** (see doorrmyayray), si **durmieres,** si **durmiere** etc., *if I shall sleep etc.* Cond. I. de Subj. si **durmiera,** si **durmieras,** si **durmiera** etc., *if I should sleep etc.* Imperat. **¡Duerme!** (dooerrmay), *sleep* (familiar to one person). **¡Duerma Vd.!** (dooerrma oostayth), *sleep* (formal to one person). **¡Duramamos!** (doorrmamoss), *let us sleep!* **¡Dormid!** (dorrmeed), *sleep* (familiar to several persons). **¡Duerman Vds.!** (dooerrman oostaythays), *sleep* (formal to several persons). Gerund. **durmiendo** (doorrmyayndo), *sleeping.* Part. pas. **dormido** (dorrmeedo), *slept.*

IR. **Ir** (eer), *to go.* Pres. de Indic. **voy** (voy), **vas, va, vamos, vais, van,** *I go, I am going etc.* Imperf. **iba** (eeba), **ibas, iba, íbamos, ibais, iban** and Pret. perf. **fui** (fooee), **fuiste, fué, fuimos** (fooeemoss), **fuisteis, fueron** (fooayronn), *I went, I was going etc.* Fut. I. **iré, irás, irá** (eera) etc., *I shall go etc.* Cond. I. **iría, irías, iría,** etc., *I should go etc.* Pres. de Subj. que **vaya** (vaya), que **vayas,** que **vaya,** que **vayamos,** que **vayáis,** que **vayan,** *that I may go etc.* Imperf. de Subj. que **fuese** (kay fooaysay), que **fueses,** que **fuese** etc., *that I might go etc.* Fut. I. de Subj. si **fuere** (fooayray), si **fueres,** si **fuere** etc., *if I shall go etc.* Cond. I. de Subj. si **fuera** (see fooayra), si **fueras,** si **fuera** etc., *if I should go etc.* Imperat. **¡Ve!** (vay), *go* (familiar to one person). **¡Vaya Vd.!,** *go* (formal to one person). **¡Vamos!** (vamoss), *let* *us go!* ¡Id! (eed), *go* (familiar to several persons). ¡Vayan Vds.! (vayan oostaythays), *go* (formal to several persons. Gerund. yendo (yayndo), *going*. Part. pas ido (eedo), *gone*.

MORIR. Morir (moreer), *to die*. Pres. de Indic. muero (mooayro), mueres, muere, morimos (moreemoss), morís, mueren, *I die, I am dying etc*. Imperf. moría, morías moría etc. and Pret. perf. morí (moree), moriste, murió (mooryo), morimos, moristeis, murieron (mooryayron), *I died, I was dying etc*. Fut. I. moriré, morirás, morirá etc., *I shall die etc*. Cond. I. moriría, morirías, moriría etc., *I should die etc*. Pres. de Subj. que muera, que mueras, que muera, que muramos, que muráis, que mueran, *that I may die etc*. Imperf. de Subj. que muriese (mooryaysay), que murieses, que muriese etc., *that I might die etc*. Fut. I. de Subj. si muriere (see mooryayray), si murieres, si muriere etc.ꓸ *if I shall die etc*. Cond. I. de Subj. si muriera, si murieras, si muriera etc., *if I should die etc*. Imperat. ¡Muere!, *die* (familiar to one person). ¡Muera Vd.! (mooaira oostayth), *die* (formal to one person). ¡Muramos! (mooramoss), *let us die!* ¡Morid! (moreed), *die* (familiar to several persons). ¡Mueran Vds.! (mooayran oostaythays), *die* (formal to several persons). Gerund. muriendo (mooryayndo), *dying*. Part. pas. muerto (mooerrto), *died*.

OIR. Oir (oeer), *to hear*. Pres. de Indic. oigo (eoogo), oyes (oyays), oye, oímos (oeemoss), oís (oees), oyen (oyayn), *I hear, I am hearing etc*. Imperf. oía (oeea), oías, oía etc. and Pret. perf. oí (oee), oiste (oeestay), oyó (oyo), oimos, oisteis, oyeron (oyayronn), *I heard, I was hearing etc*. Fut. I. oiré (oeeray), oirás, oira etc., *I shall hear etc*. Cond. I. oiría (oeereea), oirías, oiría etc., *I should hear etc*. Pres. de Subj. que oiga (oeega), que oigas, que oiga, que oigamos, que oigáis, que oigan, *that I may hear etc*. Imperf. de Subj. que oyese (oyaysay), que oyeses, que oyese etc., *that I might hear etc*. Fut. I. de Subj. si oyere (see oyayray), si oyeres, si oyere etc., *if I shall hear etc*. Cond. I. de Subj. si oyera (see oyayra), si oyeras, si oyera etc., *if I should hear etc*. Imperat. ¡Oye! (oyay), *hear* (familiar to one person. ¡Oiga Vd.ꓹ (oeega oostayth), *hear* (formal to one person). ¡Oigamos! (oeegamoss), *let us hear!* ¡Oíd! (oeed), *hear* (familiar to several persons). ¡Oigan Vds.! (oeegan oostaythays), *hear*

(formal to several persons). Gerund. **oyendo** (oyayndo), *hearing.*
Part. pas. **oído** (oeedo), *heard.*

VENIR. **Venir** (vayneer), *to come.* Pres. de Indic. **vengo** (vayngo),
vienes (vyaynays), **viene, venimos** (vayneemoss),
venís (vaynees), **vienen** (veeaynayn), *I come, I am coming etc.*
Imperf. **venía** (vayneea) **venías, venía** etc. and Pret. perf. **vine**
(veenay), **viniste, vino, vinimos, vinisteis, vinieron** (veenyayron),
I came, I was coming etc. Fut. I. **vendré** (vayndray), **vendrás,**
vendrá etc., *I shall come etc.* Cond. I. **vendría, vendrías, vendría**
etc., *I should come etc.* Pres. de Subj. **que venga** (kay vaynga),
que vengas, que venga etc., *that I may come etc.* Imperf. de Subj.
que viniese (veenyaysay), **que vinieses, que viniese** etc., *that I*
might come etc. Fut. I. de Subj. **si viniere, si vinieres, si viniere**
etc., *if I shall come etc.* Cond. I. de Subj. **si viniera, si vinieras,**
si viniera etc., *if I should come etc.* Imperat. **¡ven!** (vayn), *come*
(familiar to one person). **¡Venga Vd.!** (vaynga oostayth), *come*
(formal to one person. **¡Vengamos!** (vayngamoss), *let us come!*
¡Venid! (vayneed), *come* (familiar to several persons). **¡Vengan**
Vds.! (vaingan oostaythays), *come* (formal to several persons).
Gerund. **viniendo** (veenyayndo), *coming.* Part. pas. **venido**
(vayneedo), *come.*

¡Haga el favor de repetir!

una lección larga	oona lekthyong larga	*a long lesson*
siento mucho	yaynto mootsho	*I am very sorry*
un diario español	oon deearyo esspangyol	*a Spanish newspaper*
la revista	la rayveesta	*the periodical*
el portero	ell portayro	*the doorman*
oferta de trabajo	oferrta thay travaho	*Help Wanted*
solicitúdes de trabajo	soleetheetoothays day trabaho	*Situations Wanted*
el taquígrafo	ell takeegraffo	*the stenographer*
el joven	ell hovayn	*the young man*
ayudar	ayoothar	*to help*
¿Qué desea Vd.?	kay thaysaya oostayth	*What do you want?*
¿Qué clase?	kay klasay	*What kind?*
¿Qué tamaño?	kay tamanyo	*What size?*
¿Qué calidad?	kay kaleethath	*What quality?*
una barra de chocolate	oona barra thay tshokolatay	*a bar of chocolate*
chocolate para cocinar	tshokolatay para kotheenar	*chocolate for cooking*
déme medio kilo	damay maythyo keelo	*give me half a kilo*
me ha tuteado	may a tootayatho	*he was very familiar with me*
después de trabajar	dayspooesz thay travahar	*after work is done*
tener reposo	taynayr rayposo	*to rest*
andando el tiempo	andando ell tyaympo	*in the course of time*
aun	aoon	*even*
todo trabajo	totho travaho	*all work*
ayudar	ayoothar	*to help*

doy un buen consejo	doy oon booayn konnsayho	*I give you good advice*
la tienda	la tyaynda	*the store*
¿Qué ha pensado Vd.?	kay a paynsatho oostayth	*What did you think?*
le digo	lay theego	*I can tell you*
mucho ruido por nada	mootsho rooeetho porr natha	*Much ado (noise) about nothing*
que sea dicho seriamente	kay saya theetsho sayryamenntay	*to be serious*
desearía	daysayareea	*you would like*
el peluquero	ell paylookayro	*the hairdresser*
la peluquería	la paylookayreea	*the hairdresser's shop*
el barbero	el barbayro	*the barber*
la barbería	la barbayreea	*the barber's shop*
enfrente de nuestra casa	ennfrenntay thay nooesstra kasa	*opposite our house*
la esquina	la ayskeena	*the corner house*
creo que iremos allá	krayo kay eeraymoss allya	*I think we'll go there*
¿Quiere Vd. afeitarme?	kyayray oostayth afayeetarmay	*Will you give me a shave?*
el cabello	ell kavellyo	*the hair*
la navaja	la navaha	*the razor*
duele un poquito	dooaylay oong pokeeto	*it hurts a little bit*
deseo un shampú seco	daysayo oong shampoo seko	*I want a dry shampoo*
corte un poco de aquí	korrtay oon poko day akee	*cut a little more here*
quiero arreglarme las uñas	kyayro arrayglarmay las oonyas	*I want a manicure*
hágame la raya	agamay la raya	*part my hair (make me the line)*
al lado derecho	al latho thayraytsho	*at the right side*
corto por detrás	korrto porr thaytras	*short in the back*
el jabón	ell habong	*the soap*
la toalla	la toallya	*the towel*
la toalla cálida	la toallya kaleetha	*the hot towel*

agua caliente o fría	agva kalyenntay o freea	*warm or cold water*
copillar y peinar	kopeellyar ee payeenar	*to brush and to comb*
el pelo	ell paylo	*the hair*
el bigote	ell veegotay	*the moustache*
un masaje facial	oon masahay fathyal	*a face massage*
la ondulación	la onndoolathyong	*the permanent wave*
déme Vd. un shampú	daymay oostayth oong shampoo	*give me a shampoo*
hoy o mañana	oy o mangyana	*today or tomorrow*
los rizos de Julia	loz reethoss day hoolya	*Julia's curls*
hace mucho tiempo	athay mootsho tyaympo	*some time ago*
había sido una experiencia	aveea seetho oona exspayryennthya	*it had been an experience*
para la gente española	para la hayntay esspangyola	*for the Spanish people*
había una discusión	aveea oona theeskoosyong	*there was a discussion*
es muy diferente	ays mooy theefayrenntay	*it is very different*
la disputa	la theespoota	*the dispute*
los boxeadores	loz boxayathorays	*the boxers*
era maravilloso	ayra maraveellyoso	*it was wonderful*
noy hay duda	no ai thootha	*there is no question, no doubt*
Pedro dijo	paythro theeho	*Peter said*
más tarde	mas tardai	*later on*
os he dicho	oss ay theetsho	*I have told you*
entre nosotros	enntray nosotross	*with us, among us*
en este mismo instante	enn aystay meezmo eenstantay	*now, in the meantime*
el estreno	ell esstrayno	
la gran primera representación	la gran preemayra raypraysaynta-thyong	*the first performance*
en verso y prosa	enn vayrso ee prosa	*in rhyme and prose*

* 246 *

todas las localidades están tomadas	tothas laz lokalee-thathays aystan tomathoss	every seat is taken
no hay despacho	no ai dayspatsho	there is no sale
el cine próximo	ell theenay proxee-mo	the nearest movie
atestado (a) de gente	llyayno, a thay hayntay	crowded
a la entrada del teatro	a la ayntratha thell tayatro	to the entrance of the theatre
entramos al teatro	enntramoss al taya-tro	we enter the theatre
¿qué localidad to-maremos?	kay lokaleethath tomaraymoss	what seat shall we take?
entramos en el bal-cón	enntramoss enn ell balkong	we enter the balcony
los palcos	loss palkoss	the boxes (in the theatre)
el vestido de eti-queta	ell vaysteetho thay ayteekayta	the evening gown
es difícil hablarle a Vd.	ayz theefeetheel avlarlay a oostayth	it is difficult to speak to you
el ruido es enorme	ell rooeetho ays aynorrmay	the chattering, the noise is tremen-dous
una canción	oona kanthyong	a song
la cantante	la kantantay	the singer
cantar	kantar	to sing
la paloma	la paloma	the pigeon
aplausos frenéticos	aplaoososs fraynay-teekoss	thunderous applause
el telón sube	ell taylong soobay	the curtain rises
el telón baja	ell taylong baha	the curtain drops
un principio magní-fico	oom preentheepyo magneefeeko	an excellent begin-ning
la temporada	la taymporatha	the season
la temporada de in-vierno	la taymporatha thay eenvyerrno	the winter season
el país	ell paees	the country

en estos países tropicales	enn **ay**stoss paee-says tropeekalays	*in these hot countries*
la cama	la **ka**ma	*the bed*
no me gusta	no may **goo**sta	*I don't like*
bastante cómodo	bastan**tay** komotho	*pretty comfortable*
una entrada independiente	**oo**na ayntratha eendaypenndyenntay	*a separate entrance*
la casera	la ka**say**ra	*the landlady*
demasiado alto	daymas**yatho al**to	*too much*
regatear	raygatayar	*to haggle*
una mesa pequeña	**oo**na **may**sa pay-**kayn**gya	*a small table*
¿Dónde vive Vd.?	**donn**day **vee**vay **oos**tayth	*Where do you live?*
todas las noches	**to**thas laz **not**shays	*every night*
servir el almuerzo	ser**veer** ell almooerr-tho	*to serve (the) breakfast*
las mejores tiendas	laz may**ho**rays **tyayn**das	*the best stores*
yo te amo	yo tay **a**mo	*I love you*
¿Quién ama?	**kyayng a**ma	*who loves?*
no sería verdad	no say**ree**a vayr-**thath**	*it would not be true*
una lengua extranjera	**oo**na **layng**va esstran**hay**ra	*a foreign language*
tenemos miedo	tay**nay**moss **myay**tho	*we are afraid*
le dice una vez	lay **thee**thay **oo**na vayth	*he tells him (one day)*
paseando en el tranvía	pasa**yan**do enn ell trambee**a**	*riding in the streetcar*
en cada parada	enn **ka**tha pa**ra**tha	*at every stop*
¡dejelos bajar!	**day**hay loz va**har**	*let them off!*
¡Cuidado!	kvee**tha**tho	*Attention! Watch your step!*
¡Sentémonos!	saynt**ay**monoss	*let us sit down!*
la reglas de movimiento	laz **ray**glaz thay moveem**yenn**to	*the traffic rules*
el movimiento	ell moveem**yenn**to	*the traffic*
el cobrador	ell kovra**thor**	*the conductor*

sin preguntarnos	seen praygoontar-noss	*without asking us*
¡Me hace Vd. el favor!	may athay oostayth ell favor	*Fares please! (do me the favor)*
paga los billetes por mí	paga loz veellyay-tays porr mee	*pay for the tickets for me*
dámelos	damayloss	*give them to me!*
el tranvía se para	ell trambeea say para	*the street car stops*
nos bajamos del tranvía	noz vahamoss thell trambeea	*we get off the street-car*
las ediciones de la noche	las aytheethyonayzth day la notshay	*the night editions*
ahora voy a decirles	aora voy a thay-theerlays	*now I am going to tell you*
sin saber ninguna regla	seen savayr neen-goona raygla	*without knowing any rule*
el almacén	ell almathayn	*the department store*
los últimos modelos	loss oolteemoss motheloss	*the latest models*
¿de qué color?	day kay kolor	*what color?*
color café marrón	kolor kafay marrong	*coffee-brown*
¿En qué puedo ser-virle a Vd.?	enn kay pooaydo serveerlay a oostayth	*what may I do for you?*
voy a probármelo	boy a provarmaylo	*I'll try it on*
¡Adiós!	atheeoss	*good bye!*
¡Qué Vd. lo pase bien!	kay oostayth lo pasay byayng	*good luck! (That you may pass well, get along very well)!*
un gran poeta es-pañol	oon grann poayta esspangyol	*a great Spanish poet*
hace casi ciento cin-cuenta años	athay kasee thyayn-to theenquennta angyoss	*almost 150 years be-fore*
aunque	aoonkay	*although*
lleno de enemis-tades	llyayno day ennay-meestathays	*full of hatred*

mucho	mootsho	much, a great deal
verdadero	vayrthathayro	real, true
la adversidad	la advayrseethath	the unhappiness
a menudo	a maynootho	often
tratar	tratar	to treat
¡Qué lástima!	kay lasteema	what a pity!
¡Cuidado!	kveethatho	Attention!
¡Por Dios!	porr theeos	for God's sake! (Goodness!)
¡Caramba!	karammba	hah, strange!
¡Cómo! ¿De veras?	komo day vayras	What! Really?
mi mejor amigo	mee mayhor ameego	my best friend
mas al fin y al cabo	mas al feen ee al kavo	but after all
tenga razón	taynga rathong	it is right, correct
acerca de ello	atherrka day ellyo	about that
sería mucho mejor	sayreea mootsho mayhor	it would be much better
el día de correspon-dencia	ell deea day korray-sponndennthya	day for correspon-dence
papel de carta	papell day karta	writing paper
un portaplumas	oon porrtaploomas	a penholder
la tinta	la teenta	the ink
lo más pronto posi-ble	lo mas pronnto poseeblay	very soon, as soon as possible
una dirección buena	oona theerekthyong booayna	a good address
la carta siguiente	la karrta seegyenn-tay	the following letter
muy señor mío	mooy sengyor meeo	dear Sir
tuve el gusto	toovay ell goosto	I had the pleasure
tengo la intención	tayngo la eentayn-thyong	I intend
la única posibilidad	la ooneeka poseevee-leethath	the only possible way
le ruego me dis-pense	le rooaygo may theespennsay	I wish to apologize
affmo.y.s.s.q.s.m.e		(instead of): very sincerely yours
en un sobre	enn oon sobray	in an envelope

la dirección	la theerekthyong	the address
por avión	porr avyong	by airmail
dirigir	deereeheer	to address
unas cartas	oonas karrtas	some letters
unas tarjetas	oonas tarhaytas	some cards
unas tarjetas ilustradas	oonas tarhaytas eeloostrathas	some picture postcards
la oficina de correos	la offetheena thay korrayoss	the post-office
el porte	ell porrtay	the postage
por cada 20 gramos	porr katha 20 gramoss	for every 20 grams
¿hay carta para mí!	ay karrta para mee	is there a letter for me?
una carta certificada	oona karrta therrteefeekatha	a registered letter
el telegrama	ell taylaygrama	a telegram
a cualquiér punto del mundo	a qualkayr poonto thell moondo	to any point in the world
los sellos	loss sellyoss	the stamps
los estancos	loss aystankoss	the tobacco stores
el buzón	ell boothong	the letter-box
el puro	ell pooro	the cigar (a pure one)
fumar en pipa	foomar enn peepa	to smoke a pipe
orgulloso	orgoollyoso	proud
pasar los aduaneros	pasar loss advanayross	to pass the custom-officers
es cómico	ays komeeko	it is funny
en la frontera	enn la frontayra	at the border
el baúl	ell baool	the trunk
¡Abra Vd. su baúl!	abra oostayth soo baool	open your trunk please!
efectos usados	ayfayktoss oosathoss	used goods
arriba de la ciudad	areeva thay la thyoothath	uptown
abajo de la ciudad	avaho thay la thyoothath	downtown
¡Sea Vd. bienvenido!	saya oostayth byangvayneetho	(Be) Welcome!

¡Qué se divierta!	kay say theevyerrta	*enjoy yourself!*
solamente poco tiempo	solamayntay poko tyaympo	*only for a short time*
el tiempo es bueno	ell tyaympo ess booayno	*the weather is good*
no nos importa	no noss eemporrta	*we don't care*
quiza	keetha	*perhaps*
hará mal tiempo	ara mal tyaympo	*the weather will be bad*
hace sol	athay sol	*the sun is shining*
hará luna	ara loona	*the moon will be shining*
debemos decir que no	daybaymoss daytheer kay no	*we must say no*
¿Dónde?	donnday	*where?*
¿De dónde?	day donnday	*from where?*
¿Por qué?	porr kay	*why?*
porque	porrkay	*because*
¡tenga Vd. la bondad!	taynga oostayth la bonndath	*be kind enough!*
¿Quién?	kyayng	*who?*
¿Qué?	kay	*what?*
¿Cuál?	kval	*which one?*
mucho gusto en conocerla	moocho goosto enn konothayrla	*very glad to meet you*
¡Vamonos al hotel!	vamonoss al otayl	*let us go to the hotel!*
unos días	oonoss deeas	*a few days, some days*
el último dinero	ell oolteemo theenayro	*the last money*
un hotel de primera clase	oon otayl day preemayra klasay	*a first class hotel*
el gerente	ayl hayrenntay	*the manager*
¿A qué hora se come?	a kay ora say komay	*when are the meals served?*
café con leche	kafay konn laytshay	*coffee with milk*
huevos fritos	ooayvoss freetoss	*fried eggs*
huevos revueltos	ooayvoz rayvooayltoss	*scrambled eggs*

hace dos semanas	athay doss say manas	*two weeks ago*
en seguida	enn saygyeetha	*at once*
Será mi mayor placer	sayra mee mayor plathayr	*it will be the greatest pleasure to me*
muy pronto	mooy pronnto	*very soon*
yo os invito a vosotros todos	yo oss eenveeto a vosotross tothoss	*I invite you all*
a la española	a la esspangyola	*in the Spanish way*
al día siguiente	al deea seegeeenntay	*the next day*
junto con la invitación	hoonto konn la eenveetathyong	*attached to this invitation*
una alimentación sana	oona aleemayntathyong sana	*healthy food*
si viene Vd. por auto	see vyaynay oostayth porr aooto	*if you go by automobile*
si viene Vd. por tren	see vyaynay porr trenn	*if you go by train*
Cervecería y restaurant	thervaythayreea ee raystaoorang	*bar and grill*
entremeses	enntremaysays	*interludes, entrées*
sopas	sopas	*soups*
platos del día	platoz thell deea	*dishes of the day, daily specials*
huevos	ooayvoss	*eggs*
pescados	payskathoss	*fishes*
entradas y asados	aynthrathas ee asathoss	*entrées and roasts*
aves	avays	*fowl*
verduras y legumbres	vayrdooras ee laygoombrays	*vegetables*
ensaladas	ennsalathas	*salads*
mermeladas	merrmaylathas	*marmalades*
quesos	kaysoss	*cheeses*
mariscos	mareeskoss	*shell-fish*
¡no me culpe!	no may koolpay	*don't blame me!*
nosotros todos	nosotross tothoss	*all of us*
sobre una terraza	sobray oona terratha	*on a terrace*

al aire libre	al aeeray leevray	*in the fresh air*
los bailes	loz vaeelays	*the dances*
en realidad	enn rayaleethath	*really*
hasta que	asta kay	*until, (when)*
la rosa	la rosa	*the rose*
la violeta	la veeolyta	*the violet*
los tulipanes	loss tooleepanays	*the tulips*
la dalia	la thaleea	*the dahlia*
los lirios	loz leereeoss	*the lilies*
los claveles	los klavaylays	*the carnations*
las orquídeas	las orrkeethayas	*the orchids*
la mesa de comida	la maysa thay komeetha	*the dinner table*
los no me olvides	loz no-may-ollvee-days	*the forget-me-nots*